MILL TOWN BOY

MILL TOWN BOY

The Biography of Raymond Margato Fosheim

by his son

Gene Raymond Fosheim

Raymond Margato Fosheim on his 1937 Harley Davidson 74 in 1939. Photo taken looking north at the Snohomish River overlook on 21st and East Grand Avenue in Everett, Washington.

Copyright © 2016 by Gene Raymond Fosheim

All rights reserved.

ISBN-13: 978-1522782407

ISBN-10: 1522782400

Library of Congress Control Number:

Imprint Name, Everett, Washington

Printed in the United States of America

Dedicated to my sons Tyler Gene and Grant Raymond Fosheim and all the future Fosheim's.

Table of Contents

	Foreword	
	Introduction	
Chapter I	From Norway to America	1
Chapter II	Settling in Everett	27
Chapter III	Childhood Memories	65
Chapter IV	The Riverside Neighborhood	77
Chapter V	Teenage Years	105
Chapter VI	The Hingston Box Company........................	135
Chapter VII	Rails, Roads, and Water	143
Chapter VIII	The Great Depression	159
Chapter IX	Motorcycles	173
Chapter X	Minnesota	189
Chapter XI	The Walton Lumber Company.....................	197
Chapter XII	The War Years	207
Chapter XIII	Back to the Sawmills	247
Chapter XIV	Married Life	259
Chapter XV	525 Pilchuck Path	273
Chapter XVI	Retirement	303
	Epilogue	323
	The Author	327

Foreword

Scandinavians migrating to the Pacific Northwest is not an unusual story. Nor is that of working men toiling the factories in mill town Everett. Enduring trials of the Great Depression and World War II is a common theme. What is uncommon is the way Gene Fosheim weaves the story of his family and that of the city of Everett into this uplifting story. Blessed by his father's diary that Fosheim rescued from the trash, a trove of family photographs, oral interviews of his father, his interest in hearing the family stories as a small child and a love of travel, he has created a unique and thorough family memento. Interspersed throughout the book are unedited passages from Raymond Fosheim's diaries. Fosheim goes on to explain the entries such as explaining movies his dad watched, places his father went and motorcycles he rode. Photos are liberally used throughout. Fosheim traces his history from Fossheim, Norway (the second s was lost in passage) to industrial Everett. Like other new Americans family members made the difficult decision of leaving the homeland behind seeking a better life - the American Dream. Like others who settled in Everett's proud working class Riverside neighborhood, they had a strong work ethic that overcame many hardships. Much of the book is the story of his father. Coming of age during the Depression Raymond Fosheim still managed to entertain himself with such activities as swimming in the forbidden Snohomish River, building camps near the mills with his friends, hitchhiking, cruising in motorcycles and riding the rails. Like many others, he sacrificed high school education and instead worked odd jobs to help support the family. He went on to marry a Swedish girl with Minnesota roots and raise his son Gene in his home town. It becomes clear that Gene Fosheim's role model and hero is his dad. Though an only child Gene had several mentors as the loving family was close on both sides. Read this heartwarming family history and learn a lot about Everett history as well.

Jack O'Donnell
Everett, Washington

Acknowledgements

Very few would attempt an endeavor like this without the help or influence of others. I'm fortunate to have so many people in my life who have helped me complete my dream of publishing this book. I would like to thank all my friends who are members of Historic Everett, the Everett Museum of History and the City of Everett Historic Commission for their support of and interest in this project. A special thank you goes to Jack O'Donnell for reading my notes and writing the foreword.

All the images in this book are from the Fosheim collection unless otherwise noted.

Introduction

I grew up spending many wonderful evenings sitting in our family home's cozy living room listening to Dad and his two older brothers telling stories of growing up in our hometown, Everett, Washington. Martin and John Fosheim were bachelors all their lives and lived together at 2620 Walnut Street. At least once a week they would show up at our home in the evening after a long day at work in the saw mills. I would usually see them drive up in Uncle John's yellow Ford pickup and get all excited as I shouted downstairs to let Dad know they were here.

Uncle John and Mart would each settle in to a comfortable chair as Dad washed the sawdust off his hands after working on one of his many carpentry projects in our basement. Dad would usually make some hot chocolate and peanut butter sandwiches as a late night snack for everyone. Mom's bachelor brother Uncle Buddy, who lived with us, would also sit down and join in on one of the inevitable conversations about the past. I usually sat in silence with open ears and a grin on my face as I worked on a plastic model or played with my toys on the floor by the fireplace.

For a couple of hours the conversation would move from early Everett to the war years to old movies and Hollywood stars. I loved every minute of it and I'm sure it was during those conversations that I developed my life-long passion for history. However it wasn't until late in Dad's life that I really cultivated my interest in early Everett history. Luckily a few years before Dad died I set up a couple of interviews with him and the wonderful historians at the local museum of history. These interviews were recorded and transcribed. I often dreamt of writing Dad's memoirs while he was still alive, but alas I was busy raising my two boys, working, and rehabilitating my growing number of historic Everett rental homes.

Dad's been gone now for eighteen years and I've finally gathered together his hundreds of historic photos, his diary, letters, and other documents into this book which I hope will be enjoyed by historians and family members alike. It's been a joy reliving family memories and learning of my past ancestors. Of course all memories are not happy ones but to complete a story they must be told. I hope this is a tale that many readers will not only find interesting but will be able to relate to.

Dad was an Everett boy through and through. He never considered living anywhere else. In addition to his story I've mixed in some of Everett's interesting history, personalities, and events that shaped the city and the lives of the people living in it. I've also added information about Dad's parents and siblings who left their homeland of Verdal, Norway to make the difficult journey to America for work and to raise their growing families.

My father, Raymond Margato Fosheim was born in a small house in Everett, Washington on January 22, 1914. Both his parents had come to America from a small farm in Norway. Dad lived his entire life in Everett and died peacefully in his sleep on July 11, 1997. He was interviewed at the Snohomish County Museum and Historical

Association on Rockefeller Avenue by Phyllis Royce. The interview was transcribed by Deborah Blake during February and March, 1994. This book was created from those interviews, his personal journal, photo albums, and the memories of his family and friends. His own words throughout this biography are quoted in italics.

Raymond Fosheim and his loyal friend Chubby at home in the late 1960s

MILL TOWN BOY

Chapter I

From Norway to America

"My parents' names were John Kristopher Fosheim and Anna Kristine Øvrum Fosheim. They came from a suburb of Trondheim, Norway."

Raymond Margato Fosheim's story has its beginnings along a beautiful river valley in one of the most scenic countries on earth, Norway. The Fosheim family came from the farming and fishing municipality of Verdal, in the county of Nord-Trondelag, in the west central part of Norway. Verdal extends from the eighty-one mile long Trondheimsfjord east about twenty-five miles to the Swedish border. The huge 2,000 foot deep fjord is comparable to the one hundred mile long Puget Sound in western Washington State where the Fosheim family now makes their home.

The surrounding area from the town of Verdalsora and up the Verdal River looks quite similar to the city of Everett and the adjoining Snohomish River Valley. Both towns of Everett and Verdalsora are bordered on three sides by water and both are just a short distance from mountains to the east. The Fosheim family surely felt quite comfortable in the familiar environment of their new American homeland.

The Verdal coat of arms taken from King Olaf's shield.

Norway with Trondheim in the center left.

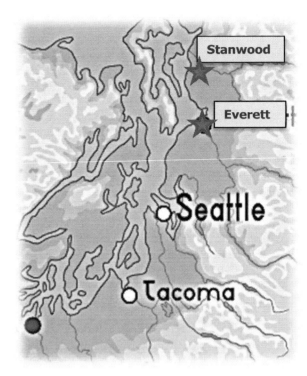
The Puget Sound area of Washington State, USA.

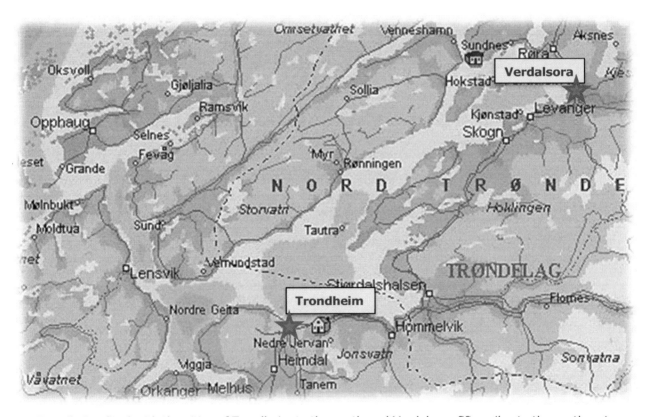
Trondheimsfjord with the cities of Trondheim to the south and Verdalsora fifty miles to the northeast.

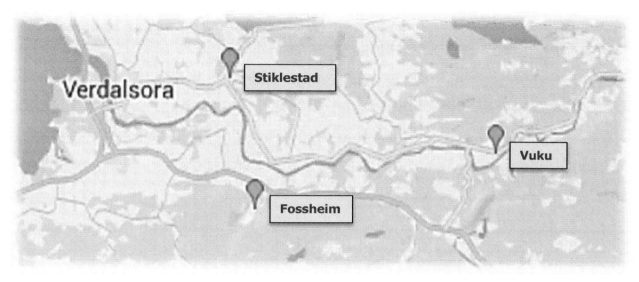

The Verdal River valley from Trondheimsfjord, left to the border of Sweden on the right.

Raymond Fosheim's father, John Kristopher Martinussen, was born on a farm called Haganesset in Reppevald, in the municipality of Verdal, on June 12, 1876. The family had one cow, two goats, and four lambs. They soon moved to a small farm named Balgaardsora where John and his six siblings took a new last name, Balgaard. John Kristopher, now Balgaard, also later lived and worked on a farm called Skogtroa.

John Kristopher's father, Martinus Bardosen Østgaarden, was born in Verdal on March 18, 1842. He married Beret Martha Halstensdotter on November 9, 1866 in Stiklestad Church. Beret was born in Oppheimsvald on May 27, 1844. They had seven children; Bernt Martin, Hans Severin, Ragnhild Birgitta, John Kristopher, Marius, Beret Martha, and Anne Marta. Of the seven, four eventually immigrated to America and three remained in Norway.

John Kristopher Martinussen Balgaard

Martinus Bardosen Østgaarden

John Kristopher Balgaard ultimately moved to a small farm that sat high up on a picturesque green hillside called Fossheim. The names of Norwegian farms can be very descriptive. Fossheim can be interpreted to mean 'waterfall home.' It was here that John met and soon married his neighbor's daughter, Anna Kristine Andersdatter Øvrum, who lived on a small farm just up the hill, on March 18, 1903. Anna was born on January 18, 1881 in Vinnesmoen, Verdal.

John and Anna Fossheim on their wedding day, March 18, 1903 in Verdal, Norway

John and Anna lived and worked on the Fossheim farm and soon started raising a family. They had followed a Norwegian tradition and took Fossheim as their last name when they got married. Their first child, Martin Andrew Fossheim, was born on June 13, 1904 but sadly died of an illness seven months later. A second son was born on December 14, 1905 and was also named Martin Andrew Fossheim. Another son, John Arthur Fossheim was born two years later on December 7, 1907.

John's family religion was Baptist but he switched to Lutheran when he married Anna. When young Martin and John Arthur Fossheim were born they were baptized in the historic Stiklestad Church, the parish church located in the tiny village of Stiklestad, not far below the Fossheim farm. The impressive grey stone church was completed in 1180. It seats about 500 people and was designed by Archbishop Øystein Erlendsson.

Beret Martha and Martinus Bardosen Østgaarden with their daughter Anne Marta Balgaard, unidentified, and their son John Kristopher Balgaard Fossheim. This is a postcard sent to the Øvrum family.

The historic Stiklestad Church and cemetery in 2006.

The village of Stiklestad is the site of the battlefield where Norwegian King Olaf II Haraldsson fell in battle on July 29, 1030. He subsequently was canonized and became known as St. Olaf of the Catholic Church. Legend says that the king died leaning against a large stone. The church building is assumed to have been erected on the exact spot where King Olaf was killed and that stone is supposedly still inside the altar of the church. The battle of Stiklestad represented the introduction of Christianity in Norway.

Olaf II Haraldsson, born in 995, was the first king of all of Norway and the country's patron saint. The son of the lord Harald Grenske and a descendant of the Norwegian ruler Harald I Fairhair, Olaf was reared as a pagan and became a Viking warrior in the Baltic region where he fought against the English and the Danes. He eventually went to France, where he was baptized at Rouen in 1013. Returning to Norway in 1015, Olaf conquered territory that had previously been held by Denmark and Sweden and by 1016 had consolidated his rule in all of Norway where he pressed relentlessly for the acceptance of Christianity, using missionaries he brought from England.

Olaf was forced to flee to Russia in 1028 when Canute, king of England and Denmark, forced him out. Olaf attempted to reconquer Norway in 1030 but was defeated by a superior Norwegian peasant and Danish army

Stiklestad Church Alter.

in the Battle of Stiklestad (1030), one of the most celebrated battles in ancient Norse history. Olaf's popularity, his church work, and the aura of legend that surrounded his death, which was supposedly accompanied by miracles, led to his canonization in 1031. His popularity spread rapidly; churches and shrines were constructed in his honor in England, Sweden, and Rome. He was the last Western saint accepted by the Eastern Orthodox Church.

King Olaf II Haraldsson. *San Carlo al Corso, Rome.*

Every year since 1954 a play based on the battle is performed in the Stiklestad amphitheater. The Saint Olav Drama is a performance that draws people from all over Europe, and other parts of the world, to what is now the largest outdoor theatre in Scandinavia.

Today the picturesque church is surrounded by shade trees and a peaceful tidy cemetery. Anna Øvrum Fossheim's parents and my great grandparents, Anders and Karen Øvrum are buried in the cemetery along with many of my cousins. Anders Bardosen Øvrum was born in Verdal on March 15, 1840 and died in 1932. Karen Elisabet Skånes Øvrum was born in Verdal in 1845 and died in 1928. They were married in 1867 and had six children; Bernt, Ragnhild, Karl, Anna, Ole, and Gustav. Three of the children immigrated to America and three remained in Norway.

Second cousins Rannveig Woll and Gene Fosheim at their great grand parents Anders and Karen Øvrum's graves in Stiklestad Church Cemetery in 2000.

My first visit to my grandparent's homeland of Norway was in the summer of 2000. As I walked the streets of historic Trondheim and drove the winding country roads in Verdal, I felt right at home. I sensed an instant connection to the beautiful country and felt as if I had been there before. My cousins drove me through the scenic countryside and up the gradually rolling hills for a view of the colorful farmlands flowing with multiple shades of green below. I thought to myself, this is just like the Stillaguamish River valley back home by Arlington or Stanwood.

The Fossheim farm with its original buildings in the early 1900s.

Ole Øvrum (see arrow) on what is believed to be the Øvrum family farm on the hillside near the Fossheim farm.

On my visit to historic Stiklestad I wandered amongst the cemetery headstones thinking of the historic events that happened on this land. As I read the names on the markers I also wondered how many of my distant cousins were here. I sat in the church and tried to picture the numerous members of my family who were baptized inside the small but impressive structure. I visited the museum and small village and wanted to learn everything I could about this amazing areas past.

The Fossheim farm on my first visit to Norway in August, 2000. Looking north over the river valley.

When we headed further up the valley along the gently winding river I was amazed at how clean and tidy everything appeared from the colorful red, yellow, and white farm buildings to the green trees majestically lining the roadways. We turned off the main road and wound up the gradual hillside and stopped at a red barn next to a small two-story grey house. I was finally at my grandparents' home, Fossheim.

There's a small attractive stream next to the little farm that gently cascades down the hillside into the green pastures that spread out along both sides of the soothingly flowing river below. It's one of the most beautiful and peaceful places I've ever seen. I wanted to explore in my grandparents footsteps and think of what it was like here a century ago. I walked across the fields to absorb as much of the view as I could. I dreamt about buying the Fossheim farm and returning to the simple life. I loved every minute of my first visit and returned again six years later.

Gene Fosheim at the Fossheim farm in 2000.

Just a few miles up the valley from Fossheim is the tiny village of Vuku. It is located at the confluence of the Helgåa and Inna rivers where they become the Verdalselva. The simple but beautiful Vuku red wooden church was built in 1654 by the architects Ole Johnsen Hindrum and Olluff Johnson Kirchebygger. John Kristopher Fossheim's parents rest in the Vuku cemetery.

The beautiful wooden Vuku Church, built in 1654, on my visit in 2000. My great grandparents, the Bardosens, are said to be buried in unmarked graves approximately where I'm standing.

A natural disaster struck Norway on May 19, 1893. The Verdal Landslide did incomprehensible damage to land and property in the valley directly below and across the river from the Fossheim farm. 750 acres and seventy-two million cubic yards of wet, slick clay slid down a hillside into the beautiful thirteen mile long Verdalselva valley and covered an area of 2,200 acres up to twenty-five feet deep.

Destroyed structures after the 1893 Verdal Landslide. *Postcard.*

The catastrophe came completely by surprise during the dark night as the valley residents peacefully slept. One hundred sixteen lives were lost in the disaster and the way of life for the survivors was changed forever. Everyone in the close knit community lost either friends or relatives. Many survivors left the area to seek a safer place to live. Homes, farms, property and jobs were lost and the local economy took many years to begin its recovery. As time and nature began to heal the wounds, people slowly moved back to reclaim the once fertile Verdalselva valley. Today one may not even recognize that the area had ever suffered a landslide or that the river had changed its channel. This tragic event certainly had an effect on the survivors as many looked for a better life and ultimately made the tough decision to leave their beloved land and come to America.

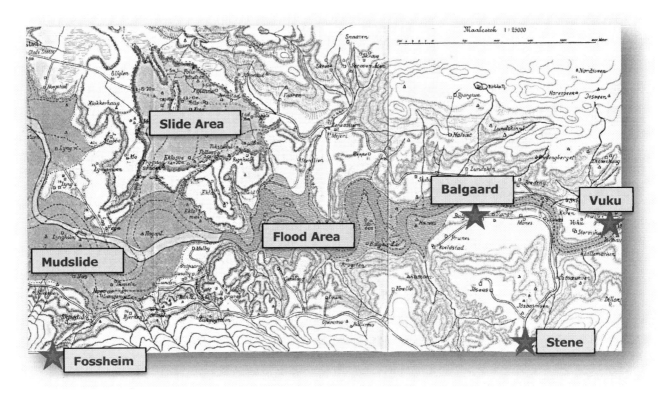

Map of the 1893 Verdal landslide and flooding showing the village of Vuku and the Balgaard, Stene, and Fossheim farms where family members lived and worked.

The 1800s were a time of turmoil and major changes for the Norwegian people. In 1813 Swedish forces invaded Denmark and a year later Denmark surrendered Norway to Sweden. In the mid eighteen hundreds the Norwegian agriculture and timber industry prospered and its merchant fleet increased swiftly so that by 1900 it was the third largest in the world after America and Britain. Population also grew rapidly during the 1800s and increased from 880,000 to 2,240,000 even with the heavy emigration to the USA. On 13 August 1905 the Norwegians declared independence from Sweden.

The Norwegian economy was hit hard during a severe depression from the mid-1870s to the early 1890s. This helped trigger the large-scale emigration from Norway to North America in the 1880s. Over 250,000 Norwegians emigrated in the period of 1879-1893 and between 1836 and 1930 over 860,000 Norwegians left their country. One major reason for the depression was the maritime industry's transformation from sailing to steam vessels. Due to a lack of capital and technological skills, Norway could not keep up and their market diminished so that by 1907 the country was no longer a major maritime power.

After a short economic boom from the early 1890s to 1899, a crash in the Norwegian building industry led to another major depression from 1900 to 1905. This undoubtedly led my grandfather John Fossheim to make the difficult choice to leave his young family behind and travel across the Ocean to America in search of a better life. John's older brother Bernt Stene had immigrated to America fourteen years earlier and was doing well working as a laborer on a farm in Minnesota. John's brother-in-law Ole Øvrum, Anna Fossheim's younger brother, had recently traveled to Canada and had found work. He sent letters encouraging his new brother-in-law to follow him. The lure of a good job in America was hard to resist.

Norwegian stamp commemorating 150 years of Norwegian emigration to America, 1825-1975. *North Dakota Studies.*

John Fossheim left his home and pregnant wife Anna in Verdal on April 25, 1907 and began his long slow journey to America. His single younger sister Beret Martha Balgaard joined John on his quest for a better life. Their travels started with a combination of horse drawn buggy and railroad southwest to Trondheim. From there they travelled by steamship along the Norwegian coast and had multiple stops including Kristiansund, Ålesund, Bergen, and Stavanger. Finally they crossed the North Sea to Kingston upon Hull their port of arrival on the east coast of England. From Hull there was a short often packed train ride across England via Leeds, Huddersfield, and Stalybridge to Liverpool, their departure point to America.

The Wilson Line steamship Tasso. *Postcard.*

John and Martha travelled on a combination ticket with the Wilson line which almost had a monopoly on the Scandinavian immigration business funneled through England. Their steamship, train, and ocean liner were all on one ticket partnered with the White Star Line. It was a crowded voyage in Steerage Class on their Wilson Line steamship, the 936 ton, 158 foot long, steel, single screw schooner Tasso. She was built in 1890 at Hull, England by Earle's Shipbuilding & Engineering Company.

It didn't take John long to get lonesome for Anna and his son. He wrote her a postcard upon his brief stop in Kristiansund and again while he had free time to visit Bergen on May 3rd. Seeing such a big city and all the new sights must have been amazing to both John and Martha.

John and Martha got lucky as they crossed the Atlantic on the brand new White Star Line ocean liner, RMS Adriatic on her maiden voyage on May 8, 1907. The RMS Adriatic was built by Harland and Wolff, Belfast, the same shipyard that built the RMS Titanic. She was one of the original 'Big Four' (Cedric, Celtic, Baltic, Adriatic) class of liners built between 1901 and 1907. The new liner was considered fast for 1907, crossing the Atlantic in only nine days, but that record would not last long when the Cunard Line's Mauritania and Lusitania arrived on the scene. The Adriatic was 726 feet long, seventy-five feet wide, and 24,541 tons. Her service speed was seventeen knots and she carried 2825 passengers: 425 first class; 500 second class; 1900 third class. Adriatic was the first ship to have a swimming bath (pool). She was scrapped in 1935.

The White Star Line ocean liner RMS Adriatic in 1907. *Postcard.*

Captain Edward John Smith was in command of the new RMS Adriatic on this maiden voyage and later was destined to command the RMS Titanic in 1912 on her ill-fated first sailing across the Atlantic. Ironically the RMS Adriatic later returned many of the RMS Titanic survivors back to England.

The following information is found on the RMS Adriatic's List or Manifest of Alien Passengers for the U. S. Immigration Officer at Port of Arrival:

Captain Edward John Smith *Postcard.*

S. S. Adriatic, sailing from Liverpool, May 8th, 1907. Arriving at Port of New York, May 18th, 1907.
Fosheim, Martinussen, J. K., laborer, able to read and write, from Verdalen, Norway, destination Nelson, B. C., to see brother Oli Fosheim, 5' 6 ½" tall, blue eyes.

The name Martinussen referred to the Scandinavian practice of taking one's father's first name and adding 'son or sen' at the end. John was going to visit his wife's brother, Ole Øvrum (not Fosheim) in Canada. Ole soon felt there would be better opportunities in the USA and subsequently moved down to the Stanwood, Washington area before John Fosheim arrived west. The mistake of spelling Fossheim with one 's' on the manifest changed our family name from that point on.

John's sister, Beret Martha Balgaard, sailed on the RMS Adriatic with him and her information was listed on the same manifest as follows:

> Balgaard, Beret, Martha, Servant, able to read and write, from Verdalen, Norway, to Underwood, Minnesota, to see brother B. M. Stene, 5' 4" tall, blue eyes. Her trip was paid for by her brother. She had ten dollars with her.

John later told his kids what a thrill it was to see the Statue of Liberty when they stopped at Ellis Island. John and his sister Martha boarded a train upon leaving New York City and headed for Underwood, Minnesota. Their older brother Bernt Stene had come to America from Trondheim via Glasgow many years earlier on May 10, 1893 and was eagerly waiting for them. Martha settled in Minnesota, got married, and raised a family, and John headed west to meet up with his brother-in-law Ole. A younger brother, Marius Balgaard also came to Minnesota later to settle.

The Statue of Liberty. *Library of Congress.*

It's difficult to trace Scandinavian family history because last names often change every generation. When the three Balgaard brothers came to America only younger brother Marius kept the family name. John Kristopher changed his name to Fossheim and older brother Bernt changed his name to Stene, which was the name of the farm he worked on before leaving Norway. Their father and my great-grandfather's name was Martinus Bardosen so in their earlier years the brothers also used Martinussen for their last name. John Kristopher was born Martinussen then he changed to Balgaard, then to Fossheim and through a misspelling at Ellis Island was now Fosheim.

Raymond M. Fosheim's family tree.

"In Norway, he worked on different farms, but he never got ahead enough to have a farm of his own. My mother's brother, Ole Øvrum, was here in Stanwood first and my dad followed him. Dad's two brothers and his sister stopped in Minnesota, and settled there. Three brothers and one sister came over, but Dad kept coming out farther west to Washington."

Underwood in west central Minnesota. *Postcard.*

After stopping for a short time in Underwood, Minnesota to visit his brother Bernt Stene, John Fosheim left his sister Martha behind and continued west on a long train ride to meet up with his brother-in-law, Ole Øvrum. Ole was living near the small town of Stanwood, Washington, a farming and logging community located in northwest Snohomish County at the mouth of the old channel of the Stillaguamish River. Stanwood was settled by Europeans beginning in about 1866 near the Coast Salish people of the Stillaguamish Tribe's encampment along the north shoreline of Port Susan in Puget Sound.

It's fascinating how John and Anna Fosheim and their brother's and sister's paths to America paralleled the pattern of immigration of so many other Scandinavians. The late 1800s and early 1900s saw a huge immigration to America from Norway, Sweden, Finland, Iceland, and Denmark. Approximately two and a half million Scandinavians, a huge percentage of the region's population, came across the Atlantic to settle in their new homeland.

When the American and Canadian economies were thriving more Scandinavians left their homeland. If the economy was bad, immigration temporarily slowed down. As the new immigrants found jobs and prosperity in America, more letters were sent home and more interest was generated in leaving for greener pastures overseas. Both Ole Øvrum and Bernt Stene undoubtedly sent letters back to their families telling of the richness of their new country and encouraged family members to join them and many did.

The majority of the Scandinavians initially ended up settling in the farmlands and forests of the upper Midwest. Many like John Fosheim eventually left Minnesota, the Dakotas, Wisconsin, and Iowa for the Puget Sound region of Washington State. With the new train lines serving the northwest, it made it even easier to travel the additional 1,500 to 2,000 mile journey to the west coast. Soon Scandinavian churches and lodges were emerging to serve the fast growing ethnic population and many of the larger communities even had Scandinavian language newspapers. By 1910 approximately eight thousand immigrants had been arriving in Washington every year for a couple of decades and they soon comprised the largest ethnic group in the state.

When Ole and later John arrived in Stanwood, Washington, it had a large Norwegian population who encouraged their relatives and friends to immigrate to the area to farm or work in the logging camps. To make farming possible, low-lying land was cleared and homesteaders constructed a series of dikes along the river and sloughs. Numerous logging camps surrounded the farmlands where farmers were growing hay and oats. Transportation was by foot, horse, train, steamboats, or even Indian canoes. By 1906, a local chapter of the Washington Good Roads Association was organized to stimulate road building in the area. Slowly at first, often muddy roads were built between villages and eventually connected to the bigger cities.

Downtown East Stanwood in 1906. *Stanwood Area Historical Society.*

In its early days Stanwood was the largest Scandinavian community in Washington State. Over one hundred years later one can still enjoy the striking beauty of the light green lowlands and the darker tree covered gently rolling hills. The city of Stanwood still reflects its Scandinavian heritage and the outlying lands are dotted with neat and tidy farms. The new immigrants cherished their heritage but were quick to adapt to the American lifestyle and eagerly learned the English language.

The 1910 United States census found John Fosheim living in a boarding house in the Utsalady area of Camano Island, just west of Stanwood. At thirty-four, he was the oldest of eight boarders residing in Dora Sather's home and the only one that was married. Boarding houses began to appear all over the Puget Sound area when single loggers and sawmill workers were present. The homes were often run by single or widowed women as a source of income. The young boarders in this case were immigrants from Norway and all had come looking for work in America during the previous five years. Forty-eight-year-old Dora Sather's occupation was listed as a cook who only spoke Norwegian. John Fosheim and the other boarders were listed as laborers in a bolt camp and most spoke English.

John Fosheim (see arrow) listed in the thirteenth census of the United States: 1910 Population, enumerated on May 4, 1910.

By the time John Fosheim arrived in Snohomish County, logging camps were operating everywhere and much of the low land forest had already been logged off. Instead of majestic forests untouched but for wind storms and fires, much of the land was now a muddy sea of stumps. The low lands and flood plains were being converted to farmland and the higher ground was mostly just left as an ugly clear-cut. The environment was taking a severe beating but jobs were plentiful.

An oxen team hauling Douglas Fir logs at the De Jorup Logging Camp over a skid road near Utsalady, Washington in the mid-1880s. *University of Washington Libraries, Special Collections, UW12331.*

Cutting cedar shingle bolts in the Puget Sound area in 1902. The Largest stump has 1380 rings indicating its age. *University of Washington Libraries, Special Collections, KIN014.*

Darius Kinsey posing with his camera. *Kinsey Collection.*

The previous photo was taken in 1902 by Darius Kinsey, possibly the foremost photographer of logging and the old-growth forests in the Pacific Northwest during the first half of the twentieth century. Kinsey and his wife Tabitha produced over 5,000 incredibly detailed photos that have been published and celebrated all over the world. They left a wonderful collection documenting a unique time in our history. He has often been referred to as the Ansel Adams of logging.

"Dad was picking up shingle bolts for shingle mills when he first came here in Stanwood, and up in the woods working for some contractor. Then he ended up in the saw mills in Everett."

Transporting cedar shingle bolts by horse and sled. *Washington State Archives.*

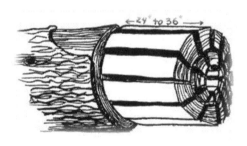

Shingle bolt cuts. *Mother Earth News.*

John Fosheim worked in a shingle bolt camp where felled cedar trees and stumps were cut to length and hauled to a nearby mill for further cutting. A shingle bolt was usually a segment of a cedar log that could have been well over a thousand years old. Cedar in the northwest was plentiful and many of the stumps were just left in place or even pulled out and burned. It was a hard, often wet and muddy job for the workers.

As the years went by and it became easier to transport whole logs to a shingle mill, the bolts were cut at the mill. Many of the logs were so big that only one could be carried at a time. The huge old-growth logs were hauled to the mills by horses, trucks and trains but the preferred way was by towing them as they floated in the water if a river, lake or Puget Sound was nearby.

As I walk the streets and parks of the Everett area today I often wonder what it would have been like to stroll amongst the two hundred foot tall twelve foot diameter trees that blanketed the land just 150 years ago. It was much like the area of the northern California coast where the redwoods forests still exist. I also wonder how sad it must have been for the native population of the Snohomish and other tribes while this clear cutting of the land was proceeding. The influx of thousands of new immigrants and the destruction of the old growth forests must have been overwhelming.

Single Douglas Fir log loads on display in downtown Snohomish, Washington. *Postcard.*

"My father wanted to better himself, and after he was here a couple of years, he sent for my mother, with the two children, the two oldest boys. She came all alone, on the boat and on the train, God bless her, it was tough going. Her brother, Ole Øvrum, was here in Everett, and my father followed him here."

Downtown Silvana, Washington from the Great Northern Railway tracks in 1914. *Great Northern Homepage.*

John Fosheim worked hard in the sawmill and logging camps in the Stanwood area for a couple of years and eventually saved enough money to send to his wife Anna and their two young boys so they could travel to America and join him. Anna, Martin, and young John left Verdal, Norway on October 26, 1910 and after a lengthy trip across the Atlantic and America finally joined John. The gathering of the young family must have been very emotional after their few years apart. John Kristopher had never seen his youngest son John Arthur as Anna was pregnant when he had left for America. The Fosheim's rented a small home in the pastoral town of Silvana just south of Stanwood a short time after Anna's arrival.

Typical steerage class upper deck area around 1900. *Postcard.*

Anna Fosheim and the two boys must have had quite an adventure travelling on a ship for the first time all the way across the Atlantic. First they had to cross the often rough North Sea to the east coast of Great Britain then take a train to Liverpool on the west coast before boarding their ocean liner. Most Scandinavian travelers couldn't afford first or second class tickets so they usually settled for third or steerage class accommodations. These weren't great but they did have their own room unlike the crowded steerage class below decks on older ships. Anna later told her family that the trip across the Atlantic by ship wasn't bad, as she had many other Norwegians to spend time with. In fact many of the ships crossing the Atlantic from England had manifests which showed that the majority of the passengers were Scandinavians.

Most female third class cabins had four berths and were private, comfortable, and clean. There was a bell to call a steward and mirrors and hooks to hang clothing on, and a private wash basin. The food was of good quality, and the open deck space allotted to the passengers was adequate. Third class accommodations on the White Star Line included dining rooms with linens and silverware, a reading room and a smoking room. Travel across the Atlantic for immigrants had improved a great deal during the late 1800s.

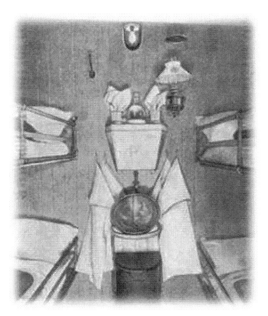

Third class four berth stateroom around 1900. *Norway Heritage.*

Sailing into New York and arriving at Ellis Island was both a thrilling experience and a cultural shock. Immigration was packed with nationalities from around the world though mostly Europeans. Anna and the two boys had to endure the crowds and the overworked and overwhelmed immigration agents. They had to be processed through with questions of health, money, and proper documentation. Luckily there would usually be someone to help interpret most of the numerous languages being spoken.

Ellis Island on February 24, 1905. *Library of Congress.*

Once Anna, Martin, and John boarded the train for the long ride to Chicago and then Everett they had to endure the lonesome trip. Neither Anna nor the boys could speak English and there was no one to talk to. She had a disturbing incident when little John disappeared and could not be found. The conductor ordered a train-wide search and eventually found him sleeping in someone's berth. There were many curiosities though with the never-ending beautiful scenery and the huge cities. They also

Immigrants arriving at Ellis Island in the early 1900s. *Library of Congress.*

probably met the first African-American they had ever seen when assisted by the black porters on board. One can imagine what they thought crossing the endless plains and ranchland of the Dakotas and Eastern Montana. When they crossed through the Cascades by Stevens Pass Anna must have been amazed by the dense green forest and trees the width of small houses.

Martin, Anna, and John Fossheim in Norway in 1909.

"My brother, Martin, was born in 1905 and brother John in 1907 in Norway. John, the youngest boy, was two years old when Mother came over from Norway, and Martin was five."

After almost three years the Fosheim family was finally together again, never to return to Norway. They quickly settled into family life in the Silvana area surrounded by fellow Norwegians with the same customs and language. Many Scandinavians took Americanized names and all were anxious to learn English as fast as they could. Assimilation into the American culture was easier for most Scandinavians in the Northwest than other ethnic groups as there were so many of them with a strong sense of community and a good support network.

Even though they were now over a thousand miles away John and Anna kept in touch with their Minnesota relatives on a regular basis. Here is a post card wishing the Fosheim's a happy new year in January 1911 sent by John's older brother Bernt in Minnesota.

Bernt Martin Stene posing in an impressive car in Murray, North Dakota, January 1911.

Anna Fosheim must have enjoyed finally seeing her brother again. Ole Martin Øvrum had come to the northwest from Norway almost a decade before. Ole left Verdal for Trondheim and then made the long journey south by rail or boat or both to Kristiansand at the far southern tip of Norway. He then sailed for New York City on April 25, 1901 and arrived on May 10th aboard the Scandinavian America Line ship SS Hekla.

Scandinavian America Line ship SS Hekla. *Postcard.*

The SS Hekla was built in 1884 by Scott & Co, in Greenock, Scotland to supersede her namesake. She was 333 feet long, forty-one feet wide and 3,260 tons. She had a single funnel and three masts and had a top speed of eleven knots. The Hekla had accommodations for forty first class, thirty second class, and 800 steerage passengers.

Anders and Karen Øvrum on the left with son Ole, his wife, and seven of their eight children in 1923. Notice that only one of the kids has a pair of shoes.

After arriving in New York, Ole took the long train ride west to Nelson, British Columbia before heading south to find work in the Stanwood, Washington area. He became a US citizen on May 4, 1908 in Seattle but then decided to return to Norway where he married Klara Marie Heieråsvald in June of 1909. Ole and Klara had one daughter, Ella, on November 1, 1909 before Ole returned to America in 1910 to work for two years. Ole returned to Norway and his wife and daughter and had seven more children. In 1924 he again returned to America where his plan was to work for a few years and then send money to his family so they could join him. Unfortunately that never happened.

Ole had a complicated life story that was kept secret from me and other family members for many years. It wasn't until the 1970s that I learned he had left his wife and eight children in Norway when he came to America and never returned. I was told that he never saved enough money to bring his family over and eventually decided to re-marry and stay in America. John Fosheim was able to bring his young family to America but Ole wasn't. Only Ole knew the real story but this was the fate of many other immigrant families at the time.

Ole Martin Øvrum.

Chapter II

Settling in Everett

"In 1909 my parents came here, to Everett, and settled at 1515 Baker Street in the north end of town."

It's easy to see why so many Norwegians and other Scandinavians settled in the Puget Sound area of Washington State. The land looks very similar to many areas of their homelands with the emerald green hills, river valleys of rich farm land, and abundance of salt water bays. There was a profusion of fish and wildlife everywhere. The location of the growing city of Everett was particularly stunning. The economy of the Everett area also matched closely what the Scandinavians were used to in their homeland with farming, logging, mills, and fishing.

Early birds eye view of Everett, Washington, looking east toward the Cascade Mountains. *Postcard.*

The Everett peninsula is surrounded by the peaceful and protected Port Gardner Bay to the west and the meandering Snohomish River and its sloughs to the north and east. From nearly every point in the downtown area one can see the sunrise over the Cascade Mountains from Mount Baker to south of Stevens Pass and the sunset over the Olympic Mountains. The Everett peninsula was also the home to some of the largest trees in the world. Western Red Cedar and Douglas Fir grew to over two hundred feet tall and over a dozen feet in diameter. The slightly smaller Western Hemlock was also plentiful. It was estimated in 1900 that Snohomish County, which included the City of Everett, had 9,000,000,000 feet of standing timber available to be harvested. And harvest they did. By the time the Fosheim family moved south from the Stanwood area to Everett the entire peninsula had been logged off and much of it was just a truncated forest of large stumps.

The Clark Park stump house was an example of the huge trees that grew on the Everett peninsula. It was sent to the St. Louis World's Fair in 1904 to represent the City of Everett. Upon its return to town it sat in Clark Park for decades before being removed when new tennis courts were built. Unfortunately this stump was a Douglas Fir so much of it had rotted away and it was eventually disposed of.

The Clark Park stump house. *Everett Public Library.*

Loggers cutting a giant Douglas Fir tree in Everett, late 1800s. *Postcard.*

In addition to the abundance of trees for the lumber industry, the nearby mountains, and the Monte Cristo area in particular, contained gold and silver bearing ores. When discovered these riches attracted the east coast mining interests. John D. Rockefeller was convinced to put up the money and the Everett & Monte Cristo Railway was created in March, 1892. Construction began almost immediately and the winding route from Puget Sound towards the center of the Cascades was completed in 1893.

The Everett & Monte Cristo Railway in the Robe Canyon showing tunnel number five in 1894. *University of Washington Libraries, Special Collections, LAR305.*

The Everett & Monte Cristo Railway started in Everett and traveled upstream following the Snohomish River to Snohomish. It then passed through Lake Stevens and Granite Falls before steeply climbing up the Robe Canyon and following the South Fork of the Stillaguamish River toward Monte Cristo. Once the route led into the Robe Canyon the construction became extremely difficult. Much rock blasting and clearing had to be completed and numerous tunnels were built. It took months just to complete the difficult route survey.

Today the Robe Canyon has an impressive hiking trail that closely follows part of the old railroad route. The rails are long gone but much of the concrete that the railroad ties and the rails were set into still remains. It's amazing that this route could have been built over a century ago. The work that went into this project is staggering and still impresses today. One can even now see the struggle that went on between some determined men and Mother Nature.

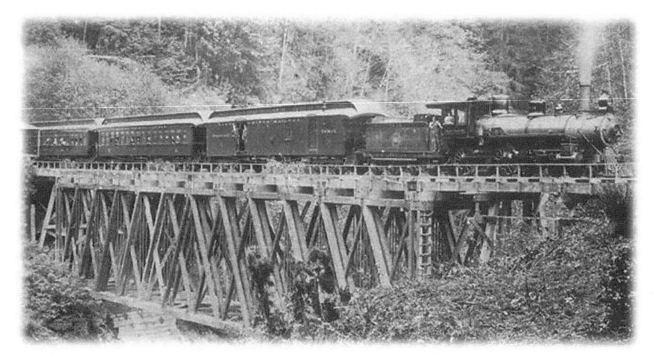

Steam locomotive and cars heading from Monte Cristo down to Granite Falls in 1904. *Postcard.*

Monte Cristo gas car entering a tunnel in 1916. *Seattle Public Library.*

The railroad soon prospered and brought in freight revenue by transporting miners, supplies and machinery to the mining camps. On the return trip the train carried ore concentrates from the mines for smelting in Everett. On May 11, 1915, the Rucker Brothers signed a ten-year lease with the Northern Pacific to use the Monte Cristo branch for their logging operations. They renamed it the Hartford Eastern Railway Company. Eventually the line also became a popular tourist route.

The Everett based Rucker Brothers built the impressive Inn at Big Four Mountain and wealthy guests were transported in gas cars or rail busses from Everett for a scenic getaway. Ultimately a slow economy, a constantly flooding river, and a reduced mining industry led to a shutdown of the Monte Cristo railroad line.

Hartford Eastern Railway car in front of the Big Four Inn in 1923. *University of Washington Libraries. Special Collections, UW2055.*

Wyatt and Bethel Rucker near Everett. *Everett Public Library.*

Dad and I drove up to the sight of the historic Big Four Inn many times but I never got to see it as it burned to the ground in an unfortunate fire in 1949 just a couple of years before I was born. We used to go up to the area every year and hike up the trail to the base of Big Four Mountain and explore the ice caves that formed at the foot of the steep cliffs. It's one of the most beautiful and easily accessible hikes in the area. All that is left at the inn site today is the large stone fireplace which still stands tall as a reminder of the past.

The Rucker Brothers, Wyatt J. Rucker (1857-1931) and Bethel J. Rucker (1862–1945), made up one of Everett's most prominent founding families. Jane Morris Rucker (1830–1907) and her sons moved from Noble County, Ohio to Tacoma, Washington in 1888.

The brothers quickly recognized that the heavily wooded peninsula that would become Everett was the ideal place to relocate to and invest in land. They combined their efforts with Tacoma lumberman Henry Hewitt Jr. (1840-1918) who brought eastern investors fronted by Charles L. Colby (1839-1896) and Colgate Hoyt (1849–1922) who represented multi-billionaire oil magnate John D. Rockefeller (1839-1937). In addition to their real estate holdings, the Rucker family had interests in several banks and prospered in the timber industry.

The Rucker family tomb in Evergreen Cemetery, Everett, Washington.

The imposing Rucker family tomb rises more than thirty feet above one of the highest points in the historic Evergreen Cemetery just south of downtown Everett. The Rucker brothers and numerous family members' remains lie inside the tomb. The large stone structure contains twenty-two crypts along three of its interior walls. In addition to being one of the most impressive private tombs in the country it also is known for its haunting presence and as a site that draws younger people who climb to its top as an Everett rite of passage.

I don't know if Dad ever climbed to the top of Rucker's Tomb, but I suspect like most Everett kids he did. I've been to the top a couple times and it is steep. Climbing up isn't too tough but once one reaches the top and realizes how steep its stepped sides really are it sends a chill up one's spine. Getting back down is the challenge. The tomb is one of a kind and deserves to be treated in a respectful manner.

Henry Hewitt Jr., Charles L. Colby, and John D. Rockefeller all had an influence on early Everett history. *Everett Public Library*.

Everett's economy had its highs and lows over the early years but the Eastern money kept rolling in. A beautiful old growth forest turned into muddy trails, eventually streets, and finally a modern looking city in just a couple of decades. Some Scandinavians became miners and fishermen but like John Fosheim, most of them worked as loggers or in the many lumber mills.

By 1900 Everett was proudly known as the 'City of Smokestacks' with fourteen lumber and shingle mills in operation. Its population had grown to almost 8,000 in less than ten years and Snohomish County had increased to 30,000. Another slogan for the young city of Everett was 'The Pittsburgh of the West.' Today Everett is proudly known by many as 'The Evergreen City.' The towering smokestacks are now gone and replaced by the roar of the many Boeing jets making their first test flight after rolling out of the largest building in the world.

Colgate and Lida Hoyt. *Library of Congress*.

Wind-Jammers loading lumber at the Clark-Nickerson Lumber Co. dock in Everett, 1901. *Everett Public Library*.

The McWilliams and Henry Mill was located at 36th Street, Everett, Washington, along the bank of the Snohomish River in 1910. *Everett Public Library*.

Sawmill workers in Everett at the time labored in a hazardous environment with long hours, low pay, and frequent shut downs. The shingle mills were often closed down during the winter months leaving workers without a paycheck. Mill worker safety was not even a consideration and accidents were almost a daily occurrence. There was no worker compensation to cover missed days, weeks, or even months. Of the 224 people who died in Everett in 1909, thirty-five were killed in accidents in the mills. John Fosheim was entering into a dangerous profession when he got his first steady job at the Clark-Nickerson mill on Everett's busy waterfront.

Seaside Shingle Mill workers in Everett in 1907. Notice the shingle weaver sawing the cedar bolt on the left. His hands are just inches from the unprotected circular saw blade. *Everett Public Library*.

By the early 1900s one could travel along the Everett peninsula from Pigeon Creek on the south end of the bay all the way around to Lowell on the Snohomish River to the east and pass nothing but mills. There were dozens of smokestacks and sawdust burning towers along the waterfront and the billowing black smoke that covered the sky was a sign of a strong economy and steady work.

Everett was a noisy town. The constant noise resonating up the bluffs from the many sawmills continued all day long. There would be a brief break for lunch but the noise sometimes didn't even let up at night if the economy was good. Huge logs were constantly being moved around the mill. The first stop would be in the bark removal area which could be deafening if it was done by a machine. Then the log would have to be sawed into various lengths and into timbers or boards. The boards would be manually stacked after coming down the green chain and readied for the dry kiln.

After lumber is dried it is often planed to a specific thickness and then it's loaded on a wagon, in a boxcar, or maybe on a ship which delivers it to its final destination. If the logs were cedar they usually ended up at the shingle mills where they were cut to length and then manually pushed past a huge circular saw by a worker called a shingle weaver. The cedar shingles were then bundled up for shipping. The population of Everett enjoyed the sounds of the saw mills as it indicated another paycheck was on the way.

The Marysville Transfer Company truck with a load of cedar shingles. *Snohomish County.*

John Fosheim like most immigrants to America was a hard worker. He worked ten hour days, six days a week at the mill. Running machinery in the mills was the most hazardous position. Often the machines were not maintained properly or were used well beyond their useful years. Saws had no safety guards like they have today and many work areas were not well lit. An employer's responsibly to his workers did not extend beyond a paycheck.

"Of course they ended up in sawmills, Weyerhaeuser, working hard. Those were the days when they walked to work; lots of walking."

John and all of his friends worked in the Everett mills. Early in the morning he walked down the hill to work and in the evening he walked back up to his home. Lunch was a simple sandwich and coffee carried in his lunch pail. Wages were around twenty cents an hour, the street car cost five cents, and postage for a letter was a penny. What little relaxing time John had was spent with the family and taking care of the home. His entire paycheck went to supporting his growing family. There was rarely any money available for enjoyment.

Anna would spend most of every day in her kitchen. Clothes needed washing and food had to be prepared for the day, the week, or the month. A walk to the corner grocery store to pick up food or other necessities got her out of the home. Shopping was usually done at the same store and a bill was paid off at the end of every month. Many of the purchased goods were delivered to a home by kids on bicycles or by horse and wagon. All the married women stayed at home taking care of their kids as the husbands worked primarily at the mills. It was common to keep a cow in the yard or nearby vacant lot for milk and a few chickens for eggs. Every day was the same except for Sunday when the family may have gone to church, visited with friends, or possibly in the summer had a picnic.

2425 Norton Avenue (see arrow) in the early 1950s looking west. *Jack C. O'Donnell Collection.*

John, Anna and the two boys moved to Everett in early 1911 and rented a small home at 2425 Norton Avenue just across the street from the railroad tracks and the waterfront. A baby sister, Emma Mathilde Fosheim, was born on January 5, 1912. One of the first things the family invested in was a new Singer sewing machine purchased at 1817 Hewitt in March of 1912. Anna paid fifty-six dollars after receiving a six dollar trade in for her old machine. She paid three dollars down and agreed to pay three dollars a month until it was paid off.

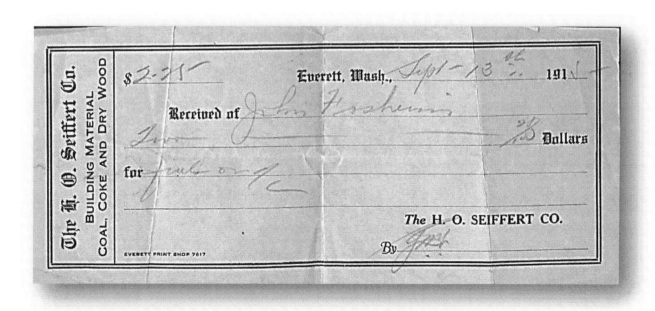

John Fosheim's receipt for fire wood from the H. O. Seiffert Company in 1912.

The Fosheim family was on a tight budget but John was finally working regularly and making more money than he ever did in his life. The lumber economy was good at the time and the family could enjoy some of life's necessities a little better than they could in Norway. Plus there was always the hope that they could afford to buy a home of their own someday. John bought fire wood from the H. O. Seiffert Company and furniture from the Barron Furniture Company and tried to save a small amount of his paycheck for the uncertain future.

John Fosheim's Barron Furniture Company receipt from July 20, 1912.

Barron Furniture Company Inc. on Hewitt Avenue and Walnut Street, Everett in 1892. *Everett Public Library*.

When one walked the streets of Everett one would hear many different languages spoken between the newly arrived Swedish, Norwegians, Germans, and others. Parents would speak to their young kids in their native language and the children would answer back in English. Society lived simpler lives with few laws and less government. No unemployment benefits or social security checks arrived by mail. Churches, family, and friends took care of any hardships that came about.

The City of Everett has no central town square and no statues dedicated to its founding fathers but as one walks its streets many important names stand out. Rucker, Hoyt, Colby, Wetmore, and Rockefeller line the central core of downtown from north to south and Everett and Hewitt are two main business routes from east to west. Other minor streets also reflect names from Everett's founding figures, including Butler, Friday, Kromer, McDougall, Smith, and Hill.

Downtown Everett in 1909. The intersection of Colby Avenue and Hewitt Avenue looking east. *Postcard.*

Andrew Carnegie. *Carnegie Corperation of New York*

Everett Washington was a rapidly growing city when the Fosheim family finally came together in America. In 1910 the impressive new Everett High School opened and the Everett to Seattle Interurban began its inaugural rail service. Another of the beautiful buildings in Everett was the new Carnegie Library built in 1905 at 3101 Oakes Avenue. Architect A. F. Heide created a design based on McKim, Mead and White's Boston Public Library and the Carnegie Library in Pomona, California. The library was built with a $25,000 Carnegie grant.

The Everett Carnegie Library at 3001 Oakes Avenue in 1905. *Postcard*.

In 1881when there were only a few public libraries in the world, multi-millionaire steel industrialist Andrew Carnegie began to promote his idea to offer to fund the building of libraries in communities across American and overseas. Carnegie went on to spend over $56 million to build 2,509 libraries in communities both large and small throughout the English-speaking world. When Carnegie died in 1919 over half of the public libraries in the United States were Carnegie Libraries. Carnegie eventually gave away ninety percent of his wealth, over $350 million to his multiple charities.

The Fosheim's were trading their rural lifestyle for one of the fastest growing small towns in the country. Though often wet with around forty inches of rain a year, the climate was mild in the winter and comfortable in the summer. The natural beauty of the area was unmatched, though there was little time for working families to enjoy it. There was usually work available at a decent wage for the times and property was readily available and fairly cheap. Early Everett had banks, restaurants, bars, and a large variety of stores to serve its citizens. Everett seemed like a good place to raise a family and maybe even move up in the world.

Everett business owner F. B. Hawes wrote an essay which appeared in the October 1907 issue of Coast Magazine which was published in Seattle. The essay was titled 'Anything to Boost Everett' and included the following suggestions on what Everett needed for the future:

good natured people only, fairly ambitious people, people who have good business sense and some money, and a limited number of women who could make good wives or until they met their 'affinity' could do a good 'stunt' at general house work.

President Taft rides in the back of a Pierce Arrow on Hewitt Avenue and Walnut Street in October 1911. *Everett Public Library*.

In 1911 President Taft visited Everett (Teddy Roosevelt had previously visited in May 1903) and the Milwaukee Road began freight service to Everett. There were more indications that Everett was becoming an important labor city as Socialist presidential candidate Eugene Debs visited in 1912. One of Everett's favorite sons, future congressman and Senator Henry M. 'Scoop' Jackson, was born in 1912. Like Raymond Fosheim, Jackson's parents also immigrated to America from Norway. News from other parts of the globe included the sinking of the RMS Titanic on her ill-fated maiden voyage with Captain Edward Smith in command.

Congressman Henry M. Jackson in 1940. *University of Washington, Special Collections, HMJ0289*.

President Taft speaking in front of Everett High School on October 9, 1911. *Everett Public Library*.

It's not known if the Fosheim family was in the large cheering crowd at Everett High School or along Hewitt Avenue when President Taft motored by on October 9, 1911, but it must have been quite a sight. The 300 plus pound Taft sat in the rear of local lumber baron David Marston Clough's Pierce Arrow touring car as it slowly motored down the street with a distinct droop at its rear.

The city of Everett was considered by many to be the leading logging, lumber, and shingle producer of not only the Northwest but the world. The city's population more than tripled from approximately 8,000 in 1900 to nearly 25,000 in 1910. In January 1900, Frederick Weyerhaeuser and his partners purchased 900,000 acres of Washington state timberland from the Northern Pacific Railway in the largest private land transaction up to that time. Weyerhaeuser built his first mill in Everett and it was the largest lumber mill in the world.

Frederick Weyerhaeuser. *The Weyerhaeuser Company*.

Several more timber industrialists had also relocated in the Everett area. The large Clough-Hartley Mill soon dominated the waterfront by the bay and others joined in. David M. Clough and Roland H. Hartley were two of the most interesting and influential business men in Everett in the early 1900s.

David Marston Clough
Minnesota Historical Society

Roland Hill Hartley
Washington State Archives

David M. Clough was Minnesota's thirteenth governor before moving to Everett in 1900 at the urging of the formidable railroad entrepreneur and fellow Minnesotan James J. Hill to establish a lumber operation. Clough arrived in one of Hill's private rail cars to search out the best location for his business. The lure of cheap timber and free land for a mill site made Everett the perfect location. The former logger and politician built a sawmill with his son-in-law Roland H. Hartley and advocated the interests of the mill owners against their employees' persistent unionization efforts.

Roland Hill Hartley served as mayor of Everett, in the Washington state legislature and as governor. He was also a major player in the logging and lumber business in Everett. He married David M. Clough's daughter Nina and was a partner in the Clough-Hartley mill, the world's largest producer of red cedar shingles. He also owned an interest in the Clark-Nickerson Lumber Company where John Fosheim worked for a short time. The Clough and Hartley families built impressive homes on Rucker Avenue overlooking their mills below.

As the bayside became the focus of industry in Everett the 14th Street Dock was built in 1892 by the Everett Land Company. The impressive wooden wharf extended approximately 2,000 feet west supported by hundreds of wood pilings above the tidelands near the mouth of the Snohomish River. The dock connected to the Seattle & Montana Railway that had been completed by James Jerome Hill in 1891.

One of the most significant events in the growth of Everett was the decision by the Great Northern Railway to come to the young city from Minneapolis and connect with the new Seattle & Montana Railway north-south route. The cross-country railroad line was the result of one man's dream, J. J. Hill. Hill was known as the 'Empire Builder' because of his capacity to create thriving businesses where none previously existed along his new railroad line. When J. J. Hill finally visited the

James Jerome Hill. *Minnesota Historical Society*

small town of Everett one can only imagine what he thought the future may look like.

Construction of the Pacific Coast extension of the Great Northern line westward from the Havre, Montana area began in 1890 just as Everett was becoming an established small town. The final spike in the line was driven up in the Cascade Mountain range near Scenic, Washington, on January 6, 1893, completing the transcontinental project. Scandinavians were known as hard workers and contributed heavily to the building of the Great Northern line to Everett. Hill said 'Give me Swedes and snoose and I'll build a railroad to hell.' Hill had 3,000 men working twelve hour days, seven days a week at two dollars a day on the Stevens Pass to Everett segment of his line.

The Great Northern Railway logo.

By the summer of 1893 Everett was linked to the East by regular service but to the dismay of the Everett investors Hill also continued his line to Seattle. Even with the competition from the larger city of Seattle, Everett became a major hub for the Great Northern line. Two dozen mills soon lined the shoreline of the Everett peninsula both on Port Gardner Bay and on the Snohomish River.

The Great Northern Railroad station on Bond Street in Everett. *Postcard.*

A small railroad station was built down on the Everett waterfront but was soon replaced by a magnificent Mission Style building in 1910. Also by 1910 the Great Northern had completed a seven block long tunnel underneath downtown Everett which bypassed the rails around the peninsula and shortened their route through town by five miles. Work on the tunnel had begun as early as 1893 but was delayed by a railway strike in 1894. Dirt was moved out of the tunnel on a short electric narrow gage line with a locomotive and cars and dumped where Norton Avenue is today. The wooden beam supported tunnel opened in 1900 and was strengthened with concrete by 1910.

James J. Hill took over the Everett Improvement Company from the Rockefeller interests in 1899 to help make Everett, his young railroad town, a more profitable community. Hill needed a good young business man he had confidence in to handle his Everett holdings. The man he chose was forty-two year old John T. McChesney (1857-1922) who had been a bank president, mayor of Aberdeen, South Dakota, and head of the syndicate that organized Chattanooga, Tennessee. McChesney's leadership focused on improving the local utilities, including water, electric light, power, and the trolley lines. After the Rucker Tomb the McChesney Columbarium is the most imposing structure in Everett's Evergreen Cemetery. It sits in a private section on a knoll at the cemetery's highest point of 229.5 feet above sea level.

The Great Northern Railway tunnel east portal in Everett in 1900. *Everett Public Library.*

The McChesney Columbarium in Evergreen Cemetery.

John T. McChesney. *Everett Public library*

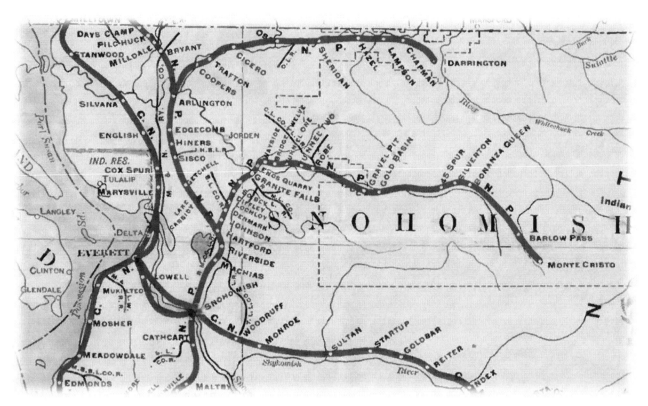

Railroad Commission Map of the State of Washington in 1908. The Great Northern Railway is shown in green passing through Everett and the Northern Pacific is shown in red to the east passing through Snohomish and Arlington. *Washington State Archives.*

The Wellington Disaster, March 1910. *Washington State Archives.*

Tragedy struck the Great Northern in late February of 1910, just a couple of years after John Fosheim travelled the same route to Everett. The seven car Great Northern passenger local #25 and the fast freight #27 were stopped heading west at Wellington, close to Stevens Pass in the center of the Cascade Mountains, by a huge snow storm. The trains were held at the siding for six long days as the storm continued and the snow piled higher.

On March 1 suddenly the entire snow drift above the parked trains came down the mountainside burying everything in the valley below. The trains were carried down the hillside, buried, and destroyed and ninety-six lives were lost in one of the worst disasters in the history of the Northwest. Anna, Martin, and John A. Fosheim traveled on the Great Northern Oriental Limited passenger train on the same route to Everett later that year.

Great Northern Railway Oriental Limited advertisement. *Great Northern Railway.*

The memories of the Wellington Disaster still haunt the area over a century later. The Great Northern built the 7.8 mile New Cascade Tunnel, the longest train tunnel in the United States, beginning in 1926 and opening in 1929, to bypass the slide area. The passenger carrying Empire Builder, the top transcontinental passenger train of the Great Northern line, began operating a daily service between Chicago and Everett the year the tunnel opened.

The Milwaukee Road and the Northern Pacific transcontinental railroads also came to Everett in the early 1900s to help move both passengers and freight through the fast growing city.

The Milwaukee Road and Northern Pacific Railway logos.

The Great Northern Railway Oriental Limited travelling along Puget Sound between Everett and Seattle in 1909. *Postcard.*

By the early 1900s, a dozen small shingle mills lined both sides of the 14th Street Dock. Numerous large mills lined the tide flats both north and south of the dock: CB Lumber and Shingle at 9th Street, Jamison Mill at 10th, Hulbert Mill at 14th, Clough-Hartley at 18th, and Robinson Mill at 21st. The mills turned out boxcar loads of cedar shingles by the day.

Saw mills soon ringed almost the entire Everett peninsula and on the bluffs above the saw mills were blocks and blocks of millworker homes built side by side. Every morning the mill whistles would blow at either six or seven a.m. to wake up the workers and an hour later they would blow to begin the work day. Each mill whistle had its own distinctive sound, easily identified by the locals. Thousands of mill workers would walk down streets or staircases to their mills to begin another grueling day. Everett became a city of stairways. The mills and industries were built on the waterfront surrounding the Everett peninsula and numerous stairways dropped down from the millworker's homes on the bluffs above. There could be just a dozen steps or the stairs could number upwards to one hundred on a long stairway such as the one gliding down from the west end of 19th street at Grand Avenue. The stairways were full in the early morning and the late evening as the workers commuted to and fro.

The 14th Street dock and shingle mills on Everett's water front looking west. *Everett Public Library*.

As workers walked back to their homes at night one could often tell what job they had. Were they covered with sawdust or were they sweaty with soot covered arms and faces? One could readily identify a group of shingle weavers by their missing fingers. I'll never forget meeting so many older men when I was a kid with a finger or even multiple fingers missing. Dad worked with lumber the majority of his life and never lost a finger. He was one of the few lucky ones.

Eighty-four inch diameter log deck swing cut-off saw erected by the Ebey Slough Shingle Company. *Everett Public Library*.

Shingle weaver with missing fingers. *I. W. W. Publishing Bureau, Chicago, Ill.*

The 14th Street dock and the railway below the bluff looking northwest. *Everett Public Library*.

Everett workers enjoying drinks after a long day at the mill. Notice the left hand of the man in front has multiple missing fingers indicating he probably was a shingle weaver. A Ringling Brothers Circus poster hangs on the rear wall advertising a performance in Everett on August 20th, 1907. *Everett Public Library*.

With three young kids now and a somewhat steady job, Anna and John Fosheim decided to move from their small one-room apartment on Norton Avenue across town to a little home on Baker Avenue in October, 1912. The home was located on the far north end of the rapidly developing city.

John, John, Martin, Anna, and Emma Fosheim at 1515 Baker Avenue in 1913.

> "They had three children: Martin, John, and Emma. Then, when they got to 15th and Baker, I was born in the house and soon after my two younger sisters, LaVern and Olivia. We lived there about fourteen years, eight people in a small four-room house."

The Fosheim family continued to grow as a third brother, Raymond Margato Fosheim was born in the little home at 1515 Baker Avenue in north Everett on Thursday January 22, 1914. How did a Norwegian get an Italian middle name? Apparently John became close friends with an Italian fellow while working at the sawmill, and Raymond was named after him. Raymond was baptized at the Evangelical Lutheran Church of America on April 25, 1915.

During Raymond Fosheim's birth month of January of 1914 the first steamboat passed through the Panama Canal and Henry Ford doubled his workers hourly pay to five dollars, reduced the work day to eight hours, and began the Model T assembly line. Woodrow Wilson was President. The French President and the German Ambassador were dining together for the first time in many years but trouble was on the horizon.

A festive occasion in front of Sheraton Ford at 2719 Colby Avenue, Everett, advertising the Princess Theater which opened in 1913 at 2822 Colby Ave. *Sheraton Collection.*

Raymond Fosheim at two years old.

In 1916, as Raymond turned two years old, the city of Everett had a claimed population of almost 35,000 and was experiencing deep labor turmoil within its huge sawmill industry. Everett was a mill town and it was run by a small but powerful group of lumber barons who owned the mills. Labor unions were active and always trying to organize the mill workers.

There were 2,000 strikes across America in the first seven months of 1916. The most out spoken and radical of the unions was the Industrial Workers of the World or Wobblies.

In 1916 union and management clashes in the mills became more and more frequent. A group of forty Seattle street-speaking members of the Industrial Workers of the World or Wobblies had been taken by deputies to an area known as Beverly Park in south Everett where they were brutally beaten and told to get out of town. Despite severe injuries, some were forced to walk the twenty-five mile interurban track route back to Seattle.

Steamboat Verona. *Pacific Steamboats, Superior Publishing 1958.*

Sunday, November 5, 1916 marked the bloodiest battle in Pacific Northwest labor history. Approximately 300 armed Wobblies boarded the passenger steamers Verona and Calista on the Seattle waterfront and headed north to Everett. The I.W.W. planned an afternoon public demonstration on the corner of Hewitt Avenue and Wetmore Avenue, a spot commonly used by street speakers. The Wobblies were showing support for Everett's workers and hoping to gain converts to their dream of one big union.

Word reached Everett that a group of armed anarchists were coming to burn down the town. 200 citizen deputies, under the authority of well-respected, Snohomish County Sheriff Donald McRae, met down on the docks at the base of Hewitt to repel the invaders. The Verona arrived first, overloaded with singing Wobblies, and pulled in alongside the dock. Suddenly a single shot was fired, directly followed by volleys of chaotic shooting. Wobblies aboard the Verona wildly rushed to the opposite side of the ship, nearly capsizing the vessel. The Captain of the Verona ducked behind a metal safe. It was a fortuitous move as later 175 bullet holes were found in the pilot house alone. The captain struggled to back the ship out of port. The Calista quickly turned around and returned to Seattle, without trying to land.

I.W.W. poster. *Industrial Workers of the World.*

On the dock, two deputies lay dying, and twenty others, including the sheriff, were wounded. While the official I.W.W. toll was listed as five dead and twenty-seven wounded, as many as twelve Wobblies probably lost their lives, their bodies disappeared into the water and were mysteriously removed at a later date. The Everett Massacre appeared in Newspapers across the country. Today it is still listed as one of the significant events in the history of the USA during 1916.

The Everett Massacre 1916. *Jay Mason Art.*

I.W.W teamster T. H. Tracy was acquitted of murdering Deputy Beard. *Everett Public Library.*

Everett was truly a union stronghold with all its blue collar jobs in the mills and supporting industries. The years leading up to the Everett Massacre marked the highpoint of union strength. The Socialist Party was also strong in Everett in the early teens. The Commonwealth newspaper, a socialist weekly, was published in Everett from 1911 to 1914. It was replaced by The Washington Socialist published from 1915 to 1917 and finally The Co-operative News in 1918 before disappearing. John Fosheim rarely spoke of politics but was a life-long union member and spent many hours on the picket line.

Deputy Jefferson Beard was killed in the Everett Massacre. *Everett Public Library.*

Everett Massacre Headline in The Everett Daily Herald. *Everett Public Library.*

IWW Massacre remembrance. *Everett Public Library.*

Industrial Worker newspaper, Seattle, November 25, 1916. *Industrial Worker.*

WOULD YOU GIVE TEN CENTS TO MAKE A SOCIALIST?

Well, Here's a Plan That Promises Well.

We want every person who reads this notice to send 10 cents to the Commonwealth by return mail, along with the name and address of some friend or neighbor. And we will send him or her a copy of the Commonwealth for one month, chock full of absolutely convincing Socialist propaganda. By the end of the month your friend or neighbor will be interested sufficiently to pay for a year's subscription on his own account, which seals his doom as an old party voter, and your Socialist is made—all for ten cents!

Will you not send it in right now?

To the Washington Socialist Publishing Co., 1612 California Ave., Everett, Wash.:

(Send the 10 cents with this coupon.)

Comrades—Enclosed find 10 cents for one month's trial subscription to the Commonwealth, which send to the address below.

From the Commonwealth newspaper in 1914. *Everett Public Library.*

Labor and management violence wasn't the only trouble the Everett workers had to endure. Everett could also be described as the city of fires. With all the lumber, sawdust, and wood chips seemingly covering most of the town, the threat of fires was very real. The Everett fire department has over the years had it work cut out for it. Dozens of fires have raged in the city resulting in the loss of small businesses all the way up to the loss of entire mills. Even the young city's new county court house burned to the ground. The Everett Theatre was also destroyed in a fire but like the court house was rebuilt.

Anna and John Fosheim were very proud of their adopted country and both learned to speak English quite well, particularly after the kids started school. One wonders what they thought of the constant labor-management clashes that dominated their newly adopted and rapidly growing town. They were after all country people from the farmlands of rural Verdal, Norway. It must have been a proud day in the Fosheim household when John and Anna became naturalized United States citizens on August 1, 1918.

> *"He worked at Clark-Nickerson mill on the bay, and Weyerhaeuser Mill B; he was there forty-three years at Mill B, a long time. He worked on the green chain, mostly taking lumber off the chain, from what I hear, and that's considered a pretty hard job."*

The Clark-Nickerson Lumber Company Everett, WA in 1915. *Everett Public Library*.

Working on the green chain was hard work for John Fosheim but even worse, it's terribly boring. After leaving the saw the 'green' rough-cut heavy boards, often eight feet long with varying widths, slide sideways down a long chain to the stacking area. Workers move fast as they grab the heavy boards off the conveyer chain and sort them onto the various piles according to the quality grade of the lumber. The boards keep coming without time for a break and one can't talk to the other workers because of the screeching noise of the saw and the nearby chipper.

A long wide green chain at Pacific Spruce Corporation, Oregon in 1924. *Pacific Spruce Corporation.*

Green chain workers can be easily distinguished by their strong, muscular arms built up as they perform the most grueling work in the mill. New hires are often put on the green chain as an entry-level position in a mill. Working on the green chain is a highly skilled position however where fast judgment is necessary. A worker goes through many heavy leather gloves on the job and one long sliver can be a dangerous proposition that can cause a painful and even permanent injury. Eight or even ten hours a day on the green chain can be tedious work leaving one's mind to wander but that can lead to trouble.

Once a stack of lumber reaches a certain height a forklift operator must be signaled for to move the lumber and make room for the next load. The stack of green lumber is then moved to a kiln for drying at high temperature.

John Fosheim, family friend Oscar Solem, and co-workers on a break at Weyerhaeuser Mill B in Everett in 1918.

When Raymond Fosheim was two years old on January 31, 1916, Everett experienced one of its largest snow storms in recorded history. The snow kept falling for three days without a pause until more than thirty inches filled the streets. Many outlying areas reported considerably more including forty-two inches in Snohomish and forty-eight inches in Marysville. The Stillaguamish and Snohomish rivers were covered with ice and businesses, schools and transportation shut down, including the Interurban trolley. One could even drive their Model T across the thick ice on Silver Lake south of Everett.

Hewitt Avenue downtown during the big snow storm of 1916. *The Everett Herald.*

The early history of Everett's growth was a story of many booms and recessions. The Great War started in Europe in 1914, the year Raymond was born. The passage of immigration restrictions during the Great War ended the massive influx of European immigrants and Everett's rapid population growth that lead to a cheap labor pool. Only 16 homes were built in Everett during 1918 but the early 1920s saw a huge demand for timber fueled by the 1923 Japan earthquake. This economic boom lasted into 1926.

The lumber industry dominated early Everett's economy but the ship building industry was also present. On December 21, 1891, the brand new freighter Charles W. Wetmore arrived in Everett with a load of machinery after a 15,000 mile journey from Wilmington, Delaware. The design of the dark, low, steel-hulled vessel was a major maritime innovation that was soon referred to as a whaleback. Her captain and designer, Alexander McDougall, backed by East Coast money, immediately announced he would set up the Pacific Steel Barge Company near the mouth of the Snohomish River where Weyerhaeuser Mill B would later sit.

Captain Alexander McDougall. *Duluth Trading Company.*

On October 24, 1894 the new whaleback, S.S. City of Everett, was launched into the Snohomish River followed by a huge ceremony. The vessel had an innovative hull made of steel, designed to carry maximum loads while resisting water and wind. The hull had a flat bottom and a rounded deck designed to shed the water of high waves as they passed over the low-lying ship. She was 346 feet long, forty-three feet wide and could haul 4,200 tons of cargo in its four holds. Unfortunately the S.S. City of Everett was the only whaleback built on the West Coast as the 1893 recession hit Everett hard. McDougall went on to build a total of forty-three whalebacks at his Great Lakes and other shipyards.

The launching of the S.S. City of Everett on October 24, 1894. *Everett Public Library.*

The S.S. City of Everett was the first American steamship to pass through the Suez Canal and had the distinction of being the first to circumnavigate the earth. She remained in service until while carrying molasses from Santiago, Cuba to New Orleans on 11 October 1923; she foundered in the Gulf of Mexico taking down her crew of twenty-six.

Early Everett's commercial fishing industry was also an important aspect of the small town's economic growth. Croatians and Norwegians were some of the earliest commercial fisherman but there were other fishing families from a broad range of cultures. Everett soon also had a local canning industry with the Everett Packing Corporation and American Packing Company operating on the waterfront around the time the Fosheim family arrived in town.

The S.S. City of Everett. *Everett Public Library.*

Part of the Everett fishing fleet on the waterfront in 1954. *The Everett Herald.*

The British three-masted schooner Bramloch loading wheat at the Everett harbor in early 1900. *Postcard.*

The Smith Shingle Mill at 11th & Hoyt Avenue in 1915. *Everett Museum of History.*

While most of the mills in the Everett area were on the waterfront to make transportation of their products easier some small mills like the Smith Shingle Mill operated up on the bluff on the outskirts of Everett. When the nearby supply of trees was finally gone the little mills soon disappeared to eventually to be replaced by the residential areas of the rapidly expanding city.

John K. Fosheim never had a chance to attend school into his teenage years in his homeland of Norway and he spent almost his entire life working hard in the mills of Everett to support his family. He had little time to get involved with politics, union activities, or social groups. Undoubtedly he would have loved to have money and the time to travel or delight in a new car and other luxuries, but he enjoyed a simple life with his wife, kids, and a handful of close friends.

I'll never know the hardships and the hard work that Dad and grandpa had to deal with. I do know what it is like to work in a sawmill though. I worked on the green chain at Smith Street Mill in Everett after I graduated from Everett High School during the summer of 1969. It was terribly boring and hard work. I made good money that summer but I swore that I would never work in a sawmill again. Thankfully I had the luxury of going to college.

The J. M. Sovde Company Skandinavisk Store. *Everett Museum of History.*

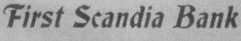

First Scandia Bank advertisement from the 1916 Everett Polk's Directory. *Polk's City Directories.*

The close-knit Scandinavian community in Everett welcomed new immigrants like the Fosheim Family. There were many resources available to make new arrivals to their new homeland welcome. Scandinavians had their own stores, churches, and social organizations to rely on as they assimilated into the American culture.

There many businesses in Everett that reflected their Scandinavian heritage such as: The Norway Hotel, The Norway Investment Company, The Norwegian-American S. S. Line, The Norway-Pacific Construction and Dry-dock Company and the First Scandia Bank.

One of Everett's main east-west streets, Pacific Avenue, in the early 1900s, about the time the Fosheim family arrived in town. The photo is looking east from Fulton Street. *Everett Public Library*.

Chapter III

Childhood Memories

"I go by where I was born, me and my two sisters, 1515 Baker, and I just stop and look around and remember things."

The Fosheim family was beginning to get a glimpse of the American dream. They still couldn't afford to buy a house of their own but their new rental home had a large yard and the children had plenty of room to play. There was even open pasture across the street that allowed them to eventually buy a cow for their daily milk. Anna Fosheim loved to garden so it wasn't long before the Fosheim's had their own fresh vegetables.

LaVern and Raymond Fosheim with Dewey at 1515 Baker Avenue in 1921

"Our address on Baker was 1515. It was pretty far north on a dead-end street, and the house we lived in, I see that they moved it in back, to the alley, and put another house in front."

The little house on Baker Avenue would be the Fosheim home for many years as the family became established in Everett. John was an excellent carpenter and he soon added a small porch for the front entryway. He and Anna put up a fence around the garden and planted a lawn. One of the first things they purchased for their new residence was furniture from the Smith & Boeshar, Inc. store. Partners M. M. Smith and L. J. Boeshar started a furniture sales business on the corner of Broadway and Hewitt avenues in 1900.

Advertisement and Receipt for furniture from Smith & Boeshar, Inc. purchased on May 10, 1913.

The Fosheim family continued to grow as sister LaVern Fosheim was born on June 13, 1915, and twins Eveline and Olivia were born on August 15, 1917. The Fosheim family's joy soon turned to despair as little Eveline died on August 31, just a couple of weeks old. It was a sad day when the family and close friends met for the memorial service. A neighbor decorated a little shoebox to use as a coffin and Eveline was laid to rest. I located Eveline's unmarked grave in the oldest part of Evergreen Cemetery in Everett a while back and her sister Olivia made arrangements to have a beautiful marker placed on it almost ninety years after Eveline's death.

The little home on Baker Avenue is still there but the address is now 1515 ½ since it has been moved to the rear of the lot adjacent to Fulton Street. A new home was then built in the front facing Baker Avenue after the Fosheim family moved. The City of Everett has expanded to the north but there is still a vacant large neighboring swampy and wooded area where Raymond used to explore and play.

Everett, Washington in about 1932, looking north of 13th street. The new Legion Memorial Golf Course is under construction in the top center. *Everett Public Library.*

"Of course we had an outdoor toilet when we first moved here. We had a cow, helped us get along, I guess; quite a few people had cows in those days. We had all that open space. Things were kind of tough then. My two oldest brothers, one of them helped, he worked delivery for the Orien Meat Market, at 19th and Broadway, and my other brother had paper routes and stuff, to help us get started. Of course they ended up working in a sawmill too, both of them, Weyerhaeuser Mill B. There was no Mill A then. Mill B was located at 5th and Walnut, down on the flats. The bridge is there still out at the point, where the street car turned around. Oh, yeah, things were pretty rough."

Andrew N. Orien had a small meat market on 1823 Broadway in the 1920s and 30s. In those days there were locally owned businesses all over Everett and one could easily walk just a short distance from home to do their shopping. These small establishments were often referred to as the corner markets. Many are still in business at the same locations.

Weyerhaeuser Mill B, Everett, Washington in 1915. *Everett Public Library*.

"When we were real little we had those cow pastures; we fooled around in those cow pastures all of the time. Me and Floyd Dahl and Billy Sullivan, in all kinds of weather, and of course we had our dogs with us. My dog was a bull terrier, I'd call it, my sister called it too, and we had him all during my really early age, 'Dewey,' nice dog. We'd always play in the woods and climb trees and all that stuff around 15th and Baker. There were no houses then, north and east of there, except 16th Street, and then Baker ended right there at 14th or 15th. So we had a lot of places to run around."

LaVern, Raymond, and Olivia Fosheim, Billy Sullivan, and Floyd and Evelen Dahl in 1919.

Ole and Della Dahl raised their family next to the Fosheim's at 1523 Baker Street and John and Josephine Sullivan lived just north on 1507 Baker Street.

Emma Fosheim, Unidentified, Unidentified, Martin, Raymond, and John A. Fosheim, Unidentified on the front porch of 1515 Baker Avenue about 1918.

"In those days, there were a lot of horses around, too. I can faintly remember the big trucks, hard rubber tires and big chain drives. That was rare, it was mostly horses hauling wood; everybody burned wood, just about. Something to keep you busy, too. I had two older brothers that stacked our wood when I was real little, and my dad, of course. There was a lot of that, and taking care of the cows, and stuff. And so we had a lot of room to run around."

Washington Stove Works at 3402 Smith Avenue was one of Everett's early industries and came to the growing city from Michigan in 1903. The company manufactured stoves, ranges, heaters, furnaces, and custom iron castings and added diversity to the local economy.

This photo was produced by the J. A. Juleen Studio, one of Everett's most prolific and significant commercial photo studios from 1908 to 1954. John Juleen operated the business until his death in 1935 when his wife Lee took over. The studio produced thousands of Everett images which included a postcard collection in the 1930s. Juleen's first studio was located on the southwest corner of Hewitt and Colby but relocated in the downtown Everett area many times over the years. In 1923 he built a new studio at 2930 Rockefeller where he employed eight people. Luckily most of his photo collection has been preserved and serves as a wonderful history of early Everett.

The Washington Stove Works delivery truck in the early 1920s *Everett Public Library*.

The new Juleen Photo Shop at 2930 Rockefeller Avenue in 1923. *Everett Public Library.*

John A. Juleen. *Everett Public Library.*

"Our neighbors included Billy Sullivan. They had six children, Mr. and Mrs. Sullivan, just to the north of us. And then we had the Freed family south of us. Another boy I played with was Floyd Dahl. He grew up as strictly a horse rider at the fairs and stuff; he took care of horse racing, he was all interested in that. This was in the early twenties and the late teens."

"Billy Sullivan's father worked at the gas plant down on lower California Street. Floyd Dahl's dad was a painter and Floyd's uncle, Charlie Stone, gave me my first automobile ride. It was in an old Oakland, I remember, and that was something. It was pretty old; I remember that real well. He took us for rides, I remember what looked like a one-way street, but it seemed to me it was out on the far end of

Oakland "6" advertisement. *Oakland Motor Co.*

Lombard, going towards the cemetery, there was a dead-end street, it cut in to the Interurban track there. It was in my mind a lot to ride in that Oakland."

The Oakland Motor Company began building cars in Pontiac, Michigan in 1907. The company was purchased by General Motors in 1909 and offered a wide range of cars including some the first closed body models. In the 1920s sales fell off sharply and the company's name was changed to The Pontiac Motor Company.

"I remember, about the last year we lived there, they took out the street, 15th and Baker. They used horses and wagons in those days, to haul dirt and everything, and build new sidewalks on both sides, and then stairways and stuff. In those days, we all had gardens, and milk delivery by Cloverleaf Dairy, horse and wagon. They'd come and pour milk into a big pan Mother would have."

Riverside Dairy Farms truck and worker. *Everett Public Library*.

Eventually horses and buggies on the streets of Everett were replaced by Model T's and trucks. Wooden and steel wheels gave way to rubber tires on newly paved streets. There were few broken wheels but still many flat tires. Instead of being delivered in big pans it was delivered in small milk bottles.

> *"I remember when my youngest sister was born in 1917; I can still remember them wearing masks and that. That was the flu epidemic, terrible. I can remember the old wood stoves, the stove pipes were red hot, going across the room. A miracle there weren't more fires. Specially the Christmas tree, with the burning candles. I can't understand how they got by with that."*

In Scandinavian custom the Fosheim's had a traditional dinner and opened their presents on Christmas Eve. The tree was decorated with burning candles and homemade ornaments and trimmings. This was a wonderful time for the kids who each received one simple present, usually a homemade toy or something special to wear or eat.

It could be dangerous to burn some types of wood. Sometimes old railroad ties, pilings, and timbers were burned that were coated with creosote which could cause an exceedingly hot fire. Cedar was always readily available but it to burned extremely hot. During the winter the Fosheim family sometimes had to buy wood for their stove. John bought two loads from the H. O. Seiffert Company in January of 1913 for four dollars and fifty cents. The Seiffert wagon could often be seen making deliveries on the streets of Everett, first by horse drawn wagon and later by truck. The Everett fire department continually kept busy during the winter months.

For years the Fosheim family bought their groceries from fellow Norwegian Edward Ecklund on 2707 Wetmore. Ecklund would send a boy by the house to pick up a list of grocery needs from Anna and then return with the delivery. All bills would be paid at the end of every month.

John and Anna Fosheim also bought furniture from the Rice Furniture Company on 2801 Hewitt Avenue. Notice the spelling of Fosheim as Fossheim on the Rice Furniture Company receipt.

A Fosheim family grocery receipt from Edw. Ecklund.

Rice Furniture Company receipt from June 1915.

Washington Elementary School at 1717 Rockefeller Avenue in north Everett. *Postcard.*

"I started at Washington School in 1919. I remember the first grade teacher, Mrs. Montague, and the room. Then, third grade, I went to Garfield School for three years, and then North Junior. I went to school with Billy Solomon and Floyd Dahl. Some of the other kids who went there were Duane Wildy, his father was a policeman, and he ended up as a policeman also in later years, and Olaf and Johnny Solem. And there was a boy named Dick Dowdy, across the street too."

"Washington was the biggest school of all the Everett schools, first three grades."

Washington Elementary School in north Everett is no longer a school but still survives as the beautiful Washington Oakes Retirement Community.

Raymond's older brother John A. Fosheim's class at Washington Elementary School in about 1917. John is seated in the center of the photo (see arrow).

Raymond Fosheim, friend Norman R., Henrietta Martinsen and mother, John, LaVern, Anna, and Olivia Fosheim enjoying a Sunday picnic in Everett about 1920.

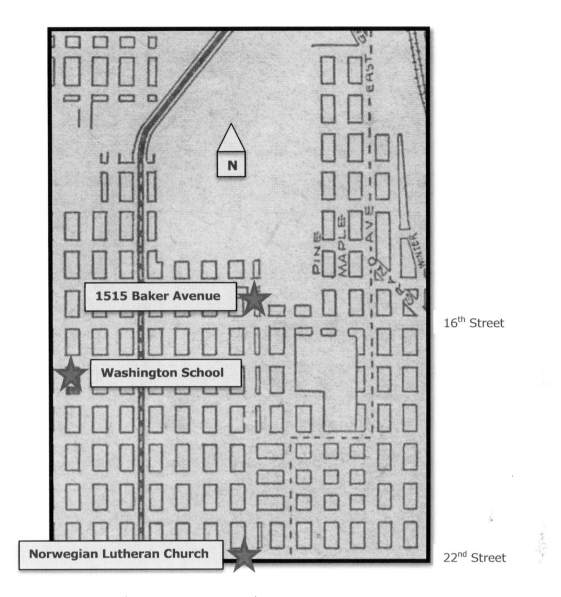

Map of north Everett from 8th Street south to 22nd Street and from Rockefeller Avenue east to State Street.

Chapter IV

The Riverside Neighborhood

"We moved in 1923 to 2202 Cleveland in the Riverside area, and that was quite a luxury for us."

The community of Riverside east of Broadway and south of 19th Street was a typical blue collar working-class neighborhood. Most of the men worked ten hour days, six days a week while the women toiled hard maintaining the home. In its early days it was quite a notorious waterfront district but soon became a genuine working-class neighborhood. Riverside is full of simple but well-built homes on single lots or if a little nicer on a lot and a half. A few larger homes were mixed in for the mill executives and managers. Almost everyone walked to work, the store, or anywhere else they needed to go.

Olivia and LaVern Fosheim with a friend at 2202 Cleveland Avenue in 1923.

John Fosheim must have been a very proud American when he purchased the home on Cleveland Avenue. This was the first piece of property he had ever owned. He was living the American dream where hard work made anything possible. I drove by 2202 Cleveland Avenue the other day and was shocked to see just a big hole in the ground. Someone tore the home down and a foundation is going in for a new house.

"It was a three-bedroom house; the three girls got one big bedroom upstairs. Us three boys got the other bedroom upstairs. There were two beds, us boys, the three of us, had two beds. I was the smallest one of the brothers, the youngest boy. I had two younger sisters, Laverne and Olivia."

LaVern, John, and Olivia Fosheim at 2202 Cleveland Avenue.

"When we moved to Cleveland, we took our cow with us, right in the nice neighborhood. The neighbors, of course I don't blame them, they made us get rid of it. But then everybody had chickens, and we brought our chickens with us in 1923. I can remember those chickens; and then we had a family of ducks, too. We got a laugh at the mother and father duck, they were the boss of all the chickens, they made the chickens all go in during the night; they were the last ones in the coop."

One of the neighborhood families was the MacGhee's from Oklahoma. They kept chickens in their bathtub and their mom chewed tobacco.

The neighborhood gang looking east at 2202 Cleveland about 1924. left to right: Wilma Anderson (later married LaVern's brother-in-law Claude), Emma Fosheim, LaVern Fosheim, Olivia Fosheim, Walt MacGhee, Sixton (Sag) Anderson, unidentified, unidentified, Raymond Fosheim with hand over his eyes, Arnold Hendrickson, and Herb (Hub) MacGhee.

We had a big yard. Then we had our wood piles; everybody was burning wood. It was my daily job, coming home from school, filling the wood box. I split it. I did a lot of work with wood. We bought a lot of mill ends from the mills. They were delivered by horse and buggy in those days, all through the twenties. I can still remember, even when we moved to 2620 up there, still was one dairy farmer who had a horse and buggy that late. Of course, that was the last one.

I'd meet George Erickson the driver for Pioneer Alpine in the restaurant once in a while, and talk to him. He died a couple of years ago, a nice fellow; we'd used to meet in the restaurant and visit awhile, all of the time. He drove a lot of truck, and horse and wagon.

Pioneer-Alpine Dairy truck on Pacific Avenue in Everett on December 23, 1925. They were located at 1905 Lombard Avenue, 26th and Broadway, and on Pacific Avenue. *Everett Public Library*.

Garfield Elementary School, 22nd and Walnut Street.
Everett Public Library.

Gertrude Jackson in the 1920s.
Jackson Family.

Life seemed simpler in Ray's childhood days. The family didn't have the time or money to travel. The best family time was spent eating together and talking. Ray attended Garfield school six hours a day and everyone walked to school. After school he would play marbles, play in the woods, take care of the woodpile, and mop the floors on Saturday. Even at a young age he loved working with wood.

> *"I can remember at the old Garfield, I had Mrs. Kopps and Scoop Jackson's sister in the fourth grade, Gertrude. In those days, there weren't hardly any men teachers, except at North Junior, there were the woodshop and the shop teachers. Otherwise, it was all women teachers. But there was one teacher at North Junior I liked so well, Mrs. Woods. She was real nice."*

Garfield was a beautiful school in its early days. It was unfortunately resurfaced over the red bricks and eventually lost to the wrecking ball. A generic modern single-story building sits adjacent to the site today. Across the intersection of 23rd and Walnut Street is the impressive two city block Garfield Park.

Raymond's school artwork dated February 11, 1930.

North Junior High School, 25th and McDougall Avenue. *Everett Public Library*.

Enoch Bagshaw *Everett Public Library*.

Dad attended North Junior High School for two years before leaving to join the workforce and help support the family. I also attended North Junior many years later. It was another magnificent three-story building that was destroyed and replaced with a new single-story plain unimaginative structure.

Adjacent to the north of North Junior High School is historic Bagshaw Field which takes up almost two city blocks. It's named for Enoch Bagshaw (1884-1930), a local football legend. Bagshaw was a Welsh immigrant and a player for Everett High School and the University of Washington before coaching football at both schools.

Bagshaw coached the Everett High School football team from 1911 to 1920 and it swiftly became powerhouse under Baggy's leadership. The 1919 team tied for the esteemed national high school football championship. During the following year, the amazing 1920 Everett team won the

Everett High School was an impressive site in 1910 and continues to be today. *Postcard*.

national title outright from Cleveland's East Tech High School. It was during that magnificent 1920 season when fans began greeting the seagulls flying over the field as symbols of certain victory. The seagull soon became the Everett High School mascot. Bagshaw went on the coach the University of Washington from 1921 to 1929 and led the team to their first-ever Rose Bowl victory. It was during the Bagshaw years that Raymond became a dedicated EHS and UW football fan even though he never had a chance to attend either school.

EHS vs Toledo on what is now Bagshaw Field on January 1, 1920. *Everett Public Library*.

1939 EHS mascot, Sammy Seagull. *Everett School District*.

Dad always dreamed of going to Everett High School but never had the chance. He constantly followed the EHS Seagulls in sports. Dad was a very intelligent guy, always reading and following world events. One would have never known that he only had an eighth grade education. Unfortunately the hard times prevented many young people from graduating from high school.

Raymond's school composition book.

"I had chores when I got home from school, always got wood in at night and then peeled potatoes. My friends were out in the street playing marbles, and I'd have to do chores first. I remember playing 'Duck on the Rock,' marbles, and then we rode our bicycles quite a bit on the empty lots and trails and stuff."

Duck on the Rock is a game that combines marksmanship and tag. It's played by placing a large rock (the 'duck') on top of a larger stone, a tree stump or a log. One player remains near the stone to guard it while the other players throw stones at the duck in an attempt to knock it off its perch. Once the duck is knocked off, the throwers all rush to retrieve their stones. If a player is tagged before returning back to the throwing line with his or her stone, they become the guard. The guard can't tag another player until he/she picks up a duck at his/her feet, nor can he/she chase anyone until he/she puts the original duck back up on its platform. The game of basketball may have been influenced by Duck on the Rock.

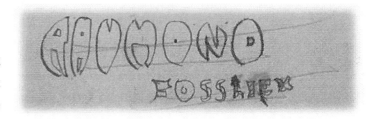

Raymond's doodling on his composition book. Even at this late date he spelled Fosheim with an extra 's'.

John, Raymond, and Emma Fosheim with friend Martha Anderson on the USS Oklahoma in 1923.

John Fosheim took full advantage of Sundays, his only day off after a hard week at the mill. He and Anna would try and enjoy time together with their family and friends. It was a big deal when the 27,500 ton battleship USS Oklahoma came into town for the 4th of July in 1923, so John took Raymond, Emma and a friend; all dressed in their Sunday best, down to tour the huge ship.

The USS Oklahoma, BB-37 at sea in 1925. *Postcard.*

The USS Oklahoma (BB-37) was a World War I era battleship. She and her sister, Nevada, were the first U.S. warships to use oil fuel instead of coal. The USS Oklahoma was commissioned in 1916 and served in World War I as an Allied convoy escort in the Atlantic. During peace time she served in both the United States Battle Fleet and Scouting Fleet and rescued American citizens and refugees from the Spanish Civil War. She visited Everett in 1923 while serving in the Pacific.

When young Raymond was on board the USS Oklahoma he was thoroughly enjoying the history that he loved. Little did he know that less than twenty years later the great ship would be destroyed in the first shots of a war that would change his life forever.

1920s celebration in the Everett harbor. Anna Fosheim is on the far right. Her close friend Henrietta Martinson is posing with the Violin. The other occupants are unidentified.

The Fosheim's were a close family and had many good friends mostly in the Scandinavian community in Everett. There were many causes for celebration to break up the monotony of the long work week. Along with the 4th of July, Thanksgiving and the other American holidays they also celebrated Norwegian holidays particularly Constitution Day. The celebration in Everett's harbor in the previous photo looks like nice break from everyday life. Henrietta H. Martinsen and her husband John H., who was a longshoreman, lived at 3431 Grand Avenue. The Martinsens were both born in Norway and were part of the close-knit Scandinavian community in Everett.

Bernt Øvrum, Henrietta Martinsen, and John and Anna Fosheim in Seattle.

Bernt Andreas Vinneval Øvrum, born in 1867, was Anna Fosheim's oldest brother and like her younger brother, Ole Øvrum, had come to America and settled in the Puget Sound area. Also like Ole, Bernt, who was called Uncle Ben by the Fosheim family, had left his wife and kids in Norway. Bernt had seven children who for various reasons ended up being adopted by different families after he stayed in America. Bernt never returned to Norway and died in Seattle, Washington in 1942.

Bernt Øvrum's youngest son, Alf was born in Verdal in 1903 and was raised by the Østmo family and took their name. Alf came to America on April 28, 1925 and married Hjordes Barbara Vestrum in 1936. They settled in Klamath Falls, Oregon where a son, Leif was born in 1937. The Østmos' later settled in the Everett area and spent a lot of time with their first cousins, the Fosheim kids.

"Then we liked to go down across the tracks in the lumber yard and run on the log rafts. It was dangerous, but then nothing bad ever happened. Mother was too busy to tell us not to go down there. She might have told me, but I can't remember."

The Snohomish River was lined with log rafts from its mouth in Port Gardner Bay all the way around the Everett peninsula and upriver to Snohomish. Thousands of logs were stored and transported on the river before being hoisted out and cut into lumber by the many mills in the area. Playing on the log rafts tied to the pilings along the Snohomish River was dangerous but exciting for kids. Raymond and his friends were naturally drawn to the river as there was so much down there to entertain them.

Logs floating at the Clough-Hartley Mill west of the bluff at 18th and Grand Ave. 1915. *Everett Public Library.*

The lower Snohomish River runs with the tides. On the incoming tide the water flows upriver all the way to the town of Snohomish. Before the river was dredged out to the depth it is today one could wade across in many places or play on the many exposed sand bars at low tide. Raymond and his friends would wade across the river in the area close to where Interstate 5 crosses now and explore Smith Island. Of course one had to time the visit right or he would be forced to swim the deeper water on the rising tide on the way back. Raymond spent a lot of time swimming in either the river or Silver Lake. He was an excellent swimmer.

There was always boat traffic on the busy river with tug boats and the large stern wheelers like the Black Prince and the Forester pulling log booms for the mills. Many passengers would ride the boats upriver from

Everett or Lowell to Snohomish. Raymond always had a love of boats and he probably got it while playing on the river and watching the variety of interesting water crafts travelling by.

The Black Prince. *Postcard.*

Stern wheel freighters and passenger steamers like the Black Prince provided particularly important methods of transportation along the Snohomish River. The wide river was a natural highway into the interior of growing Snohomish County well before roads and railways were built.

The Black Prince was built in Everett for the Snohomish and Skagit River Navigation Company. She was 112 feet long by nineteen feet wide and weighed 159 gross tons. In 1910 the Black Prince was sold to the Washington Towing Company and then the Puget Sound and Baker River Railroad Company. In 1923 the American Tug Boat Company bought her and in 1936 she was dismantled in Everett. Her upper works was removed and used as a clubhouse at the Everett Yacht Club until 1956.

The W. T. Preston in 1950. *The Seattle Times Inc.*

The snag boat sternwheeler the W. T. Preston patrolled the local rivers for deadheads and other hazards. She was launched in 1929 and completely rebuilt in 1939. Luckily the Preston was saved and serves as a wonderful museum in Anacortes, Washington, just north of Everett.

"Ray Hall, I remember he lived on the river, him and his brother and dad in one of the boathouses. So many of my friends died young. Three or four years ago, Leo Hall died, Ray Hall's brother on Camano Island, I was so surprised, I just had talked to him, not long before."

The Snohomish River and the sloughs had numerous boat houses tied up to docks or just pilings. One of the larger communities was just below East Grand at 21st street, just north of Canyon Mill. A narrow road went a short way down the bank and then access was by a tall wooden stairway down to the railroad tracks. On the east side of the tracks was a boardwalk that led one past swampy area to a small bridge with led to the boat houses. They were mostly just little floating shacks put together with whatever lumber floated down the river. They provided a cheap shelter for the families and individuals that resided there. In the early days some just had an outhouse mounted over the water. A few of the little homes were there into the sixties.

"I went down to the spring on Riverside to bring home water. Mother would want a gallon of water. We did that quite often, my brother did that too. That was a running spring. During the flu epidemic, or influenza, there was quite a line-up there, getting water. After that, in '24 or '25 of course we only lived one, two, three, four blocks from the spring. But I remember that spring real well, I don't know if it's still there or not. I think that trail down there is gone, the trail to the steps, there used to be steps going down, that's gone, I think. It's got a sign there, 'No Trespassing.'"

The natural spring was in a swampy area at the base of 21st street just east of East Grand Avenue. It was a well-known and popular place for the Riverside residents. In later years someone even built a fence around it and left a tin drinking cup there on a post for visitors to use. Some kneeled over and drank right out of the bubbling spring; others took the water home in jugs and boiled it first. The steep wooden steps went down the bluff to the edge of the railroad tracks below. A wooden

Friends Ethel and Nora Haugen with LaVern, Olivia, and Raymond Fosheim in 1924.

walkway crossed a large swampy area ringed by salmon berry bushes and alder trees to the spring. The entire swampy area is now covered with sand that was dredged out of the river and spread over the whole area. There appears to be nothing remaining of the once popular spring in that location today.

Dad often talked about the many Hobo camps on the flats between the railroad tracks and the Snohomish River. He called the men that lived down in that area bums. Today they are called homeless but either way they lived in tents or wooden shacks pieced together from anything that could be found. Dad and his friends kept their distance from the bums as they played by the tracks and on the river.

John, Emma & Raymond Fosheim, Ole Øvrum & Alf Østmo in 1928.

"Us boys spent a lot of time there on the railroad tracks. We spent time on the Great Northern yards. Those days, they had a bunch of old engines there, waiting to be scrapped, and we'd go through them, pretending to be running them. Then we'd stand on the bridge and look right down the chimney while it was smoking up. Lots to do."

In Raymond's younger days great clouds of smoke followed the steam engines as the chugged up and down the Everett rail lines. Trains were busily travelling back and forth along the edge of the entire Everett peninsula. Rail yards and siding lined most of the length of the Everett side of the Snohomish river bank. It was a busy and exciting time for railroad buffs and kids who enjoyed the excitement of watching the trains.

Great Northern locomotive #3359 in the Delta Yard in the late 1920s. *Everett Public Library*

The arrival and eventually expansion of the Great Northern Railroad changed much of the landscape of Everett. The Delta Yard was built in the floodplain and marshy area on the northeast side of the Everett peninsula. A small winding slough was filled in and the river was eventually dredged and the sand was spread to raise the area so multiple tracks could be laid for the switch yard. Some of the steep sandy cliffs along the tracks were dug out to provide more fill.

Dad also told stories of hitching rides on and in the boxcars. He and his friends would hop on a car as it slowly rolled past and ride around the rail yard. It could be a dangerous thing to do. Occasionally someone would fall off and scrape their legs and arms up on the gravel by the rails. Unfortunately worse accidents did happen over the years such as losing a

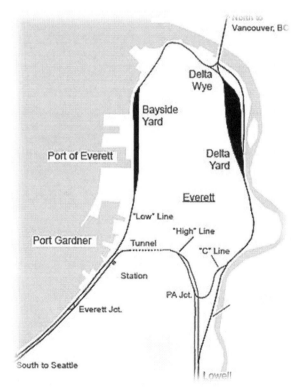

Map of Everett's railroads and switch yards

leg or even one's life. Sometimes the railroad workers would kick everyone off the cars, other times they would just look the other way. Dad was not one to be reckless or take risks but he said riding the train was fun.

The whole area along the river bank was an exciting place for kids. Before the area was filled in with sand, there were channels cut across the marshy areas by the river. Canyon Mill had a mill pond full of logs in storage just waiting for adventurous kids to play on. There were hobo trails crisscrossing through the grassy areas and skunk cabbage leading to all kinds of thrilling places to play.

Raymond Fosheim, unidentified, Olivia Fosheim, and cousin Alf Østmo in about 1928.

"We hitchhiked a lot in those days. I remember going to Snohomish and there were cherry trees right out in the street in the parking strips. I remember we'd go there during cherry time and pick cherries. And then our friend, Dale Jensen, our neighbor on Cleveland, we went with him a lot. He come from Granite Falls, and we'd go back up there and visit his friends, hitchhike, so we hitchhiked quite a bit. And you never heard of bad things in those days, as much. But that's something you can't do now, but we did it quite a bit."

"On Halloween, I can't remember doing anything bad. I remember we had a rattler we'd hold up against the window and make a noise. We did soap some windows, but not very much. I remember just going around, walking around. I can't remember doing anything bad, breaking up anything, fences or not. I knew kids that tipped over outhouses. But our house never had anything damaged from Halloween. But we had an older gang there, I don't know what they did, they might have been kind of rough in the neighborhood, but not around our house."

"There were neighborhood gangs, and they all had their own names. Our gang was called the 'MJB Gang,' 'Mike, Jack and Bill.' That was Ray Hall and Dale Jensen and me. Delta Gang was kind of rough, I guess, down on Delta. I knew some of those guys. But we spent quite a bit of time over on Spencer's farm, across the river. Ray Hall worked for Spencer a lot, and he'd take us over there quite a

bit and ride horses there, we had a lot of fun over there. That was Frank Spencer; he was commissioner of public works in Everett later, for years after that. He had a dairy farm there. He had a couple daughters, I knew one of them, and she writes sometimes in The Herald about things. She's kind of a deformed girl, her neck is stiff. And then she had a sister; I think one of them did marry, but I can't remember."

Raymond's two brothers were both born in Norway and were almost eight and six years older than him. Martin was the oldest and then John. Martin loved movies and talked about them and the Hollywood stars all the time. He also had a love of history like his younger brothers but he didn't have their interest in cars and motorcycles. Martin lived in the family home all his life and never married.

John K., Anna, and Martin Fosheim around 1925.

John Arthur Fosheim on June 29, 1930 in Everett.

John Arthur Fosheim was the nicest guy one could ever meet and like older brother Martin was a bachelor all his life. He loved working on carpentry projects around his home and was also good with mechanical repairs. John was wonderful with kids and all his nieces and nephews loved him. He was said to resemble his father in many ways. He always looked like a tough guy to me, with his sleeves rolled up showing off his muscular arms, but he was a very gentle man.

John Arthur Fosheim was musically inclined and kept a piano at his home on Walnut Street in his later years. He also played the saxophone and was an excellent guitar player.

A friend with John A. Fosheim in about 1928.

John K., Raymond & Martin Fosheim around 1930.

John Arthur Fosheim (see arrow) with his guitar group in the late 1920s in Everett.

"Sundays, we weren't church people. I remember me and my sister going to church when we lived on Baker, I was six, seven years old maybe. Me and my sister would walk to church on 22nd and Baker, some kind of Free Church, I think. The churches didn't entertain much for the children that I can remember. I did go a few times with Dad and Mom, but, like kids nowadays I was restless, I remember. The preacher spoke Norwegian, and it was all Greek to us, you know. Mom and Dad spoke Norwegian all the time, we understood them, but it was kind of monotonous for children. It was tiresome to us. We could understand some of it. We sat with the grownups in church, now days they got them separated."

The church the family attended was the Norwegian Lutheran Church at 2208 Baker Avenue. Later the family belonged to the Calvary Lutheran Church at 1711 26th Street. Raymond was not a real religious man. He certainly believed in God and was a Christian but he would much rather work on his wood projects around the home instead of sitting in church on a Sunday morning.

"I took my boy to that church on Hoyt and Everett Avenue when he was little. They did things for the little fellows; they drew pictures and painted things. That's something, years ago, they didn't let the kids do, of course it was a poor church."

First Swedish Baptist Church at 2625 Hoyt. *Everett Public Library.*

In my early years I loved going to Sunday school at Bethel Baptist Church at 2625 Hoyt. In its early years it was the First Swedish Baptist Church. Attending church was very important to my mother. She wanted to go every Sunday and sometimes in the evenings. Dad was not so interested. As I got a little older, I hated to go. I wanted to stay home and play with my toys.

"We answered in English, and our folks spoke in Norwegian at home. They could speak English. I wish they had made us answer them in Norwegian so we knew a little bit about it, but our relatives from Norway, they talked good English, but us younger kids can't talk Norwegian. The Norwegian cousins had to talk English to us, and they knew English pretty well, all of them. That's the way we should have been."

Alf Østmo, Olivia and John K. Fosheim, unidentified, LaVern Fosheim, and Stuart Solem in about 1925.

Today so many immigrants teach their children their native country's language. In my parents day everyone wanted to forget the 'old country' and adapt as quick as possible to American ways. They did not want their kids to speak their native language, only English. When I was a kid Mom and Dad would speak a little Norwegian and Swedish when they didn't want me to understand what was going on. I wish today that I could have learned the languages of my ancestors. A few years ago when I went to Norway and Sweden to visit my cousins I heard many words that I remembered hearing when I was young. One of the few regrets that I have about my upbringing was not being taught more Norwegian or Swedish.

"There were six children, and I don't know how we ever got along, but we ate common, just potatoes and everything. When I went to school, I saw other kids with lettuce and mayonnaise sandwiches, and I envied them so much. I usually ate peanut butter and margarine. In those days, you were kind of ashamed to use margarine. Even in junior high, they'd look at me, it was white, before it came colored."

"Mother made potatoes and fish so much in those days. We used so much grease on the potatoes and stuff, so you got along. I used to love that Swiss steak with gravy, you had to have that for a big family, potatoes and gravy. We had that, of course, every night. Of course there were so many families the same way, bigger families, even. We'd have oatmeal, lots of oatmeal. Up until I married, we'd have oatmeal all the time. Then, of course, Mother would make bread all the time, constantly. Others did the same; a woman in those days really had it rough. We sold milk to neighbors. I can remember, I'd deliver milk."

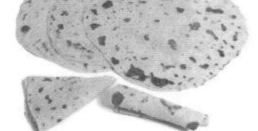

"Every Christmas my mom would make lefse and I loved it. Lutefisk was another matter though; I just could not bear to taste it. My dad didn't eat it either but the Swedes, my mom and

uncle, loved it. I remember having all different kinds of great tasting cookies too."

Lefse is a traditional soft, Norwegian flatbread usually made with potatoes and flour. It's cooked on a griddle and a special rolling pin with grooves is used to flatten each piece into a pancake shape.

Lutefisk is a time-honored Scandinavian dish made from aged or dried and salted codfish and lye. It has a gelatinous texture.

Christmas was the one time of year that we enjoyed the Scandinavian traditions and food when I was young. I loved lefse and the wonderful cookies. Mom and Uncle Buddy ate the lutefisk but Dad and I didn't. They all loved canned fish balls but I didn't like those either. When I later visited my cousins in Norway I loved all the fresh food that my cousins cooked.

"Mother cooked traditional Norwegian things like lefse and little cookies and it was all so good. She used cardamom seed, that was traditional; made lots of cookies and little cakes, coffee cake. In those days, she had women friends come over all the time, and they'd have their coffee. I've never seen people drink coffee like they did, the foreigners. Norwegians like coffee and sweets. Mother made 'klub,' a potato dumpling, quite often and it was good. My two older brothers and sister, they'd eat that lutefisk, but us three younger, never did get us to eat it. Still, to this day, my wife fixed it all the time, and her and her brother ate it, he lived with us. But I never did eat it. I just don't go for much fish at all, although we were raised on it and ate it as kids, thought nothing of it. They bought lots of herring and potatoes."

"We hardly ever had any vegetables, like peas and carrots and that. I don't know why, but very seldom, until later years. We always had a garden and my family grew its own potatoes and in later years, peas and carrots. Our neighbors had chickens. We had a few chickens too. We had our eggs and up until 1930, people started getting rid of their chickens and everything in the towns. Up until

then, we had chickens in 1930, '31, during the Depression."

"When I was young I remember walking or riding my bike to the little stores that were still on many of the street corners in Everett. We didn't usually buy any groceries mostly just gum or candy."

"There were lots of little grocery stores; everybody had their charge account at the local, little stores. I went to Pilon, at 17th and Baker Avenue. I know one of the boys is still in town, I read about in the paper. The kids that were brought up with us, so many of them are still around. And then there's that little store on 16th and Baker, I used to go there a lot. But we usually went to Pilon's, one block farther."

The White & Muzzall Transfer Company was one of Everett's early family owned businesses that used a heavy truck for moving and hauling. They were located on 2938 Broadway.

Braaten's Grocery Store at 1532 Broadway in 1923. *Everett Public Library.*

Olaus Braaten's Grocery Store at 1532 Broadway was typical of the many corner grocery stores that popped up every few blocks throughout Everett. The Braatens were Norwegian immigrants like the Fosheim's.

Some things hadn't changed from my father's childhood to mine. I walked or rode my bicycle to all the little stores that still remained in north Everett, including the one at 16th and Baker. I bought gum, candy and as I got older maybe even a plastic model. In the early 1900s neighborhood grocery stores and other businesses popped up every few blocks. Some of the stores are still around today.

A busy Hewitt Avenue looking east up toward Colby Avenue in Everett in 1924. *Everett Public Library*.

Brown the Plumber had a successful business at 2923 Oakes in 1925. *Everett Public Library*.

"When we moved to Cleveland, there were about six blocks there, a dead-end street. There were one or two stores on just about every corner. They all lived on people charging. Some of them lived above their stores. Once in a while, I'd see a picture of 25th and Summit, a family, little store, but I don't remember that one. But there were two grocery stores on 25th and Summit."

I Cover the Waterfront. Dir. James Cruze. United Artists, 1934.

White and Muzzall Transfer Co. truck in 1923. *Everett Public Library*

"I remember Max Miller's father. Did he have a store, too? We'd go in there, across from Duffy's, and I remember him driving his car, he'd run it in low gear all the time. He was deaf. Wouldn't hear anything, and that thing would be racing in low gear all the time."

Max Carlton Miller (1899-1967) spent his younger years in Everett and went on to be a famous author writing twenty seven books. He grew up in the Riverside neighborhood on 2303 Summit Avenue and some of his books covered his boyhood adventures in early Everett. Miller's best-selling book, 'I Cover the Waterfront' was made into two movies. The major film starred Claudette Colbert and Ben Lyon, and is credited with the phrase, 'Not tonight, Josephine.'

Reporter Joe Miller is positive that local fisherman Eli Kirk is smuggling illegal Chinese immigrants into America, but can't find enough evidence to placate his newspaper editor. Chance plays into his hands in the lovely form of Kirk's daughter, Julie, whom he catches swimming in the nude and pumps for information. But she's fiercely loyal to her dad, and may be too attractive for Joe's own good. Max Miller's autobiography provided the basis for the film.

The Solem family was the Fosheim family's life-long friends. Oscar Johansen Jjolgan and his wife Anna Caroline were from the Trondheim area of Norway and came to America about the time Raymond Fosheim was born in 1914. Like many immigrants they Americanized their name and it became Solem. The two families had known each other in Norway. Anna Solem and Anna Fosheim became close friends and spent time together whenever they could. The Solem's had nine children: Olaf Alfred 9-26-13, Johan Melvin 5-31-16, Olga Louise 2-5-19, Lillie Olena 2-5-19, Helen Sophie 11-25-22, Harold Stanley 4-21-24, Agnes Mayetta 7-26-28, Robert Oscar 11-

19-29, and William Arnold 2-27-31. Their family home was at 2202 Harrison Street, next to the Fosheim's, and later at 2717 21st Street and then at 1931 Rainier Avenue in the Riverside neighborhood.

Olaf and John Solem, Raymond Fosheim, and Maynard Kendal in East Everett in 1927.

John A. Fosheim with friend Anna Lindstrom.

The Fosheim family home in east Everett during 1926 & 1927.

The Fosheim family left their home on 2202 Cleveland Avenue and moved to a house in the country in East Everett up on Cavalero Hill. It was a move of just a few miles but it was like a different world. They lived there for just one year from 1926-27 before moving back to their old home in the Riverside area of Everett. It's not known today why they moved for only a short time but the city life may have suited them better than the country life.

The Fosheim family cow in a pasture by East Everett in 1926.

Some significant events were happening around the Everett area while the Fosheim's were living outside of town. In mid-1926 the huge Medical and Dental Building opened downtown and it was announced a third floor would be added to the Interurban building on Pacific Avenue and Colby Avenue. South Junior High School opened on Rucker Avenue and in 1927 the Marysville-Everett cutoff opened making a direct road between the two towns for the first time. The big event in the spring of 1928 was the dedication of Everett's first airport as an 'aviation field.' The Ebey Island Airport opened on the east side and adjacent to the new highway between Everett and Marysville between Union and Steamboat Slough.

The Everett aviation field under construction adjacent to the Everett-Marysville highway in 1927. *Postcard.*

A new Birney Company street car on Summit Avenue at 23rd Street in the Riverside Neighborhood. *Everett Public Library.*

The eastern portion of the Riverside Neighborhood adjacent to the Snohomish River. A new Highway 2 bridge at the east end of Hewitt Avenue was built to replace the dangerous original bridge off of Everett Avenue to the right in the photo. *Everett Public Library.*

Jack Norberg, Unidentified, L. Solem and LaVern Fosheim.

John A. and Martin Fosheim acting out a movie scene.

Olivia Fosheim on a friends pony.

John A. Fosheim and Friend in 1932.

Chapter V

Teenage Years

I always appreciated Dad's stories and could listen to them for hours. When the three Fosheim brothers got together and talked about old Everett I loved it. If I could relive those days I would record every conversation.

One story from his teenage years that I still find fascinating and hard to believe today was Dad's trip to Minnesota by train. Dad was just sixteen and the Great Depression was hitting Everett hard when he and a couple of friends hopped in an empty boxcar and rode the train all the way to see Aunt Martha near Fergus Falls in west central Minnesota. This seems amazing and rather scary nowadays, but back in the summer of 1930 it was quite common to ride the rails. Usually the workers on the train just looked the other way as long as no one was doing any damage or causing any trouble.

Raymond Fosheim at sixteen years old in 1930.

Dad said there were a quite a few hobos on the train but mostly just working men out of a job. They rode the rails of Montana and the Dakotas watching the beautiful scenery fly by. He packed food and had a sleeping bag so he could be fairly comfortable at night. Dad felt a real connection to his Aunt Martha, John K. Fosheim's sister, and always spoke of her kindly. Years later he made several trips on his motorcycle back to Minnesota to visit her.

Raymond and Emma Fosheim with Chuby around 1928.

Martin Fosheim and friend Jack Norberg atop a Northern Pacific boxcar during the depression years.

At the height of the great depression there were as many as a quarter million American teenagers not only riding the rails but actually living on the trains. It's estimated that over two million adults were making their homes on the rails in the empty boxcars and in the hobo camps. During those hard times the empty boxcars were tempting as a way to travel the country looking for work.

During his teenage years Dad kept a diary with entries starting on July 19, 1931 and ending on July 4, 1933. I stopped by Dad's home on 525 Pilchuck Path just a few years before he died and he had his pickup bed packed full of books, boxes and miscellaneous items. He was heading for the city dump! I was shocked as I looked through the boxes and found his diary, letters, and homework from grade school. I quickly retrieved the items and put them in safe keeping at my house. I don't know what got into him as he usually saved and treasured everything. Thank goodness I just happened to stop by that morning.

Recently I found some separate notebook sheets with entries that started May 2, 1929 when Dad was fifteen years old, living at 2202 Cleveland Avenue, and attending North Junior High School. I've left some of the less interesting entries out and transcribed the writing just as it appears on the pages, spelling errors and all.

These dated diary entries give us an interesting perspective on what it was like growing up during the depression years.

3-2-29 "I got my bycicle fixed at Hack's a wheel that costs $2.20. We went down to the Wherhouser, int the filing room and rode back with Mason's dad."

3-3-29 "Sunday. It was damp, and I went down and got some cruches. I then went with Mr. Southard out to Home Acres."

Home Acres is the primarily farming area on Ebey Island just east of Everett, across the Snohomish River and south of Highway 2.

3-4-29 "At school we heard Hoover's anguration for 1.30 minutes. After school me and Mason went to Hack's and he got and new bike."

3-5-29 "After school me and Mason went to look for a job, we went down to the docks, and then to his gramas and home. I'm reading Ivanhoe. Gold Cache. Wilderness Castaway."

Ivanhoe is a popular historical novel set in 12th-century England and written by Sir Walter Scott in 1820. Ivanhoe is often credited for increasing interest in medievalism and romance in America. Raymond was an avid reader and had a life-long interest in history.

3-8-29 "I didn't go to school, my tire went flat but I fixed it. Jack got a new bike today."

3-21-29 "I built on the camp then went over to alfred's and made candles."

3-23-29 "Me and pa went up to East Everett. and sawed some wood then I just about finished the camp. I'm reading The Longer Trail. Story of the Great War. And a hilltop on the Marne."

3-24-29 "Me and Ole Solem went to see Rough House Rosie."

The great Clara Bow stars as a poor but ambitious young girl determined to crash high society, but she isn't prepared for the reception she receives. Sadly this sixty-six minute silent black and white 1927 film is presumed lost. Clara Bow was the classic 'Flapper' of the 1920s and Americas first sex symbol. She made fifty-eight films between 1922 and 1933.

Rough House Rosie. Dir. Richard Strayer. Paramount,

7-19-31 "Me and Clint went swimming at Basslero (Lake Stevens).

Clint Hill was Raymond's life-long friend. They met while working at the Hingston Box Company at the foot of Everett Avenue in Riverside.

7-20-31 "After work me and Clint went to Maces place, he took us in at Purple Pennant, had a fine time."

Purple Pennant was a very popular dining, dancing, and swimming resort on the east side of Lake Stevens. All that remains today is a road by that name. Raymond was a good swimmer and obviously loved it.

3-26-29 "Got out of school at 1:00 today and don't go back until Monday. Me and Alfred got a lamp and kerosin and went up into the camp."

Clint Hill and Raymond Fosheim visiting Chilliwack, Canada on May 10, 1931.

The interior of the Purple Pennant at Lake Stevens, Washington. *Postcard.*

The Purple Pennant advertisement in the 1946 Everett phone book.

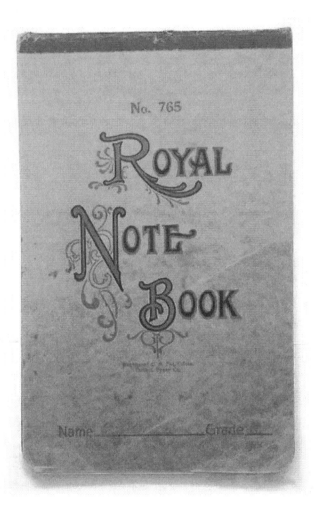
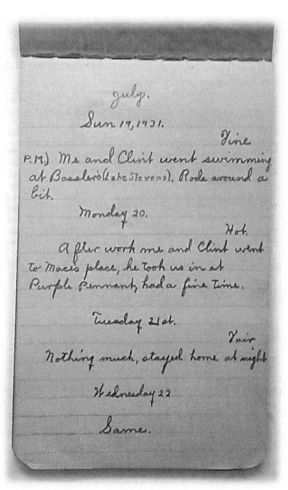

Ray Fosheim's diary from July 19, 1931 to July 4, 1933

7-26-31 Sunday "Went swimming at Purple Pennant, then went to Arlington 17 miles in 18 minutes, we (me and Clint) certainly did travel."

Raymond's friend Clint Hill always loved tinkering with cars and built a real speedster out of his model 'A' Ford. Raymond nick-named it the 'bug.' Travelling from Everett to Arlington in the pre-highway days of the thirties in eighteen minutes seemed to be quite a feat. Raymond never exaggerated so it must have happened. He and Clint soon did everything together from fishing to hiking to exploring around Everett.

Ray Fosheim, LaVern Fosheim, and Clint Hill in his Ford 'bug' on June 12, 1932.

7-29-31 Wednesday "Went after the girls at Basslero, had a fine swim. Ole, Clint, Gladys, Marie and LaVern. Got laid off until Monday."

8-20-31 "Me and Clint and John S. went down to the Ferry Baker Mill and made a raft and went fishing, waters fine."

The Ferry Baker Mill was at the east end of 15th Street, just off of East Grand Avenue, on the Snohomish River. There is a good sized Island in the river close to where the mill used to sit. Fred K. Baker came to Everett from New York in 1901 and founded the Ferry-Baker Lumber Company which was formerly the Rice Lumber Company.

The Snohomish River east of Everett is known for its great fall runs of pink, Coho, and chum salmon. It also provides excellent fishing for steelhead, sea-run cutthroat and Dolly Varden trout. More than likely Raymond and his friends ended up catching bullheads and chubs that are plentiful in the lower part of the river.

The Ferry Baker Lumber Company on the Snohomish River in Everett. *Everett Public Library.*

12-24-31 "Hingston gave us all an extra bonus check, mine was $15.69. I bought Clint and Gladys a present. Alf came here Monday. Had a good Christmas."

1-3-32 "Introduced to Gertrude Wymer, nice girl."

1-8-32 "Me and Clinton went to see 'The Millionaire' at the Granada."

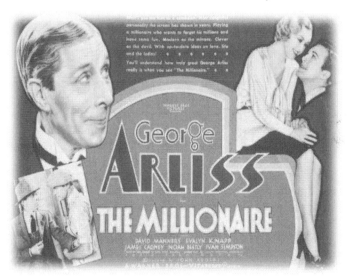

The Millionaire. Dir. John G. Adolfi. Warner Bros, 1931.

In the 1931 comedy 'The Millionaire', George Arliss is a retired auto industry millionaire who's been instructed by his doctor to rest and avoid exercise. He is awakened out of his inactive life by an insurance salesman (brilliantly played by James Cagney) who advises him to begin enjoying life again. Arliss heads to California, and conceals his identity while he works in a gas station. With a new lease on life, the millionaire entertains himself by playing matchmaker with his daughter (Evelyn Knapp) and the gas station manager (David Manners).

Raymond was a lifelong lover of movies. In the middle 1920s thru the 1930s the city of Everett had no less than nine movie theaters: Apollo, Balboa, Everett, Granada, Liberty, Orpheum, Rose, Roxy, and Star. Some were open for just a few years, others for decades, and the Everett Theater is still operating today. Since the settlement of Everett in the early 1890s there have been almost fifty theaters in town. Many of the theaters were later converted to different uses. The Granada Theater was converted into a swimming school.

Interior of the Granada Theater, 2926 Wetmore, December 1927. *Everett Public Library.*

Chuck Lee's Swim School in the old Granada Theater in April 1957. *The Everett Herald.*

The Everett Theatre opened on Nov 4, 1901 as the curtain rose for an evening performance of the musical comedy 'The Casino Girl.' Everett's impressive new playhouse was designed by the distinguished architect Charles Herbert Bebb who had worked under Adler & Sullivan's on Chicago's Auditorium Building, one of America's greatest theatrical structures. The $70,000 Everett Theatre seated 1200 people, about a sixth of the entire population of the city at the time.

The Everett Theater on 2911 Colby Avenue in 1929. *Everett Public Library.*

The Everett Theater when new in 1901 and with its wonderful marquee in 1961. *Everett Public Library.*

Tragedy struck the Everett Theatre on December 11, 1923 when a fire destroyed the building leaving just the side and rear walls standing. The theatre was soon rebuilt with the new formal Renaissance façade that remains today. After boom and bust years the theatre was again drastically changed when the prestigious firm of B. Marcus Priteca was hired in 1952 to add a new plate-glass entrance with a freestanding octagonal ticket kiosk below a commanding triangular neon marquee which extended out over the sidewalk. More than a mile of neon tubing went into this remarkable display.

Like my father, I grew up watching films at the historic Everett Theatre. It was and still is one of the most beautiful buildings in Everett. Unfortunately the building went through some very tough times in the 1980s and 90s and the beautiful one of a kind marquee was removed and destroyed. Luckily the rest of the building is still standing.

1-30-32 "Went up to 16th street, went down once."

On 16th street between Cedar Street and Pine Street there's a steep hill that has often been used for sledding if Everett gets enough snow in the winter.

2-27-32 "We had to shut down at 9:30 o'clock this morning on account of the flood."

2-28-32 "I got up early this morning and went down to the track, the water was over tracks. Clint and I fell in."

LaVern Fosheim with Chuby in 1932.

4-9-32 "I bought Donald Joyce's car today, paid $13.00 for it."

4-16-32 "Clint and I took a trip around the lake at night, we certainly did travel fast."

5-24-32 "The Akron came over today. The whole gang at the factory got on the roof."

USS Akron ZRS-4 above San Francisco. *Postcard.*

USS Akron (ZRS-4) was a helium-filled rigid United States Navy airship that was commissioned on November 2, 1931 and lost in a weather-related accident off the coast of New Jersey on April 4, 1933, killing seventy-three of the seventy-six crew and passengers on board. She was 785 feet long, just twenty feet shorter than the German Hindenburg. Akron and her sister ship, Macon were among the largest flying objects in the world at the time. She left Lakehurst, New Jersey on May 8, 1932 for her first Coast to Coast flight carrying mail for the US Post Office. The Akron arrived in San Diego on May 11th and then 'showed the flag' all up the West Coast as far north as the Canadian border before returning to California. When she flew over Everett at low altitude she must have been quite a sight to see.

6-10-32 "Bought a new swimming suit today cost $3.00, went swimming with Clint and Larson's. In for the first time this year, waters fine."

The USS Akron over 2130 Rucker Avenue on May 24. 1932. *Photograph by Doris Bell. Jeanne Hartley Anderson Collection.*

LaVern and Oliva Fosheim and John and Anna Fosheim on June 12, 1932

Raymond always seemed to have a camera with on his adventures. He certainly didn't have much money but he managed to take photos of his family and his travels. He kept many of the photos in albums with names, dates and locations. Before Raymond died he sorted out his hundreds of negatives and put them in labeled envelopes.

6-19-32 "Hingstons team went to Machias to play indoor, we lost 5-1. Clint and I then went swimming."

7-1-32 "Me, Olive and Chub took a few pictures."

7-4-32 "Clint, Kennedy and I went over to Bill S. house and shot explosives. We then went swimming and took pictures. Had dinner at Bills. Saw the fireworks and went to the carnival."

8-15-32 "Olive celebrated her 15 birthday tonight. Harry, Hub, Mart, John, Sag and I sang songs and drank root beer."

8-20/21-32 "Sag letting us use his car we started for Pilchuck at 15 minutes to eleven. I was left behind two or three times while climbing, we arrived at the timberline at 3 o'clock and camped overnight. Had a great time. We got up at 5:40 am started climbing at 6:25 and reaching the top at 7:55 am, we stayed up there about one hour and a half, took pictures and then went down, stopping at the 3 mile cabin, then down to the car."

Martin Fosheim and his friend Hub MacGhee on top of Mt Pilchuck on August 20, 1932.

The trail to the top of Mount Pilchuck today is just under three miles long with an elevation gain of 2,200 feet to the Forest Service lookout. When Raymond and his family and friends hiked to the top in 1932, it was quite a task as the trail started at the Stillaguamish River in Verlot just up the road from Granite Falls and wandered seven miles up to the top. The elevation gain was over 4,000 feet. To cross the river, they had to pull themselves across in a metal basket which hung from a heavy cable stretched between trees on either side.

LaVern and Raymond Fosheim with Louise Solem near the top of Mt. Pilchuck on July 11, 1937.

Raymond Fosheim near the top of Mt. Pilchuck on July 11, 1937.

Raymond's favorite mountain; Mt. Pilchuck in the fall of 2011 taken from south Everett.

Raymond had a life-long love of the Cascade Mountains, particularly the impressive peaks that can be seen from Everett. In his younger days he did a lot of hiking and camping along the Mountain Loop Highway leading up to Monte Cristo. Raymond loved to brag about the height and beauty of Mt. Rainier to his Midwest and eastern relatives and friends. He took his family on weekend trips to Paradise Lodge to enjoy the beauty. But by far his favorite mountain was Mt. Pilchuck the most prominent peak in the spectacular view from downtown Everett.

8-23-32 "Hub, Mart and I went down to the Canyon and caught 40 bullheads."

The Canyon Lumber Company on the Snohomish River on the east side of Everett. *Everett Public Library.*

The Canyon Lumber Company is one of the last remaining sawmills in Everett. It's at the east end of Everett Avenue in the Riverside neighborhood. Steamboat Slough originates as it branches off from the Snohomish River where it bends around the wide Canyon Mill peninsula. Raymond spent many hours down there playing and fishing on the log booms that lined the river.

It's not surprising that my youth growing up in Everett paralleled Dad's in some ways. My friends and I often went down to the Snohomish River to fish. We tried to catch the native cutthroat trout but usually just caught dozens of bullheads and chubs. We always had a fun time though. There's something fascinating about fishing on the river that still draws me down there even today.

Raymond loved fishing when he had the time which wasn't too often. After the war he did a lot of salmon fishing in Port Gardner Bay off of Everett's waterfront. He was not a hunter though. He went on many hunting trips with Clint Hill and other friends but he could never bring himself to shoot an animal. Raymond loved animals and always had a pet dog that he treated like a best friend.

8-26-32 "Clint and I drove up to Jim Creek Dam and fished. No luck!"

9-1-32 "Clint and I went at Lake Silver and cut down two snags."

Raymond spent his whole life cutting wood. The Fosheim home was heated with wood when he was a boy and his home seventy years later was too. Everett was not only the city of smokestacks but also of scrap wood burning towers at the mills and chimneys on nearly every home and business. Home heating wood had to be collected from the woods or the sawmills for kitchen stoves and the larger stoves. Much of the wood was collected by the homeowners but there were also wood wagons pulled by horses travelling the streets of Everett making deliveries.

9-8-32 "We went down to the dock and watched the U.S.S. New York come in. We got on the first boat over."

The USS New York BB34 in 1931 the year before visiting Everett. *Postcard.*

The USS New York BB-34 was a United States Navy battleship, commissioned on April 15, 1914, the same year Raymond was born. The USS New York saw action in both World Wars, providing gunfire support for numerous amphibious landings. She was decommissioned in 1946 and sunk as a target. Here displacement was 27,000 tons and she was 573 feet long by ninety-five feet wide. She had ten fourteen inch guns, a speed of twenty-one Knots, and a crew of 1052.

Dad had a life-long love of ships and we talked about them often. When I was young, he took me on tours of all the navy ships when they made an Everett or Seattle visit.

9-11-32 "Clint and I went down to the Great Northern oil docks and fished. Not a bad place!"

The Great Northern oil dock in the Everett harbor 1907. *Everett Public Library.*

9-15-32 *"Clint, Hub, Mart and I went to Mill 'A' dock and fished. Not a bad place."*

Weyerhaeuser Mill A on the Everett waterfront in 1912. *National Oceanic and Atmospheric Administration*

9-25-32 *"Painted the boats, had dinner at Clint's then went shooting rats at the dump. Got 5."*

When Raymond talks about going to the dump to shoot rats one can bet that Clint did the killing. Clint loved to shoot and anything was fair game. Raymond loved to target practice but wouldn't harm and animal, even a rat at the city dump.

The City of Everett garbage dump next to the Snohomish River at the east end of 36th Street was a wonderful place for kids to explore but it wasn't the first dump in Everett. In the early days garbage was disposed of wherever vacant space was available. This quickly became a problem so the City leaders came up with a plan for disposal in Port Gardner Bay. A small barge or scow was tied up to the south side of the City Dock at the base of Hewitt Avenue so wagons could drive up to the edge and dump their loads. The little garbage barge was then towed out halfway to Hat Island by a tugboat and dumped in the bay. Dozens of excited seagulls would always follow the action.

9-27-32 "Clint traded his single shot pistol for a shot gun."

9-28-32 "Clint and I dug spuds at Alvin farm."

9-29-32 "Took the shotgun down to the dump and shot rats. Jim got a bad beating up. Could hardly recognize him."

10-1-32 "Listened to the football games then went over to Hills. Gladys fixed us supper."

Raymond picking potatoes at the Alvin farm in October 1936.

10-2-32 "Got up at 5:30 o'clock to go hunting with Clint. Ma made me go back to bed Clint went alone and got smashed up near Silver Lake. Gladys and him came here about 7:30 am and Mart and I went and took the parts we could (hit a Austin sedan). Then went out and we all four shot the shotgun."

When Clint Hill crashed into an Austin he hit a pretty rare car. American Austin's were only manufactured a few years and it may very well have been the only one in Everett at the time. The American Austin Car Company

American Austin advertisement from 1930. *American Austin Automobile Company.*

founded in 1929, and produced cars under license from the British Austin Motor Company from 1930 through 1934, when it went bankrupt. In 1935 the company was reorganized under the name American Bantam and production resumed from 1937 to 1941. The company built the first prototype of what later became the WWII Jeep.

10-9-32 "Clint, Bill J. and I rowed over to Ferry Baker Island and hunted for game, no luck."

Clint Hill always had his guns with him everywhere he went. I even remember him wearing a gun in a holster while he walked the streets of Everett. My favorite Dad and Clint story, though a little frightening, was when Dad said he and Clint would stand on the shore of Lake Twenty-two up on Mt. Pilchuck and take turns shooting their twenty-two caliber rifles straight up in the air. They stood and waited for the bullets to fall to earth and who ever got their bullet to fall closest to them was the winner.

10-18-32 "Worked on the pontoons. Played football out in front."

10-22-32 "We went down to the river and celebrated Mrs Haugens 40th birthday. Had a good time."

11-1-32 "Heard that Lester Mildbraon was hurt last night."

11-4-32 "Hear that Lester's hurt rather bad."

11-5-32 "Lester died at 2 am this morning. Worked all day on lettuce."

11-6-32 "Me and Clint went down to the tracks and shot pa's 38 revolver and John's 22. Later we went up to see Lester at Challacombe's, hardly recognized him."

Family friend Mrs. Haugen, Martin, Anna, and John Fosheim by the Snohomish River on October 22, 1932.

Challacombe and Fickle Building at 2727 Oakes Avenue in 1934. *Everett Public Library*.

The Challacombe and Fickle funeral home at Oakes Avenue and California Street was designed by one of Everett's most prominent architects, Benjamin Turnbull in 1923. The beautiful historic structure is still there today and is now used as an office building.

11-10-32 "Clint, John, and I went to the Gay Cabralero. George Obrien."

George O'Brien stars in The Gay Caballero, a 1932 B-Western as an eastern football star who inherits a cattle ranch. Unfortunately, he soon discovers that much of the fortune has been wasted by a cattle baron attempting to build an empire of his own. He joins forces with outlaw El Coyote to defeat the greedy cattle baron but he falls in love with the villain's daughter.

The Gay Caballero. Dir. Alfred L. Werker. Fox Film Corp, 1932.

11-18-32 "Got off half a day today because the flood came up its highest. Took pictures of the plant."

The land below the bluffs in Everett is part of the Snohomish River flood plain. The river has flooded the low-lying areas on a regular basis over the years in a constant fight between man and nature. Much of the area was raised by dredging the river and depositing the sand in the regularly flooded areas.

Home Acres Road just east of Everett on November 18, 1932

11-25-32 "Hurt my back at noon, went home."

11-26-32 "Ma took me up to the clinic. They x-rayed my back then took me to Dentist Weber, he pulled 4 of my teeth out (payed 5 dollars)."

11-27-32 "Didn't sleep much last night because my tooth hurt. Stayed home today."

11-29-32 "pulled 4 more teeth."

12-2-32 "pulled 10 teeth today, hurt pretty bad when I got home. Took my loggers to the shoemaker."

12-3-32 "went up to Weber to stop my tooth from bleeding."

Silver lake wheel slide. *Everett Public Library.*

12-11-32 "Clint and I went to Lake Silver and cut some wood for Hills."

Raymond visited Silver Lake in south Everett quite often. He collected fire wood there and drove around the lake in his cars and on his motorcycle. He learned how to swim at the big amusement park at the southeast end of the lake. Silver Lake was quite an attraction as visitors came from Seattle, often on the interurban, and other nearby communities to swim, boat, picnic, and enjoy the huge water slide.

12-12-32 "*Started work today. Felt rather punk.*"

12-17-32 "*Went to the dentists , then stayed at Clint's a few hours.*"

12-22-32 "*I got my teeth tonight.*"

12-23-32 "*Worked half a day today. Got the Christmas tree and Clint, ma and I decorated it.*"

12-24-32 "*I went up town with Clint. Bought Gladys a stationary and Clint a deck of cards.*"

12-25-32 "*Ole and Ben came over and stayed all day. Played cards with John, Harold, and Bill. Won 43 cents.*"

Raymond was a really good poker player. In later years he played casino all the time with his wife and her brother.

12-29-32 "*Clint, John, Mart and I went out to Silver Lake and cut a load of wood. LaVern, Clint and I went to see Passionate Plumber at the Granada.*"

In Passionate Plumber, Paris plumber Elmer Tuttle (Buster Keaton) is recruited by socialite Patricia Alden to help make her lover Tony Lagorce (Gilbert Roland) jealous. With the help of his friend Julius J. McCracken (Jimmy Durante) and through the high society contacts he has made through Patricia, Elmer hopes to find financing for his latest invention, a pistol with a range-finding light. Comic complications arise when Elmer's effort to interest a military leader is misinterpreted as an assassination attempt.

The Passionate Plumber. Dir. Edward Sedgwick. Metro-Goldwyn-Mayer, 1932.

12-31-32 "*Last day of the year today. I and Clint went down to the tracks today and shot the gun. Jim and I went to Marysville after Seluh met Hank. Stayed up until 12:30 and listened to the new year come in.*"

2-24-33 "*Me, Clint, and Alfred went down in the swamps and found some pencil cedar.*"

2-27-33 "Clint had his trial today and won. I got on the witness stand twice."

3-7-33 "Went to North Junior High School with Clint and Harry, saw United Producers Program."

4-2-33 "Played ball for Hingston today against W. Uniforms and lost 4-12. Lonny-catcher, Louie Locher-pitcher, Lamon A.-ss, Ray Friend-3rd, V. Nelson-2nd, Joe Borroughs-1st, Ray Fossheim-left f, A Canary – center, and Harry (Hungary) Walton-rf.

Note the spelling of Fossheim with 'ss.' Even at this late date.

4-6-33 "Went to see Harold Loyd tonight with Clint."

Harold Lloyd was an American actor, comedian, filmmaker, screenwriter, and stuntman who is most famous for his comedy films. Harold Lloyd made nearly 200 films and rates alongside Charlie Chaplin and Buster Keaton as one of the most popular and influential film comedians of the silent film era. Here is Lloyd in one of the most famous film images of the silent years in 'Safety Last' where he swings on the hands of a giant clock.

Safety Last. Dir. Fred Neymeyer. Hal Roach Studios, 1923.

Raymond loved movies and his favorite star was the beautiful and talented French-born American actress Claudette Colbert. She was an academy award winning star of the 1930s and 1940s. Raymond also loved music. His favorite singer was Bing Crosby.

7-4-33 "Clint and I saw the parade. Clint, Harry and I went up to the carnival. We had a fairly good time."

"Hingston's opponents during the season: Summit Barbers, Marysville, Machias, Delta Merchants, Great Northern, Reform Church, Blue Streaks, County Commissary, Mukilteo, Duffy Drugs, and Stroms Implement".

Claudette Colbert in Cleopatra. Dir. Cecil B. DeMille. Paramount Pictures, 1934.

The following diary entries covering from late 1933 through 1936 were written on loose notebook pages.

11-10-33 "Factory worked half day, I worked all day with Lyle on single resaw, got payed $14.86. The folks gave me five of it. Clint and I went to the football game and saw Everett beat Tacoma 9-6."

Most mills have a resaw which is a large band saw used to cut rough lumber into smaller sizes.

11-11-33 "Cloudy day but cleared up a little in the afternoon. Took ma and Mrs Coldbeck up town and waited for a couple of hours. Bought malted milk and cream puffs. Kicked the football with the boys."

Sawmill resaw bandsaw.

11-20-33 "Went with a church party to the Rink. Dale and I had a swell time. Clint stayed home because he was to tired."

11-25-33 "Worked all day. Got paid 45 give the folks 25. Bought shaving brush."

Raymond and his brothers shared their paychecks with the family to help make payments during the slow times. Often only one person in the family was lucky enough to have a full-time job.

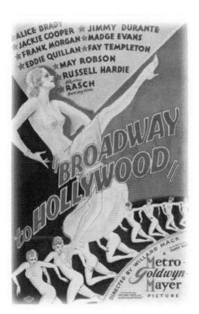
Broadway to Hollywood. Dir. Willard Mack. Metro-Goldwyn-Mayer, 1933.

11-27-33 "Jim, LaVern, and I went to the Granada to see the Broadway to Hollywood."

Broadway to Hollywood is a rather minor pre-code 1933 MGM musical with some notable up and coming stars including Frank Morgan, Jackie Cooper, Jimmy Durante, Nelson Eddy, and Moe and Curly Howard of the Three Stooges. The film follows three generations of a family of vaudevillians, from the

1880s through the 1920s. The most celebrated scene features a twelve-year-old Mickey Rooney doing an exceptionally vigorous tap dance.

12-21-33 "The boss came over. Got me out of bed about eight thirty, went to the factory and worked with J. Rhoads, J. Bennett and Clint. We had to move stock to higher flooring because of higher water."

12-22-33 "Pa, Mart, Clint, John and I went down after our checks. The water was the highest I ever saw it. Shot the guns awhile."

12-23-33 "Took ma and the girls uptown, bought a mouth organ, stationary, and copper set for ma. Went down to the dump and shot rats. Ole came over."

12-24-33 "Worked on shaving box all day, went to church with Clint. We all had Christmas dinner. Alf sent greetings telegram."

4-1-34 "Clint and I took the motorcycle to peaces, put new rings and ground the valves and painted her up."

4-26-34 "Clint's tearing his car apart. Harold Nygard and I went all over looking for John. Wata Ride."

8-26-34 "Lavern, Olive, Nora, Clint and I went up to Lake 22 had a fine time."

LaVern, Raymond and Olivia Fosheim with friend Nora by Lake 22 on August 26, 1934.

Raymond Fosheim at Lake 22.

Raymond on Green Mountain in November 1934

The Fosheim kids loved hiking in the Cascade Mountains. They enjoyed the area up past Granite Falls on the Mountain Loop Highway. Mount Pilchuck, Lake 22, Heather Lake, and the Big Four ice caves were some of their favorite destinations.

2-24-35 "Went riding with Jean B., Russ Brendage, Johny W. and Harmond W. went to Granite Falls me and Russ took two girls for a ride. Met Lois Hunnycut and Kate Walters in Lake Stevens went for a ride."

3-19-35 "Didn't work today. Played cards with Harold N. Jean B. and John. and played again at night with Clint, Wilma, and Olive. We took a spill yesterday."

9-7-35 "We started back east Wednesday August 14 at 4:30 in the morning and come back Saturday September 7, at 9:30 A.M."

Dodge Brothers Inc. advertisement.

9-11-35 "Me and Harold Laymon and Mart went up and traded the Essex for a 1926 Dodge."

9-12-35 "Me and Harold worked on the car, went out to Island service station looking for work, none, went home and had a meal in the restaurant, went over to Storks house in the evening."

1-3-36 "Stayed home all day because of rain, wrote a letter to Morrice. Played cards with Orvell."

1-2-36 "Worked on sink awhile, went over to Laymon's played marbles with Laymon John S and Joe. Went down to Walton's but no work."

LaVern Fosheim, Chuby, Louise Solem, Clint Hill, Olivia Fosheim, Lilly and Helen Solem on June 12, 1932 at 2202 Cleveland Avenue with the Fosheim's 1926 Dodge.

1-5-36 "Played football and marbles with Johnny and Laymon up at Laymon's place the went to show in the afternoon, Saw the Roxy The Wonder Bar."

Wonder Bar is a 1934 pre-code movie adaptation of a Broadway musical of the same name directed by Lloyd Bacon with musical numbers created by Busby Berkeley. It stars Al Jolson, Kay Francis, Dolores del Río, Ricardo Cortez, Dick Powell, Guy Kibbee, and Ruth Donnelly, in the main roles. For its time, Wonder Bar was considered risqué, barely passing the censors at the Hays Office.

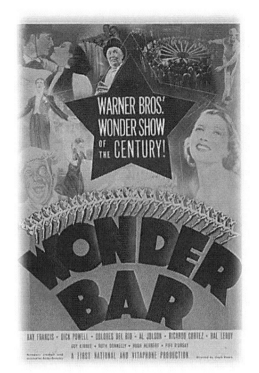

Wonder Bar. Dir. Lloyd Bacon. Warner Bros, 1934.

1-6-36 "Me and Johnny went out to see the new bridge met Sag A. and Joe L."

1-10-36 "Worked on 2 desk rained all day. Stork got drunk and had a row. Went to show."

Stuart 'Sturk' Solem like all the Solem family members was a good friend and spent a lot of time together with the Fosheim's in the 1920s and 30s. He was the younger brother of Oscar Solem and lived at 2634 Oakes Avenue and later at 2519 Harrison Street.

1-12-36 "Me and Laymond walked all over looking for work. Played Pinocle. Going down to Weyerhausers now. With John and Laymond."

3-2-36 "Went down to Walton's again but no luck. Went over to the pipe line, Jim Myers and I went to show, saw Diamond Jim and Ken Maynard at the Roxy."

Martin Fosheim and Stuart 'Sturk' Solem in 1936.

Diamond Jim. Dir. A. Edward Sutherland. Universal Pictures, 1935

Ken Maynard western book. *Fawcett Publications.*

Edward Arnold starred in over 150 Hollywood films and this story of legendary gambler Diamond Jim Brady and his romance with entertainer Lillian Russell was one of his best films. The wonderful Jean Arthur also stars.

1920s and early 1930s western superstar Ken Maynard was a trick rider with the Buffalo Bill Wild West Show and Ringling Brothers. He was celebrated for the stunts he could perform with his horse Tarzan. Maynard was the first singing cowboy in the movies. By the late 1930s he suffered heavily from alcoholism and soon disappeared from Hollywood.

Raymond loved movies and enjoyed going downtown to the theaters whenever he had time or could afford it. Some of the top female movie stars of the 1930s who Raymond enjoyed were Jean Harlow, Greta Garbo, Carole Lombard, Marlene Dietrich, and Myrna Loy. Some of the most popular male movie stars included Clark Gable, Jimmy Stewart, Spencer Tracy, James Cagney, and Leslie Howard.

Double boiler for cooking.

3-12-36 "Went out to Waltons. John and I went up town. Bought ma double boilers, got our pictures."

3-13-36 "Worked on the car awhile Lavern is a little worse today. Emma's sick spaded some more of the garden. I wished I could get a job at Waltons. Me and Johnny S. is figuring on going down to see Hingston and Lyle maybe the first of next month."

Raymond was without steady work all of 1936. He was twenty-two years old and a hard worker. He already had many years of experience in the lumber industry but he had little education and no advanced skills to fall back on. It wasn't until the first day of 1937 that he finally was hired by The Walton Lumber Company next to the Snohomish River in Lowell just southeast of Everett.

A friend with John K. Fosheim, his brother-in-law Ole Øvrum, and Anna Øvrum Fosheim in Everett around 1932.

John A. Fosheim swimming with a friend at one of the local lakes about 1932.

John Norberg at 2202 Cleveland Avenue with the Fosheim family dog, Chuby about 1932.

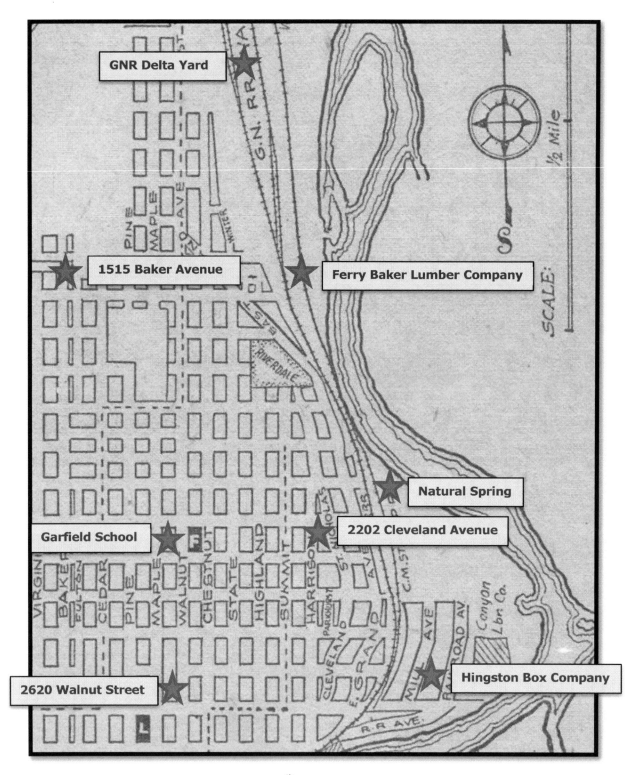

Map of the Riverside area of Everett from 8th Street south to California Avenue and from Virginia Avenue east to the Snohomish River.

Chapter VI

The Hingston Box Company

"Us three boys, ended up in the mill, and we paid our room and board, and that helped. I was fifteen years old when I started. I quit school in the ninth grade; I didn't finish the ninth grade."

Raymond's first job in the mills was at the Hingston Box Company at the east end of Everett Avenue in Riverside, just a short walk from home. Hingston used to be part of the adjacent Canyon Lumber Company and was built in a low-lying marsh along a bend on the Snohomish River. Raymond made twenty-five cents an hour and worked ten hour days five or six days a week.

Raymond and Chuby at 2202 Cleveland Avenue looking east about 1930.

"I ended up in the Hingston box factory down there, over the bank, on 22nd and Cleveland, we lived. Fifteen years old, and then I worked there six years. Then they went out of business in 1935."

Getting to work for Raymond was just a short walk down 22nd street to East Grand Avenue and then down the wooden stairway at the east end of 24th street. Then he had to safely cross the busy railroad tracks, and walk a short distance to the mill on a sometimes muddy road. Raymond usually brought his lunch with in a small metal lunchbox, but when the weather was nice in the summer he enjoyed a short respite from the noise and sawdust by walking home for lunch. Most of the older workers stayed in the crowded lunch room to play cards or visit while they ate. When Raymond got his paycheck he turned it over to his parents to help support the family. He did get to keep a little of it to enjoy at a Sunday movie or to buy candy.

The Hingston Box Company in the lower right center by the sawdust pile. The Canyon Mill is upper left. *Everett Public Library.*

Hingston Box Company: Ole, Clint Hill, Ed, Palmer, Hub MacGhee, and Ray in 1931

Raymond took the photo of his co-workers at Hingston during their work break. He met Clint Hill at the mill and they became life-long friends. Hub MacGhee was a childhood friend from the Riverside neighborhood.

"I was living at 2202 Cleveland when I started at the mill. Most of my neighbors were mill workers. We had a policeman across the street, Tiff and we had a bus driver across the street, also, Morrison. Otherwise, most of them were sawmill workers. A lot from Canyon Mill were right there, neighbors, and some fishermen, of course: Stuart Solem, he went to Alaska, worked in the fishing business in Alaska, then he came back. He came from the family that we knew all our lives; the folks knew them in Norway, too. Sixton Anderson lived across the street. He worked with me down at the box factory; he ended up in the cabinet shop. That was a pretty nice neighborhood."

Orange Clinton Hill was Raymond's best friend. Clint was a north Everett boy and his dad, Orange K. Hill, owned the OK Fixit Shop, on 2811 Rockefeller Avenue. Clint loved to tinker with cars and always had a hot rod when he was young. For years, in the 1930s Raymond and Clint worked, went hiking, went shooting, and hung out together. Clint married Esther May in 1937 and had two boys early in life, Raymond and Kenneth. They lived at 1823 Lombard Avenue and he worked as an electrician at Weyerhaeuser Mill B after he left the box company.

Clint Hill in his heavily modified Ford at 2620 Walnut on April 5, 1936.

Raymond Fosheim and Esther, Raymond, and Clint Hill on June 6, 1937.

When I was young we took a few family camping trips with Clint and Esther. Clint always had his guns with him and he would shoot at targets and anything that moved in the woods. I loved riding on the back of his trail bike and hung on tight as we explored the old steep logging roads. Clint was one of the cockiest and self-assured guys I ever met. He never walked, he strutted down the sidewalk. He and Dad were certainly two opposites. Clint was born on September 23, 1912 and died on May 14, 2002.

"When I first started at the mills, of course the box factory was all easy work, small stuff. That was six years of that. I was what they call off-bearer, off a machine. I went from one machine to another, wherever they wanted me; my steady job was on the printing machine, I was off-bearer on the printing machine. Printing labels on wooden panels. And then I worked on a nailing machine, putting in forms, for the nailer to nail together. It was all kids' work, you know. Then running little machines, staplers, and little, tiny planers, stuff like that. A lot of our orders went to Australia, cauliflower boxes and stuff. And we made boxes for the egg cases, too; nowadays, it's all cardboard."

Boxes in the 1930s were made out of wood, not cardboard like today. The sawyers would cut different length thin boards and the workers would stack and bundle the pieces for shipment by boxcar. The wood pieces were later assembled into four-sided boxes with bottoms after shipment.

As in the larger sawmills, work at the box factory could be dangerous and Raymond had to always be alert. The saws, chains, planer, and other equipment had no safety guards and the sawed pieces moved away from the saws pretty fast. The enemy of everyone who had a menial job in the sawmill was boredom which could quickly lead to a costly mistake. Many workers knew each other before they worked in the mill as there was a tendency to hire relatives and friends.

Raymond's co-workers unloading wood scraps at the Hingston Box Company in November 1932

The box factory was a busy, noisy mill and everyone working inside was covered from head to toe with sawdust. Only about two dozen employees worked in the building and a good percentage were teenagers.

> *"I was in the Lumber and Sawmill Workers' Union, located on Lombard, between California and Hewitt. I remember that in '35, and there was lots going on then, a big strike."*

Like most of the mill workers in Everett, Raymond spent months on the picket lines for sometimes little gain. By the time Raymond entered the work force Everett had already had a long history of management and labor clashes.

Dawn, Elliot, Raymond, and Esther enjoying a day off at 18th and Lombard Avenue on May 4, 1936.

1920s Wooden box factory interior similar to Hingston. *Lars Andersson.*

"I worked at a box factory then during the strike, and we'd picket line down at the end of Everett Avenue, east end. I can remember, we were picketing there, twenty or thirty of us, and some of the head men at Canyon made it awful dangerous. They wouldn't stop or blow the horn, and they'd come pretty fast right through the picket line. I often thought somebody could have gotten hurt pretty bad. Just lucky they weren't. We were picketing for higher wages, but we were out three months, and we only got about a nickel, when we went back. Terrible."

"The least we made at the box plant was fifteen cents an hour. That was more than they were making in the sawmill; seems strange. When we started, we were making so much, piecework; that is, on certain machines, like the printer, but they quit that. In 1935, the unions started; I think they had a union there about a year before I joined it, then they went out of business. He had a box factory in Goldendale; he just moved over there. They used mostly hemlock for the boxes, that's the cheapest lumber; he got his lumber from Canyon Mill, the sawmill right next door. When we first started, they worked you the way they wanted to. If they wanted you to work ten hours, they'd just put it up on the *board; you didn't have no say-so. We put in a lot of ten-hour work days; we were paid just so much an hour. It got down to fifteen cents an hour. When we went back, I think we went back after the big strike in '35, I think we went back to work for thirty-five cents an hour."*

Picketers blocking the road to Weyerhaeuser Mill A in Everett on August 2, 1954. *Everett Public Library.*

Raymond spent many hours on the picket line trying to improve wages and working conditions for him and his fellow workers. It was sometimes productive but more often than not frustrating.

There were many problems in Everett that led to lost wages for the mill workers from fires to labor disputes, but for the mills close to the Snohomish River, flooding was also a big issue. Spring and fall often brought high water but the flood of November 1932 was an exceptionally bad one. Hingston was built on the low lying marsh land that had been filled in over the early years of Everett. The buildings were built up on slightly higher fill but the railroad tracks were a few feet lower. The mill was shut down for half a day so Raymond took his dog Chuby down to take photos of the flood. The railroad tracks in front of the loading dock were four feet under water.

Chuby standing on the Hingston Box Company loading dock on November 18, 1932.

When Raymond began working at Hingston he was following his brothers and his dad into the sawmill business. There were other options for employment in early Everett but for a boy with a good work ethic but little education, working in the mills was usually the inevitable choice. By 1930 Raymond's father John K. Fosheim was making five dollars and twenty cents a day or twenty-six dollars for a forty hour work week. On rare occasions he worked a few overtime hours at the same pay rate. He also missed a few hours for various reasons at no pay. John kept meticulous pay records all his life and did his best to support his family. After leaving the farm in Norway, John had spent his entire American life in the lumber industry.

"Poor Dad, he worked hard in the sawmill all his life, until he got real old, and then they put him on clean-up crew."

John Kristopher Fosheim with daughter LaVern and friend Louise Solem on August 15, 1933 and later in life.

Chapter VII

Rails, Roads, and Water

"Dad, all his life, had no car. Some neighbors never had a car. It's strange. But he did drive a Model T in later years, thank goodness, he never learned how, real well."

John Fosheim like most of the working class in Everett of the early 1900s relied on public transportation or their legs to get around town. Having the money to purchase a car for most was a luxury that one couldn't afford.

"I can faintly remember him driving, I guess he borrowed the car--I don't know how he happened to be driving it. It was kind of dangerous, I remember, he never did really get on to driving a car. But he probably just liked it, but he should never have had any kids in there with him."

Here is a photo that is a mystery. Raymond states that his dad, John K. Fosheim never owned a car yet he labeled this photo, with a 1925 Essex as the Fosheim family's first car. The Essex shows up in many photos from the same period.

The Essex was produced by the Essex Motor Company between 1918 and 1922 and then by the

Martin, Anna, and John Fosheim with a friend, Mrs. Haugen in 1930.

Hudson Motor Company of Detroit between 1922 and 1932. It was an affordable smaller car and very successful as more than a million were sold before the brand was discontinued due to dropping sales. In 1929 Essex sold more cars in America than any brand but Ford and Chevrolet.

Hawkins-Allen Essex and Hudson Dealer at 3020 Colby Avenue in Everett in 1932. *Everett Public Library.*

> *"Of course there wasn't the traffic in those days. The roads then were full of potholes and gravel, all over town, and wooden sidewalks, especially where we lived on north Baker. I remember getting slivers in our feet from the wooden planks; me and my sister would be barefoot a lot of the time."*

The early streets of Everett were dirt, mud, and later gravel. Some of the main streets like Broadway and Walnut were covered with wood planks as were the sidewalks. Eventually many of the wood planks in the streets were replaced by six by six wooden blocks and sealed with tar. Many of the gravel streets were oiled as a sealant. A few of the main streets were covered with bricks. Finally in later years the city used concrete on the main streets and asphalt on the others.

In the early 1900s roads were being built throughout Snohomish County connecting the growing city of Everett to the many other rapidly expanding towns. Horse or horse and buggy were still the best ways to get around but the few that could afford to own a car were eager to try new routes.

Street work looking west on Hewitt Avenue from State Street, January 14, 1892. *Everett Museum of History.*

A wood covered street and sidewalks in early downtown Everett. *Everett Museum of History.*

The first car owned by an Everett citizen was Wilde Knisely's Grout Brothers Automobile Company steamer which appeared on the streets in 1902. By the time the Fosheim family moved to Everett in 1911 there were enough cars on the streets to cause the city leaders to enact laws requiring lights, warning bells and a twelve mph speed limit. Some of the early cars sold in Everett were the Mason, Orient, Reo, Buick, Oldsmobile, and Ford.

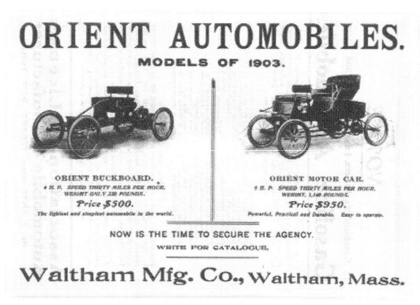

Early Orient auto advertisement from 1903. *Watham Manufacturing Company.*

By the early 1900s automobile clubs began forming across the USA. These were social clubs that advocated rules and safety for drivers on the rapidly expanding system of roads. In 1917 all Washington automobile clubs west of the Cascade Mountains joined under the name the Automobile Club of Western Washington. In 1923 this organization was incorporated under the name The Automobile Club of Washington and eventually became AAA Washington.

The road marking crew for the Automobile Club of Western Washington erecting a mileage post at the base of Cavalero Hill by East Everett. *Skagit River Journal.*

From 1900 to 1910 it seemed like every fire and police department in the country was switching from horse transport to the new automobiles that were starting to appear in greater numbers on the mostly dirt roads. The City of Everett was determined to have the best transportation it could afford.

Everett Fire Department chief Taro and driver in front of their station in 1909. *Everett Public Library.*

The City of Everett has always had a well-financed fire department and has dealt well with numerous fires throughout the city over the years. One of the strangest and most tragic stories involving the department happened on the evening of October 29, 1923. The department fire engine, speeding west on Hewitt Avenue from the riverside station, and the fire chief's car, travelling north on Colby Avenue, collided. Both vehicles were responding to an alarm for a house fire south on Grand Avenue. The huge crash was reportedly heard throughout the downtown. Injured firemen were strewn around the busy street. The fire engine continued on and crashed into the large glass front window of Brewster's Cigar Store on the corner of Hewitt Avenue and Colby Avenue. Chief William A. Taro and Lieutenant Denny P. Boyle were killed in the vehicles and in a hard to

Fire Chief Taro. *Everett Public Library.*

imagine coincidence, bystander and former Everett Fire Chief Daniel H. Michel was struck and killed on the sidewalk. The fire call was a false alarm.

Chief Taro had a checkered past. Tragically in November 1919 decorated Civil War veteran Daniel Bennett who had retired in Everett stepped off the curb at Twentieth and Broadway and was struck by a car driven on the rainy evening by Fire Chief Taro. Bennett's legs were both broken, one arm was fractured, and he suffered a scalp wound and internal injuries which led to his death the next morning.

Everett police posing with their new Oldsmobile in front of the station in 1910. *Everett Public Library.*

In 1911 a saloon owner in the tiny mining and lumber town of Index in eastern Snohomish County offered a case of champagne to the first motorist to drive to his town. After a long just under four-hour journey that included driving on the Great Northern railroad tracks, the first driver to arrive and claim the prize was W. C. Pabst piloting a red Hupmobile. He was closely followed by a muddy black Ford. In 1912 the first paved county road was built near Stanwood and by the time Raymond drove his first car there were over 150 miles of paved roads in the county.

The new highway from Everett to Index in 1911. *Everett Public Library*.

The Hupmobile was manufactured from 1909 to 1940 by the Hupp Motor Company in Detroit, Michigan. The company initially produced 500 vehicles and by 1928 was producing 65,000 cars a year. The Great Depression and other internal problems led to the company's demise in 1940.

With more and more cars on Everett's roads the danger to drivers, passengers and pedestrians was increasing significantly. One of the most tragic early accidents occurred on March 4, 1917 on the road from Everett to East Everett and Cavalero Hill. The highway was built from the east end of Everett Avenue and across the Snohomish River on a wooden bridge and trestle. It was narrow and often slippery with just simple wooden railings on each side.

The winning red Hupmobile entering Index on April 15, 1911. *Pickett*

The scene of the March 4, 1917 two-car accident on the trestle crossing Deadwater Slough. *Postcard.*

Six people in a Ford touring car were heading home to Everett at 2am after attending a dance in Snohomish. They came up behind two people in an Abbott-Detroit car and attempted to pass just as they were crossing Deadwater Slough. Just as the Ford came up beside the other car at fifteen to twenty-five miles an hour, the front car unfortunately swerved slightly to the left and the two cars locked front wheels, sending both through the railing and into the fifteen foot deep water at high tide. Rescue efforts with ropes from the bridge and later row boats saved four people in the Ford but two female passengers drowned along with the two men in the Abbott-Detroit.

A Buick with two passengers that was following slowly behind with its headlights out had just been passed by both cars, giving the driver a view of the accident. By mid- morning the next day the trestle was closed and filled with on lookers as the four bodies were pulled from the slough. When the two cars were retrieved they were still locked together from the contact.

1911 Abbott-Detroit four passenger touring car advertisement. *Abbott-Detroit Motor Company.*

The Abbott-Detroit Motor Company produced its first car in 1909. The company used four cylinder and six cylinder Continental and eight cylinder Herschell-Spillman engines. By 1916 the company moved from Detroit, Michigan to Cleveland, Ohio and changed its name to the Consolidated Car Company. Production ran at five to twenty cars per day but the company filed for bankruptcy in 1917. The Abbott-Detroit was a fast, expensive, and luxurious car so there probably were very few on the streets of Everett.

Raymond said that his first time behind the wheel of a car was at age fourteen in 1928 with older brother John in his model T. They drove around Everett for about five miles until the brakes started failing. John carefully drove it back home with little or no brakes. The Fosheim boys were very good mechanics and loved to tinker with their cars and motorcycles.

John also had a motorcycle but soon switched over to driving cars. Raymond bought John's motorcycle and that was his major form of transportation during the 1930s. Martin Fosheim stuck to owning cars and never rode motorcycles.

John Fosheim in 1928 with his Ford Model T.

"My first car was a Model A Ford coupe that I had quite a while. I got it in 1939 it was a 1930 model. Then, after we got married, I got a '46 Plymouth; it was nice, I liked that car very well, of course I liked most of them. A Model A was your 'Depression Ford,' so many people had them they were pretty cheap. I think for four or five hundred dollars, the new ones, those days, in the depression. Mine was second-hand when I bought it; I made payments, I think about eighteen dollars a month. Hard-earned money. I got it in Seattle at a General Motors firm."

The Ford Model A was the second huge success for the Ford Motor Company, after its predecessor, the Model T, which was produced for eighteen years. The Model A was manufactured from 1928 through 1932. By February 1929, over one million Model A's had been sold and when production ended in March, 1932, there were nearly five million Model A's on the American roads.

Ford Model A. *Ford Motor Company.*

Alf Østmo, John K. Fosheim, Ole Øvrum, and Emma Fosheim in 1928.

The Charles Edeen Automotive Service station at Everett Avenue and Rockefeller in 1932. *Everett Public Library.*

"Clarence DeMars the policeman, he arrested me once. My sister was in a sanatorium during '37 TB, and her girlfriend up there, her mother asked me if I wouldn't go to Seattle and take her daughter to Seattle to this doctor. I did that, and coming home, I came down Rucker, then I turned at Everett Avenue and going back to the sanatorium by Snohomish, and he stopped me down on lower Everett Avenue. He had the book out and everything, was going to stop me for speeding. I was going about forty, I guess. In those days, there wasn't too much traffic on the road. Anyhow, he says, 'Where you going in such a hurry?' And I said, 'I'm going to the sanatorium.' And of course, Faye was laying in the back seat with her mother, laying down on her mother's lap. He looked in there and seen that; he was going to give me a ticket, but he didn't."

The Aldercrest Sanatorium hospital building in 1937.

"He arrested my friend, we were both on a motorcycle, for making too much noise. He was around Everett quite a bit, Clarence DeMars."

Aldercrest Sanatorium in Snohomish was the first site in the northwest built to treat patients suffering from tuberculosis. It was built on a twenty-five acre site about two miles north of the city beginning in 1915 and was open to patients in 1918. A two story administration building was built which included the physicians and nurses rooms, a clinic, a superintendent's office, an x-ray room, a kitchen, and an auditorium. The basement contained the building water system. The buildings for the patients had screened porches so they could get as much fresh air as possible to aid in the healing process. Raymond took these photos in 1937 while his sister Olivia was a patient. The Sanatorium was open until May of 1954 when it closed due to lack of patients.

The Aldercrest Sanatorium administration building in 1937.

The Everett interurban station at Pacific Avenue and Colby Avenue. *Postcard.*

"I enjoyed riding the Interurban to Seattle. I faintly remember the folks riding the Interurban to a picnic at Silver Lake. Those days, things seemed to be such a long trip. Farthest I got otherwise was Mukilteo and Stanwood."

Everett-Seattle Interurban train. *Everett Public Library.*

The line from Seattle north to Everett had its first run in the spring of 1910. There were thirty stations along the twenty-nine-mile route and the trains ran regularly from early morning until late evening. All the stops between the depot stations were 'flag stops' where passengers waved down the oncoming train. The Interurban line was popular at first, but soon passengers switched to buses because of the more flexible routes. The park and activities near Silver Lake increased ridership from Everett in the summer months. Buses and more importantly cars eventually won out and February 20, 1939 was Interurban line's last day. Today much of the original Interurban line has been preserved as a popular walking and biking trail.

Everett to Seattle Interurban schedule in 1938.

Interurban trains were larger, more powerful versions of the electric street cars or trolleys that worked the streets of downtown Everett. Strong electric motors powered from overhead lines allowed the interurban to reach speeds up to seventy miles per hour on straight flat stretches and to climb steep hills. The larger cars had leather seats for forty passengers and were luxurious with leaded glass windows, brass fixtures, and mahogany lined interiors.

When Raymond was growing up Everett had an extensive electric street car that ran on rails through much of the city. One could ride the rails all the way from Lowell to the north Everett Smelter. The service was frequent and the fares were low but it was a very special occasion when Raymond could afford five cents to ride the street cars. The cars were smaller than the interurban and had a two man crew with the conductor collecting fares and calling out stops and the motorman standing up front controlling the speed and applying the brakes. The electric cars had four wheels, open entrance platforms on both ends and two long wooden seats facing each other on each side of the car. Later larger cars were added with closed platforms with entry doors.

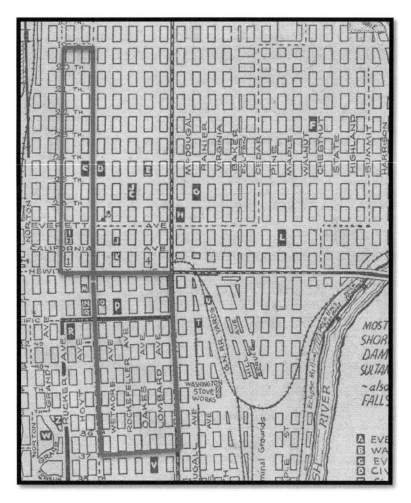

The downtown Everett figure eight trolley line in red.

The downtown figure-eight line opened on July 3, 1893 and ran south on Broadway to 37th, up to Colby Avenue and then north to 19th Street, west to Grand Avenue, then south to Hewitt Avenue and east back to Broadway. The lines were expanded north, south and east to cover much of the young, fast growing city.

The Everett leaders were proud that it was one of the first cities in the United States to dispose of its streetcar system. As cars and busses replaced them, the electric wires were taken down and the rails were pulled up or paved over. Ironically today many cities are bringing back streetcars and light rail like the Interurban at a steep price.

Everett-Seattle Interurban car

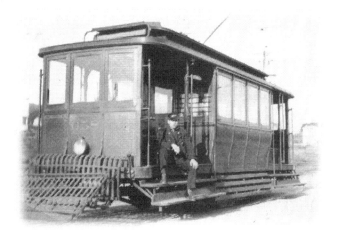

Everett trolley car

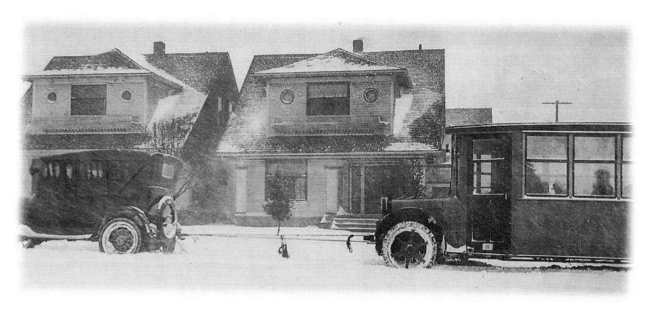

One of Everett's Fageol Motors Company busses being towed on Colby Avenue on February 15, 1923. *Postcard*.

Fageol Motors Company advertisement.

When the City of Everett decided to switch from rail trollies to gas busses the Fageol Motors Company was the obvious choice to partner with. The company was founded in Oakland, California by Rollie, William, Frank and Claude Fageol in 1916 to manufacture motor trucks, farm tractors, and automobiles. Initially the company produced luxury automobiles and tractors but busses and trucks became its big seller.

In 1921, Fageol became the first company to market busses built from the ground up. The company's goal was to build a vehicle that was resistant to overturning when cornering so the new bus had a wide track and was low to the ground for easy entry and exit. The busses were referred to as 'Safety Coaches.' Unfortunately the successful company did not survive the Great Depression and its assets were sold in

1939 to the Peterbilt Motors Company.

Another option for travel in early Everett was by water, and there was plenty of it. Steam powered ships ran from the City Dock at the base of Hewitt in Everett to Seattle regularly and stern wheelers went up the river on regular runs to Snohomish. They were often slow but the fares were inexpensive and the ride was pleasant and scenic.

The City of Everett built in Everett in 1900 for the Everett to Seattle run. *Everett Public Library*.

The first steamboat on the Everett to Seattle run was the Greyhound. Later the wooden passenger steamer City of Everett was built for the run. The Puget Sound and river steamers soon lost their business to the interurban, buses, and later the automobiles, but their memories live on.

The City of Everett passenger steamer was built in Everett in 1900. She was 134 feet long and weighed 212 gross tons. In 1924 she was stripped down to her hull and rebuilt as the car ferry Liberty and then was changed over to the diesel ferry Ballard. After her service at sea she spent the last years of her life tied up in Lake Union as a floating restaurant, The Four Winds. In 1966 she flooded and sank and was soon after broken up.

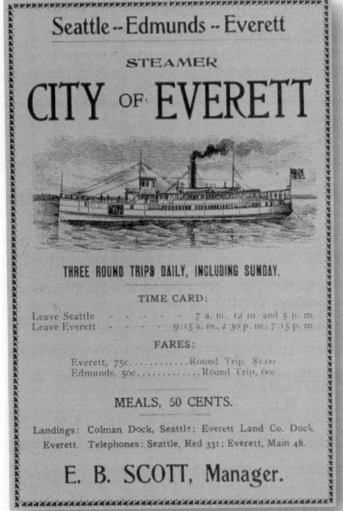

Seattle-Edmonds-Everett route information.

Chapter VIII

The Great Depression

"I grew up during the Depression, that was our bad times, very bad times."

Beginning in October 1929, the Everett area and most of the world suffered from the largest economic depression in modern history. The United States economy withered, after eight years of unparalleled growth. On Black Friday, October 29, the Stock Market plunged and lost forty percent of its value in eight weeks. It took about a year for the full effect of the economic downturn to strike the Everett area but the Great Depression soon ruined the local economy. The lumber industry quickly reduced production as the construction trade came to a dead stop. Exports from the Port of Everett fell dramatically, leaving dock and maritime workers unemployed. It is estimated that the Puget Sound area went from about eleven percent unemployment in 1930 to twenty-five percent in 1935. Homelessness was rampant with shacks and camps popping up everywhere.

The Fosheim's were fortunate to have a home, though they were forced to move several times. Many families and individuals were not as lucky as homelessness became rampant. So called Hoovervilles or shack towns sprang up in many cities across the country as people erected huts made of tin, wood and cardboard for housing.

"Those days, you were with friends a lot more. If you had to go any place, you did a lot of walking. Then you had your gardens. The

Hooverville at the foot of South Atlantic Street, Seattle in 1933. *University of Washington Libraries. Special Collections Division, UW2129.*

city had places for people to raise food and stuff. Then those that worked, worked for little or nothing, so it was tough, real tough. My dad had a steady job, but even he was out of work, not too long, but he did get out of work. None of my family was in the CCC or the WPA."

The Civilian Conservation Corps (CCC) was a public work relief program that operated during the Great Depression from 1933 to 1942. It was set up as part of the New Deal to provide unskilled manual labor jobs in the conservation field for unemployed, unmarried, young men ages seventeen to twenty-eight. Over three million men participated in the CCC, which provided shelter, clothing, and a small wage of thirty dollars a month of which twenty-five dollars had to be sent home to their families.

The Works Progress Administration was the largest American New Deal agency, employing millions of unemployed and mostly unskilled men and women to carry out public works projects. Almost every community in the United States has a park, bridge, or school built by the WPA. The WPA also employed actors, artists, musicians, writers, and directors in arts, drama, literacy, and media projects.

The Great Depression hit Everett hard but some relief was provided by a few Works Progress Administration projects that employed a number of people. Forest, Legion, Garfield, and what is now Senator Henry M. Jackson Park all had major WPA projects during the 1930s. Forest Park's Floral Hall was designed and built by the WPA in 1939. It was built of unhewn timbers from the Verlot area in the Classic National Parks Rustic style and is now on the National Register of Historic Places. None of the Fosheim family had a chance to work in either the CCC or WPA.

An undated photo of Floral Hall in Forest Park in Everett. *Everett Public Library.*

"My dad worked at Weyerhaeuser during the Depression. I remember they were laid off for a while, not very long, and then I was the only one in the family that was working for a while. I was fifteen years old, working at the Hingston Box Factory, down there next to the Canyon

Mill. During the Depression, all six of us kids lived at home."

The depression was tough on the Fosheim family. In 1933 they lost the home that they bought at 2202 Cleveland Avenue ten years before. They rented a home close to their best friends, the Solem family, at 2917 Leonard Drive for the next two years. Family and friends stuck together more than ever as the rough times continued.

"The Depression affected my family terribly. Even my dad was off work, and we'd go down and get railroad ties to heat the house. Him and us three brothers. You can imagine, the ties were tarred and everything, what an awful mess that was. But we just had to keep warm. Then, of course, the Red Cross gave us some clothes, like overalls and stuff. Our grocery bill went up, but one good thing about those family grocery stores, Clark Patterson, they kept you on for food, and of course Dad paid it up later, after things got going good."

"My mother took care of us kids during the Depression. One can imagine a woman with six kids doing the washing and food in those days. She cooked three meals a day. She didn't have it easy

Olivia and Emma Fosheim at 2202 Cleveland Avenue in 1928.

at all, but she had three girls to help her housecleaning. I can remember Saturdays, their jobs. She had a washing machine that made so much noise it was terrible. It was kind of a dangerous rig for little kids, but then in those days, it was a luxury. That's in the late '20s, you know. When we got over on 2620 Walnut in 1935, they got a little more modern one. But all the water came from heated water, from a wood stove. She had a big boiler on the stove on wash days. She had the three girls to help her a lot, thank goodness."

1920s wooden electric washing machine.

Jack Norberg and Emma Fosheim at 2202 Cleveland Avenue in 1930.

Emma Mathilde was the oldest of the three Fosheim girls and the first child of the family to be born in the USA. She was born in Everett on January 5, 1912. Emma married John Aron Norberg on May 31, 1930 in Seattle when she was only eighteen years old. John, also called Jack, was born in Alnön, Västernorrland, Sweden on January 27, 1904 and lived at 2826 ½ Walnut Street in Everett when they meet. He had immigrated to America on October 9, 1926.

The Norberg's moved into 1702 Cedar Street and had three kids soon after their marriage; John (Jackie) Aron Jr. born March 25, 1931, Dolores Jean born March 12, 1932, and Donna Marie born May 7, 1933. A few years later, they completed their family with two more children; Sharon Ann born November 29, 1939, and Raymond Martin born November 6, 1942.

LaVern, Chuby, Anna, and Olivia Fosheim with young Jackie Norberg Jr. in 1931

"My oldest sister, Emma, got married in 1931. She started her family in the Depression. She lived all over town in little shacky houses, and Mom used to bring groceries to her. Even though we were hard up. Boy, it was rough. Emma married Jack Norberg. He was working with us at Walton's mill. He was a nice fellow except for the drinking. He got mean when he drank, so my oldest sister spent most of her married life to him in terrible conditions. But when he was sober, which wasn't very often, he was nice. She lived in the old Sumner office, down in Lowell, for a few years. I'd stop there and visit quite a bit. She was eighteen when she got married."

The Fosheim's were a very close family. Even after Emma was married she shared her time with her parents, brothers, and sisters. Olivia and LaVern were more than happy to help with babysitting and Anna loved her grandchildren. Martin and John were in their twenties but still lived at home to help with expenses.

Raymond was wonderful with kids even when he was young. He spent a lot of time with the Norberg family and took dozens of photos of his nieces and nephews as they were growing up. When he got his first movie camera before the war he also took several reels of home movies of the kids. He made sure that during the tough times all the Norberg kids got a birthday and a Christmas present.

Raymond Fosheim and nephew Jackie Norberg at 2917 Leonard Drive on January 1, 1934.

Emma spent her younger years working as a maid for different families around Everett. She also worked at Providence Hospital for a short time. In 1905 the Sisters of Providence purchased the grand Monte Cristo Hotel, which had been built in 1891, for $50,000 and converted it into a hospital with seventy-five beds. It was staffed by three employees and eleven Sisters. Over 400 patients were treated during the first year it was open.

Original Providence Hospital. *Everett Public Library.*

In 1923 the Sisters of Providence borrowed $200,000 to build a new brick 126-bed hospital at the base of Rucker Hill over the waterfront just east of their original building. Sadly the original historic wooden

The Monte Cristo Hotel in 1936. *Everett Public Library*

Monte Cristo Hotel was destroyed. A wonderful new brick Monte Cristo Hotel opened in downtown Everett in May of 1925 using 500 recycled bricks from the original structure and still stands as one of the most beautiful buildings in the city. It was built for $535,000 and had 136 fairly small guest rooms on its second through sixth floors. The first floor had a barber shop, kitchen, cigar store, coffee shop, candy counter and dining room.

Everett City Hall in the early 1950s. *Everett Public Library.*

Another one of the attractive buildings in town was the new Everett City Hall built on the corner of Wetmore Avenue and Wall Street just before the Great Depression in 1929. The wonderful Art Deco structure was designed by architect A. H. Albertson.

One of the few buildings to go up in Everett during the Great Depression was the Everett Public Library which opened in 1934. The stunning Art Moderne building at 2702 Hoyt Avenue was designed by the famous architecture firm of Bebb & Gould. Particularly impressive are the front entry glass and the decorative details above the entry.

Other than the new library there was little construction activity in either the public or private sector in Everett. Most families were just fighting day to day to survive. Many families did have a strong support system between friends and the church but that was strained to the fullest by the time the economy finally showed a little growth in 1934.

The Everett Public Library in 1934. *Everett Public Library.*

LaVern and John Fosheim, unidentified, Emma, Jack, and Jackie Norberg at 2202 Cleveland Avenue in 1931.

While the Fosheim men were working or more often than not looking for work, Anna and the two remaining sisters still living at home had their hands full taking care of the household.

"She cooked lots of potatoes and gravy. She'd send me to the meat market on 23rd and Summit. For twenty-five and thirty cents, we had a lot of Swiss steak and stuff like that. There was a lot of gravy and potatoes and I can remember sometimes I'd keep a nickel out and buy candy. Still, we got enough meat for twenty-five and thirty-five cents, but then, that's a whole hour's work too in those days. We had homemade bread all the time, that was another one of her chores. I remember the neighbors' also made homemade bread. She made Norwegian sweets quite often, and especially at Thanksgiving and Christmas time, she was constantly making stuff, which was all so good."

1935 was a big year for the Fosheim family. They had survived the deepest part of the Great Depression and had managed to save enough money to buy a house. The big beautiful home on 2620 Walnut Street was purchased by John K. Fosheim for $1,500.

Anna Solem, Olivia and Anna Fosheim at 2202 Cleveland Avenue on September 1, 1933.

"We moved to 2620 Walnut, and I lived there quite a while until I got married. Most of my livelihood I remember was at 2620 Walnut."

The Fosheim House at 2620 Walnut Street was built in 1910 by a highly skilled German carpenter named Schapler. It's a classic example of the American Four Square style which is related to Frank Lloyd Wright's trademark Prairie style. American Four Squares, or sometimes called the Classic Box, were common throughout America from about 1900 to 1925. Schapler also built the smaller one story home next door. The robust home John Fosheim purchased was built without plumbing and like the other early homes in Everett had an outhouse in the backyard. Before long indoor plumbing was installed and a small storage room off of the kitchen was converted to a bathroom.

Raymond in front of 2620 Walnut Street and with sister LaVern and Weezer in May 1936.

The Schapler family lived in their home until 1935 when John bought it. The challenge for the Fosheim's during the remainder of the depression was making the fifteen dollar monthly mortgage payment which was not easy.

A historic home is not just built of wood, plaster, and bricks; it's built with love and a whole lot of memories, some good and some bad. Some of my earliest memories were of playing on the linoleum floor of the Fosheim home. I distinctly remember the small checkerboard pattern on the brown linoleum living room floor. It's still there underneath the new carpet I installed when I remodeled the house many years ago. I just couldn't bear to remove it.

Over the years the Fosheim family re-built the garage, and added a chicken coop and a wood storage shed at the rear of the house adjoining the alley. The buildings had been remodeled and rebuilt a few times but were in bad shape by the time I purchased the home in 1984. Dad told me the neighbor across the alley, Boitano always backed into the garage with his car. Finally the garage was not worth saving with leaning walls and a sagging roof when the City of Everett told me to tear it down. It was a sad day taking away all those memories but some of the old-growth lumber was reused in a friend's project.

Anna and John Fosheim at 2620 Walnut in July 1937.

Three generations of the Fosheim family made 2620 Walnut Street their home. It became a gathering place for family reunions and for visiting friends and relatives from all over the country.

Raymond Fosheim with sister Emma and Donna, Dolores and Jackie Norberg at 2620 Walnut in October 1936.

Donna and Dolores Norberg.

Raymond and John K. Fosheim, Jack Norberg, and John A. Fosheim at 2620 Walnut Street in 1936.

Martin and Anna Fosheim by the garage at 2620 Walnut Street in 1936.

Martin and John K. Fosheim with their wood supply at 2620 Walnut Street on July 12, 1937.

Anna Fosheim was a wonderful gardener and spent many of her few hours of spare time working with her beloved rosebushes that lined the edge of the sidewalk along the house on Walnut Street. She, along with many women of her day, had hard lives with little time for pleasure or vacations. Anna loved her children. She had eight children, lost two in infancy to illness, and raised the other six to be adults that she was proud of. She enjoyed the last decade of her life with her growing group of grandchildren. When Anna wasn't working in her kitchen, cleaning the house, or shopping for household items, she enjoyed time talking to her friends in the close-knit Everett Norwegian community. Sunday was a day of rest when family and friends spent some relaxing time together.

Ray Fosheim and Ole Øvrum at 515 23rd Street in Seattle in May 1936.

"I was twenty-two years old and Frances was fifteen. We went together all summer of 1936 and we wrote letters together for the next nine years. She wrote to me all the time I was in the army. I liked her very much."

The sentences above were written on the back of the photo of Frances below. Raymond met Frances Mitchell in Seattle when he lived with uncle Ole Øvrum at 23rd Avenue and East Jefferson Street during the summer of 1936. She was the early love of his life. Raymond often said that the war ruined everything. When he was drafted and was sent overseas, she met another man and got married. Even after Frances married, she sent Raymond letters.

Frances Mitchell

Anna and John Fosheim at 2620 Walnut Street.

Ray Fosheim and Frances Mitchell in July 1936 and in January 1938.

Raymond Fosheim with Frances Mitchell and friend Mary Keene on June 6, 1936 in Seattle.

Jack Norberg, Martin, Raymond, Emma, Olivia, John K. and Anna Fosheim, Ben Øvrum, and John Fosheim with Dolores, Jackie, and Donna Norberg outside 2620 Walnut Street about 1937.

In 1937 just as most Americans felt the hard times were finally over, Everett and the rest of the country plunged into another downturn in the economy. National unemployment rose to nineteen percent and Everett sawmills began cutting their workforce. The Fosheim's were again struggling to stay employed and make their house payment. Finally in 1939 the United States began permanently emerging from the Great Depression as it borrowed and spent over a billion dollars to build up its armed forces. By the time of the Japanese attack on Pearl Harbor in December of 1941 U.S. manufacturing had risen an extraordinary fifty percent. After over a decade of economic turmoil the world was finally free from the Great Depression but soon would be mired in an even worse crisis.

Raymond and Olivia Fosheim in 1938 at 2620 Walnut Street.

Headline on November 11, 1938. *The New York Times.*

Chapter IX

Motorcycles

"I took up motorcycle riding from my brother."

aymond's older brother John begin riding motorcycles in 1929. By the late 1920s motorcycles were quite popular on the streets of Everett.

"He was riding with certain guys, and I was that age, fifteen, and I'd sit on his motorcycle all the time, just to see what it was like to sit on it. I ended up owning it; I think I paid one hundred twenty-five dollars for it quite a bit of money. I doubt if I ever went over seventy-five or eighty miles an hour, but my friends, they hit up to ninety, which is very dangerous."

Raymond, John & Emma Fosheim looking northeast at 22nd and Cleveland around 1930 with John's 1927 Harley-Davidson.

"Before I got my car, my main transportation was a motorcycle I had. I bought the motorcycle from my brother, John. I was seventeen years old when I got the first motorcycle, a Harley-Davidson, and I had that until I got the car, that Model A."

"The Harley-Davidson was a 1927 and after I had it awhile, I took it all apart and painted it, put it together; it looked pretty nice. They were pretty small in those days, sort of between a bicycle and a motorcycle in size."

Raymond was an excellent mechanic. Even though working with wood was his first love he also enjoyed modifying his motorcycle and later his cars. One had to be a fairly good mechanic back in the 1930s as the bikes were constantly breaking down or getting damaged by the rough streets in Everett and Snohomish County. Flat tires were a frequent occurrence. Motorcycle injuries were also common. No one wore helmets and a spill on the gravel or uneven wooden street could remove a lot of skin if one didn't wear leather clothes.

John K. Fosheim posing on his son John's Harley-Davidson at 2202 Cleveland Avenue in 1929.

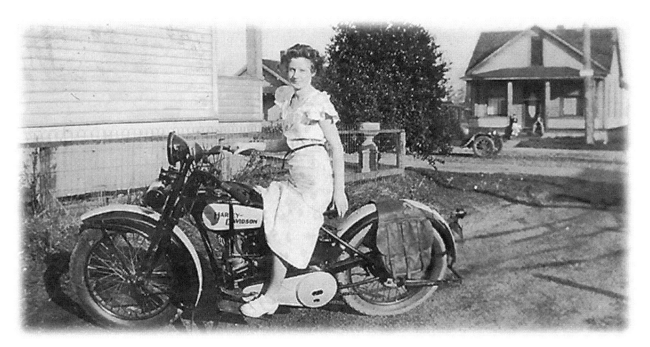

Olivia Fosheim on Ray Fosheim's Harley-Davidson at 2620 Walnut in November 1934.

"I'm lucky; I had my sister riding, we were going south on Broadway on those wooden blocks, the frost had heaved them up a bit, and we hit one of those mounds and we fell down, my younger sister, Olivia, and I. We slid quite a way, but we didn't get hurt, I'm so happy. But that was dangerous, those wooden blocks, about Broadway and Wall Street."

Raymond Fosheim on his Harley-Davidson in July 1934.

"It's like it is now, of course it's worse now, I think, traffic. And so many times people drive too fast. Motorcycles get the worst of the deal all the time. I can remember, a guy apparently didn't see me, or he was drunk or something. We were going about thirty-five or forty miles an hour on Evergreen Way, and he came up and banged me; I could have fallen down, but I didn't. He took off, and I didn't think much of it; just banged up the motorcycle a little bit. That could have been serious, too. A lot of them don't see the motorcycle. So, I was awful lucky during the twelve years I was riding a motorcycle."

Dad was always a safe driver but some of his motorcycle stories were fairly scary. He told me in the winter the wooden Highway 2 trestle to Snohomish would be frozen and covered with ice so he would ride his bike with both feet sliding on the ground for balance. He also had a lot of success picking up girls on his bike. They all loved to ride on the back with their hair flying in the wind.

When I was in my early twenties, I followed in Dad's footsteps and started riding motorcycles. First I had a little mini-bike which I built and then I worked my way up to a Honda 90 and then a 125 mostly for off-road use but I also licensed it for the street. I remember Dad was very upset when I started riding the bigger motorcycles. After his experiences as a rider, he was concerned for my safety.

"There were three people that I rode with, Johnny White and M. McGuire, course they died during the war, in the South Pacific. I rode with them a lot, and Sam King, he was the dealer; rode with him a lot. And Bob Dusheen and Ray Frank, and we called him 'Deacon' McDaniels I can't think of his first name. We had a lot of fun, we had a club, the Everett Motorcycle Club. We'd put on dances and everything, really had fun. In '36, '37, '38, '39 and '40 before I went into the service."

Raymond Fosheim and Mac on their Harley-Davidson at 2620 Walnut Street in May of 1938 left and May of 1939 right.

The Everett Motorcycle Club at Forest Park in the late 1930s. Ray Fosheim fourth and future brother-in-law Frank Marsh third from the right.

An early photo of the Everett Motorcycle Club in 1915. *Everett Public Library.*

Raymond's friend Betty Hensley sitting on his Harley-Davidson in 1939 and with her bike on the 3400 block of Broadway in July 1941.

Along with his many photos, Raymond also had an album with many high quality cartoons drawn by one of the Everett Motorcycle Club members. The cartoonist was Raymond's close friend, Jack Keeler. The cartoon with the broken bike is obviously meant as a joke on Raymond.

One of many cartoons in Raymond's Everett Motorcycle Club album.

The Everett Motorcycle Club had its origins back at least as early as 1915 but I haven't but there is little information about it. Raymond was the treasurer in the late 1930s until World War II. The club may have disbanded during the war and never started again.

> "Before I started riding, Windy Morrow rode with Eugene Boitano, my neighbor. Boitano was pretty young when he started. But he kind of retired when I was riding."

One of Raymond's many fun stories was the one he told about tying a board lengthwise on the seat of his Harley so sisters LaVern and Olivia could both ride with him. He also could pick up girls as he rode around Silver Lake. Two girls, not just one! His first date was Lois from Lake Stevens. They rode around Everett on his Harley.

This cartoon identifies the Everett Motorcycle Club members. Raymond was the treasurer.

"When I rode my motorcycle around here we visited motorcycle clubs in Vancouver and Wenatchee. On a Sunday, we'd take off. They'd put us up for the night, and when they'd come here, we'd put them up for the night. And a lot of small towns, Wenatchee and these little towns south of Seattle. Motorcycle clubs invite one another, you know. Then you put on dances and stuff. We did that quite a bit. And we put up visitors for the night. We just looked over each other's motorcycles. That was my, a lot of adventures in those days, on my motorcycle."

Advertisement in the July 1, 1939 Everett Herald newspaper. *The Everett Herald.*

When I was digging through Dad's photo albums, I found a clipping from the Everett Herald on July 1, 1939. It was a story about Dad performing a motorcycle stunt called the 'dual-flaming board wall crash.' He jumped his bike over a ramp and through a burning wall of fire while another rider did the same while riding toward him from the other side. Dad was the most cautious and safest person that I have ever known so I was pretty shocked when I read this.

Motorcycle Rodeo Set for Bagshaw Field Sunday

With practically every outstanding motorcycle rider of the Pacific Northwest on hand, both riders and fans are awaiting the motorcycle rodeo to be held at Bagshaw field Sunday evening, starting at 7:30 o'clock.

Many races, stunts and thrills have been arranged for the evening's entertainment, which is a part of the Fourth of July celebration. It will be the largest event of its kind ever held in Everett.

About 35 top riders will compete, including the greatest dirt track and trick cyclists available. The famed Cossack troups will provide additional stunts to the regular program. Bob Duchine and Ray Fashiem, two Everett youths, will attempt a dual board wall crash from opposite directions. It is the first time that this has been tried.

Outstanding Canadian stars such as Deeley, Taylor and Saint will be present and Portland will send a large delegation, including such star performers as Roy Burke, Bob Dillon, Ole Olson and Red Rice. Olson holds the dirt track championship.

Many from Seattle are included in the events, including the oversize Heavy Taylor, Aurora speedway titlist, and the Skeel brothers. Aberdeen sends George White, expert hill climber, in addition to others.

Everett will have plenty of entries itself, including two in the board wall crash, Bill Jensen, Frank Marsh, Harry Stephens and Emmet Redeen. These boys have been placing high in a number of the events held about the Northwest.

The show runs for three hours and includes an Australian pursuit race, balloon breaking contest, club relay race, tourist trophy race and others.

The Everett Herald on July 1, 1939. *The Everett Herald.*

The story in the Everett Herald makes the motorcycle rodeo sound pretty exciting. Unfortunately there are no photos or movies of Raymond jumping his motorcycle through the burning board wall. This was so out of character for him. He was always so overly cautious and safe with everything he did. The Seattle Cossacks group is still riding and performing stunts in parades around the northwest. I love watching them every year in the Fourth of July parade and think of Dad. Frank Marsh listed in the last paragraph was Raymond's Arlington friend who he introduced to his younger sister Olivia. They later got married.

A cartoon making fun of Raymond in the Everett Motorcycle Club album.

The Everett and Arlington Motorcycle Clubs in action on a local dirt track in 1939.

The Everett Motorcycle Club family picnic in Lake Stevens in 1939. Raymond Fosheim is in the center wearing the Everett shirt.

The Everett Motorcycle Club at Mitchell's garage at 22nd and Broadway in March of 1938. Raymond Fosheim is in the center.

The late 1930s were certainly some of the best years for Raymond. He made many friends in the Everett and the other motorcycle clubs and enjoyed numerous adventures around the area. The club hosted and participated in dozens of races and exciting programs.

WARD'S 'CRASH' SHOW THRILLS OVER 6000

Crash! Crash! Crash! Thus went automobiles and motorcycles Monday evening at Bagshaw field as, under the sponsorship of Earl Faulkner post of the American Legion, Captain Bob Ward presented his Hollywood Daredevil Aces in a two and one-half hour program. More than 6000 people were in the stands and grouped around the edges of the big arena to witness the daring drivers in their thrilling performances.

One of the greatest of the crowd pleasers was a free-for-all wrecking bee staged by four men piloting old "jaloppies." From the four corners of the field the four cars were driven full tilt at one another and the slamming and banging continued until but one car was able to limp about the field under its own power.

But the free-for-all was only one event on a long list of thrilling acts staged by the Hollywood stuntmen, assisted by members of the Everett Motorcycle club, who put on a zigzag race and a game of motorized musical chairs. At high speeds two automobiles were driven together in headon collision, meeting with such force that it was only with difficulty that the two badly wrecked automobiles could be pried apart. In another thriller, the concluding event on the program, a car was driven right through a 24-inch brick wall.

In still other events a car was spun over at high speeds, doing a tail spin and rolling completely over before landing again on all four wheels. Dynamite was exploded under a speeding car; a stuntman, his head projecting out in front of the car, was driven through three successive board walls, and other drivers demonstrated remarkable skill in handling their automobiles.

Story in The Everett Herald in 1939.
The Everett Herald.

Raymond's friend Ray Frink trying to decide which direction the club ride should take in January 1938.

Raymond showing off his Harley-Davidson at 2620 Walnut Street.

Raymond always rode Harley-Davidson motorcycles. William S. Harley and Arthur Davidson begin work on their motor-bicycle in a Milwaukee, Wisconsin machine shop in 1901. Arthur's brother, Walter Davidson also joined in on the project. In 1906, Harley and the Davidson brothers built their first factory and produced about fifty motorcycles. The company continued to grow until the Great Depression when sales fell from over 21,000 motorcycles in 1929 to under 4,000 in 1933. To survive the Depression, the company produced industrial power plants based on their motorcycle engines. By the beginning of World War II Harley-Davidson and Indian were the only two surviving American motorcycle companies.

Raymond Fosheim and Frances Mitchell overlooking Mt. Rainier in August 1939.

This photo of Dad with his longtime girlfriend Frances Mitchell on a road trip around Mt. Rainier is one of my favorite photos from his albums. He obviously loved her very much and he always enjoyed riding and driving in the mountains.

Riding Motorcycles was Raymond's life for half a decade at the end of the 1930s. Bikes were cheaper than cars to operate and maintain and all of the motorcycle club activities and camaraderie helped take one's mind off the seemingly never-ending Great Depression. Work still wasn't steady but Raymond was living at home with his family and there was enough money to enjoy some of the good things in life.

Raymond made many friends in not only the Everett Motorcycle Club but in the various other local riding clubs. Every community seemed to have an active club during the 1930s and up until the war broke out. One of the riders that he became close friends with was Frank Hall Marsh of the Arlington club. He was an excellent rider who participated in stunt riding and racing. He also was a very nice guy.

Raymond Fosheim in 1939.

Raymond often brought his younger sisters with when he attended the local motorcycle races and shows. Both LaVern and Olivia enjoyed riding with Raymond on the back of his Harley-Davidson and watching him race and perform stunts. He introduced Frank Marsh to Olivia Fosheim and they soon became close friends. Frank Marsh and Olivia Fosheim were married on June 8, 1940, a marriage that would last sixty-five years.

Newlyweds Frank and Olivia Marsh in 1940 and Sandra and Frank Marsh in the early 1940s at 2620 Walnut Street.

LaVern and Olivia Fosheim in their motorcycle riding gear at 2620 Walnut Street in about 1940.

Raymond Fosheim in Lake Stevens in 1940 and friend Mercedes Phelps in 1939.

Chapter X

Minnesota

"My aunt's name was Martha Lyng. She lived in Battle Lake, Minnesota. She lived on the outside, on a little farm. My dad's sister."

The Fosheim family had a close connection to Minnesota as did numerous Scandinavians who came to America. Many settled in Minnesota and other parts of the Midwest. Some stayed and others moved on, often to the Puget Sound area of Washington State. John Fosheim and his sister Martha Balgaard followed their older brother Bernt Stene to the Battle Lake area close to Fergus Falls, Minnesota. Brother Marius Balgaard also immigrated to America and settled in the same area. John continued on to Washington to meet up with his uncle Ole Øvrum while the others were satisfied to stay in the rolling farmland and lake country.

Raymond Fosheim had adventure and the need for travel in his blood from a young age. That combined with a love of family led him on numerous adventures including six trips to see his relatives in Minnesota before World War II. Here is a photo of Raymond on the family farm after a long ride across the west.

Raymond's first travel adventure was his trip by boxcar at sixteen years old in 1930 to see his aunt, uncles and cousins. He followed that endeavor with four trips east alone on his motorcycle in the late 1930s.

Raymond Fosheim and friend Betty in Minnesota, June of 1940.

"I went to Minnesota three or four times on a motorcycle. I just took off. One year, I had twelve dollars in my pocket. Another year, I had twenty-five dollars. That would be my food and my room, I remember paying fifty cents a room. A lot of them were pretty nice rooms, in nice little homes, you know. And then in Jamestown, North Dakota, I ended up with so many cockroaches when I turned on the light, the wall was just full of cockroaches, and of course they scattered. I left the light on all night while I was sleeping. It was down in a kind of basement."

Raymond Fosheim behind sheep clogging the highway outside Livingston, Montana in June of 1938.

"But you'd end up in different things like that. In Montana, I ended up in a restaurant and I had about thirty miles to go to another little town. I should have stayed there; it was getting dark; I ended up in the dark, and the road was thirty miles of twisted road--I shouldn't have done it in the nighttime, that's the only bad thing that happened to me while traveling alone on my motorcycle."

It was roughly 1,600 miles from Everett to Fergus Falls, Minnesota in the late 1930s when Raymond rode his motorcycle east to visit his relatives. There were no freeways back in those days and even the main highways, 2, 10, or 12 were not built for speed. Usually Raymond rode on Highway 10 and it was quite an adventure in those days. Much of the route was unpaved and full of ruts. He travelled during the summer but even though the roads were in decent shape he still had to brave a few thunder and wind storms. One of the main hazards was dodging the cars on the roads on his heavy bike.

"Then I fell down in Beach, North Dakota. They were repairing a road, and there were so many ruts in the road, I hit the rut and broke part of my motorcycle. I had to run to get it started, and when I got to my aunt Martha's, I sent away for the part for it. That was the only bad thing."

Raymond Fosheim's Harley parked near Bozeman, Montana in June of 1938.

"Then, I had a flat tire in Montana. You know, that's an awful job, fixing a flat tire on a motorcycle. In those days, you had tubes in the tires. The roads were so bumpy and crooked in those days. It'd been a pleasure nowadays. Of course, now you'd go faster, which is dangerous, too."

"I went from here to Spokane, and then to the middle of Montana, and then to the border of North Dakota in about four days. It was during the Depression '34, '36, '38 and '40. I ate in just little beaneries and stuff like that. You know, twenty-five dollars, you can't spend much of course you got a good meal for thirty-five cents, in a lot of places. In Montana, I got a steak, thirty-five cents, then you got your coffee and that with it."

Raymond wrote a couple of postcards home to his parents in Everett. One was mailed in Wilber, Washington on May 31, 1938:

"Couldn't find any post office open. Swell weather here and feeling fine. Going on to Spokane 60 miles from here. Good roads and very few cars on the road. Will write to Em and you both tomorrow."

A second postcard was mailed from Medora, North Dakota on 2 June, 1938 as Raymond continued his ride east:

"Hello again. Just crossed into N. D. Bad roads. Had little trouble with clutch, have to get it fixed in Fargo. Feel fine. I'll get there tomorrow sometime. Ray"

"Gas was about eighteen cents a gallon; I'd go seventy miles or eighty miles on the little motorcycle, sixty on the bigger one. I can imagine, my mother worried a lot, but then, young kids never think about that."

"In North Dakota, I stopped and got a room. And while I was taking my belongings off my motorcycle, a kid, came by and talked to me. He asked if he could take my motorcycle for a little ride, which I never should have done, but I did, anyhow. Nowadays, they'd never bring it back again. He just went around the block or so. Of course in those days they were different than in these days. So many people you can't trust, you know. I think people were more honest then. I

Raymond Fosheim with his uncle Bernt Martin Stene in Minnesota in June, 1938.

think on account of the T.V., people don't visit like they did in the olden days. Good Lord, now days, your neighbors, of course we do, too--just stay in the house, and watch the T.V. 'Them days, neighbors visited one another and took care of each other. I tell you, that T.V. is terrible."

First cousins Marie Balgaard Windom and Edna Lyng in Minnesota, June 1938.

Richard and Marie Windom with Raymond's motorcycle In Minnesota, June 1938.

John's sister Martha Lyng with Martin, John K, Raymond, and Anna Fosheim with their 1937 Oldsmobile sedan in Montana on their trip to Minnesota in June 1941.

Raymond's final pre-war journey to Minnesota was a 1941 road-trip with his family. Father John, mother Anna, brothers Martin and John, and his aunt Martha Lyng, who had taken the train west to Everett to visit the family, all hopped in their car and headed east on the long drive to Martha's farm in Battle Lake. It must have been a cozy drive with six people in the car.

The SS State of Nebraska. *Postcard.*

One can just imagine the wonderful feeling the three brothers, John, Bernt, and Marius had when they finally were together for the first time in over thirty years. John's oldest brother Bernt Martin Stene was born on February 15, 1867 in Østgaardsvald and left for America from Trondheim, Norway on April 19, 1893. He arrived in Scotland and boarded the SS State of Nebraska, Allan Line steam ship, and arrived in New York on May 10th. Bernt boarded a train to Underwood, Minnesota to meet some Norwegian friends and that's where he stayed the reset of his life. He was a farm laborer and a bachelor all his life and died on January 8, 1963 in Underwood.

John's younger brother Marius Balgaard was born in July 14, 1879 and made the hard decision to join his older brother Bernt in America. He left Norway and traveled to Liverpool where he sailed on June 13, 1906 on the SS Teutonic. Marius arrived in New York on June 21st and passed through immigration on Ellis Island. He married Laura Anæusdatter Byna (bakken) and had three children: Arne Balgaard, Marie Emilia Balgaard Windom, and Ingolf B. Balgaard. Marius died on June 16, 1951 in Underwood.

The SS Teutonic. *Postcard.*

The steamship, SS Teutonic which Marius Balgaard crossed the Atlantic on was a White Star Line ship with an interesting history. She was the first ship built under the British Auxiliary Armed Cruiser Agreement, and was Great Britain's first armed merchant cruiser, sporting eight 4.7" guns. These were removed long before Marius sailed on her, but the 10,000 ton ship returned to duty as a convoy escort during World War I. The Teutonic had a close call and just missed hitting an iceberg in 1913 a year after the Titanic disaster.

John's younger sister Beret Martha Balgaard was born in February 13, 1886 in Verdal and travelled to America with her brother John Kristopher Fosheim in 1907. She married Johannes Lyng in Underwood and had three children: Maurice Lyng, Borghild M. Lyng Wilson, and Edna Lyng Miller. Martha died on July 20, 1980 in Fergus Falls, Minnesota.

Brothers John K. Fosheim and Marius Balgaard in Minnesota in 1941.

John K. Fosheim, friend Orwell, Martin Fosheim, Edna Lyng, and Raymond Fosheim at Martha Lyng's home in Ottertail County, Minnesota in 1941.

In the summer of 2012 after visiting Mom's relatives in Alexandria, Minnesota I drove west to Battle Lake searching for the Tordenskjold Free Mission Church Cemetery where Dad's Balgaard family was buried. I drove through typically beautiful Minnesota country with gently rolling farmland and more lakes than I could count. I watched the many John Deere tractors in the fields and dreamed about fishing in every little lake as I passed by.

Tordenskjold Free Mission Church in Ottertail County, Minnesota in 2012.

I followed a winding two-lane road with great anticipation until I spotted a tranquil small white church along the road. Sure enough, this was the little Norwegian church I was looking for. I pulled my truck and boat into the grassy field and searched the small cemetery behind the church for my relative's graves. There were probably only about a hundred markers in the field so it didn't take long to find what I was looking for. I found my grandpa's family and spent time alone thinking of what it would have been like to have been in this area seventy years ago. I would have loved to have sat back in a comfortable chair on their farm and listen to stories of Norway and coming to America. As I left and began my long lonely drive home across the open spaces of North Dakota I was content but a little sad.

Tordenskjold Free Mission Church Cemetery in Ottertail County, Minnesota in 2012.

Balgaard family markers in Tordenskjold Free Mission Church Cemetery in Ottertail County, Minnesota in 2012.

Chapter XI

The Walton Lumber Company

"I was out of work until 1937, when I started at Walton Lumber Company. I was twenty-one, and I worked there about twenty years; about four years, 'til I went in the service."

The Walton Lumber Company was on the Snohomish River in Lowell, a neighborhood in southeast Everett at the foot of 47th street. Clyde Walton moved to Everett in 1912 and bought a bankrupt mill, naming it the Walton Lumber Company. He renovated the mill and soon added the Walton Veneer Company next door in July 1924. The adjacent river allowed adequate log storage and a lift facility, giving access to three railroads; Great Northern, Northern Pacific, and Milwaukee. The mill employed more than 300 workers.

Aerial view of the Walton Lumber Mill in Lowell, Washington. *Everett Public Library.*

"Walton's Lumber was just at the entrance to Lowell, on the east side, right by the paper mill and the plywood mill. Today, it's just an open field; the park is on the west side of the tracks, and Walton's was on the east side--the tracks were in between. There was a lot of business there, the plywood mill and the paper mill. Walton's had two crews, a night and a day shift going."

Raymond loved giving his co-workers nicknames. Raymond's nickname was Yogi at the mill. It's not known how he got that nickname but even in later years friends would call him that. Raymond seemed to get along with everyone he met. He was popular with his co-workers and often told funny stories about his friends. He had a wonderful sense of humor. He used to love telling his brothers stories about working at Walton.

"Mack Barley, he sold shoes on the side, I ordered shoes from him sometimes. I worked with a nice bunch, Big Red, and Pinky Lee. Lots of the tally men were the old fellows, the foreman's friends, you know. The foreman, Axel Nordgren, had two sons, and his two sons hired younger fellows all the time, through their dad. Herbert Nordgren was in the army with me, up in the Aleutian Islands. Clyde Nordgren, lives over on the north end of Hoyt. They were Swedish, nice people. There were lots of Swedes at the mill, it was mostly Swedes and some Norwegians. But most of the tally men were Swedish, friends of the foreman. They belonged to the Vasa Lodge, Swedish organization, all nice fellows."

Raymond Fosheim and Mac at 2620 Walnut Street in 1939.

The Vasa Order of America is a Fraternal Society originally established in the 1900s for the benefit of Swedish immigrants. Today the group is dedicated to preserving and sharing Nordic culture and heritage. Raymond was a member of the Sons of Norway at the Normanna Lodge in Everett.

"They chewed snus! That lumber went to North Dakota. They'd spit right on this lumber, certain ones, you know. That's filthy. I didn't chew snus. Funny, I grew up with kids that smoked heavily, but I don't know why I never got in the habit of it. There was a lot of snus chewing, because they couldn't smoke on the job."

1930s Swedish snus box.

"At the box factory, we worked eight and ten hours a day. At the sawmill, it was all eight hours, and lots of times, Saturday work too. Even Sunday, when I first started, they were busy. They wouldn't ask you, you just came to work. The union wouldn't care, this was after the war; the economy seemed to be pretty good then."

"There was a picket line at Walton's a few times, too. But that Walton's was such an old-fashioned mill, and I can't understand, they had such an up keep; everything was on planks, and you can imagine all the repairing, all the time. Then, every time there was a flood, it would ruin a lot of things around there, the planks and stuff. But that one flood really set them back, it was all the flooring and everything was upheaved. I can remember, they brought in gravel for a month or two, just hauling in gravel, taking the planks out. But that's an awful expense. I guess if it weren't for Walton owning so much timber, they couldn't afford to run that thing."

"They closed the plant because of expense and it was never modernized, all old-fashioned. That old mill was a fire hazard. They'd burn all their rubbish out in back. Nowadays, they'd never allow that. But you can imagine, sparks flying all over from that, just a miracle. Their rubbish included a lot of their stuff out of the sawmill, and a lot of their planks from the whole mill. A lot of sawdust, a lot of rubbish. They had a conveyor coming up and dumping on the fire, open fire. That's the only mill that didn't have a regular burner."

"Mr. Walton himself, Clyde owned the mill, and the two boys worked there in the office. Pete Walton was the older one, they called him Bud Walton; I don't know what the younger one was named. You'd see him there all the time. Of course the old man, he'd walk around a lot, you'd see him quite often. They had a firing range out in the back there, too, and the owner and his friends were out there shooting a lot. Even met my doctor out there shooting with the crowd."

The Rucker Mansion in 1980. *Everett Public Library.*

Clyde Walton did very well in the lumber business and purchased one of Everett's finest homes from the Rucker family for a reported $32,500 in 1923. The fabulous home at 412 Laurel Drive is known as the Rucker Mansion and sits high on Rucker Hill overlooking the Everett waterfront.

"We had, in our outfit, a good friend, he was a former wrestler; I nicknamed him, 'The Whale.' He was kind of chunky, had a big stomach. We had these valve houses they kept warm all the time so the valves didn't freeze. I had a sign out there, 'Bomb Shelter, room for one whale.' And then we had another carrier, kind of a big kid, 'Pinky' was his name. 'Two Pinkies.' And then another heavy-set driver, we called him 'Big Red.' And I put down, 'three Big Reds.'"

"I started in making up orders for a few years...they'd give us a slip, and we'd go up in the yard and make up orders. And then I'd work in a boxcar, too, loading the boxcars, until I got the carrier job. Walton's never did modernize, that's one reason it went out of business. In the last year or two, they started to modernize a little bit, but it was too late."

Raymond with his dog and his motorcycle at 2620 Walnut Street in 1940. Perl Williamson, John A. and John K. Fosheim, Frank Marsh, and Martin Fosheim are on the Porch behind him.

By the late 1930s Raymond and his brothers were making a decent living working in the mills. They were all single and could finally afford a few luxuries like newer cars or motorcycles. Most of the residents of Everett were now confident about the economy and jobs but were well aware of the constant depressing news coming from both Europe and Asia.

Martin Fosheim, Frank Marsh, John A., Olivia, Anna, John K. Raymond, and LaVern Fosheim at 2620 Walnut Street in 1940.

"When I went in the service, I made fifty cents an hour; I don't think I was making that when I started. After the service, we got more raises and stuff, 'course, the unions after 'em all the time. I ended up at the casket mill making a little over six dollars an hour all through the sixties and half of the seventies. I retired in 1976; I was making a little over six dollars an hour then, 'course I ended up running a big machine."

"The unions improved our overtime pay a lot. We worked overtime; we'd get a raise every once in a while, you know, we'd negotiate. Ended up at fifty cents an hour. Them days, you'd get a raise, five cents, you know. You'd be on the picket line for a month, and then you'd only get five cents. It didn't amount to anything. We picketed in front of the mill, before you come across the railroad tracks. You couldn't picket on company property, so we had to picket out there. I was on the picket line quite a few times. We had our leaders, and we just kind of took orders from them. You're bound to have a few radicals in a big bunch like that, but they weren't dominant, nobody got hurt."

Ray was a member of the sawmill workers union pretty much all his working life. He believed the unions were good for workers like him, but he disagreed with many of the union hotheads that advocated violence. He talked about some union members throwing nails on the road at the entrance to the mill and threatening workers with violence if they crossed the picket line. He was on strike numerous times during his career and lost many weeks and months of pay with sometimes little to show for it, but he stuck with the union through it all.

Olivia, LaVern Fosheim, Ole Øvrum, and John A. Fosheim in his work clothes at 2620 Walnut Street.

"I remember so many of the people that I worked with that are gone now. They were quite a bit older than me; 'course I was only twenty-one when I went there. One of my good friends just now died; he'd been there many years, too. My middle brother, John, worked there, he went there from Weyerhaeuser. Otherwise, there's so many of them gone. Burl Scott, he's still alive, I see him once in a while. He worked with us; otherwise, I don't meet anybody."

"I started at Walton's New Years' Day, 1937, first day of the year. In those days, holidays didn't mean much. I can remember even Thanksgiving Day, at the box factory, I worked half a day. There was a union when I went into Walton's, but not the box factory. Then they hadn't got their holidays and stuff, just starting in."

One of the many waterfront mills that prospered in the pre-depression years was the Hulbert Mill Company at the foot of 12th Street, which employed almost 200 workers who cut over 80,000 feet of lumber and 50,000 shingles daily. In 1926 the Hulbert Mill also began a casket making business called the North Coast Casket Company. A huge new building was constructed to produce caskets from the left over lumber scraps. The Hulbert Mill Company survived the Great Depression and the casket business became the Collins Casket Company.

The Collins Building construction was typical of many industrial buildings of the time with a robust timber frame. It was three stories tall, built on pilings over the Port Gardner Bay mud flats and surrounded by water at high tide. Each floor of the huge building was 100 feet by 200 feet, and 60,000 square feet overall. Raymond ended his career working at the Collins Casket Company.

"The National Recovery Act, that was what, 1936? I think we got thirty-five cents an hour, and when I left Walton's, I was fifty cents, I think. That was in 1942 when I went into the military. Then I didn't make much for the first two or three months, twenty-one dollars a month. But then it got more and more."

Hulbert Mill and North Coast Casket Company, Everett, 1938. *Everett Public Library*

President Roosevelt pushed the National Industrial Recovery Act (NIRA) through Congress in 1933 to give him the power to regulate industry in an effort to raise prices after severe deflation and to stimulate an economic recovery during the Great Depression. It also established the Public Works Administration which went on the build major projects like Grand Coulee Dam. The National Recovery Administration (NRA) portion of NIRA had a goal of eliminating ruthless competition by bringing labor, industry and government agencies together to create codes of just practices and set prices.

By 1941 the Fosheim family was doing fairly well economically. Huge military spending programs had brought on prosperous times in many industries. The Fosheim brothers finally could afford fairly decent cars and all three sisters were married and had kids. Life always has its difficulties though as John K. Fosheim had suffered from a stroke and was slowly recovering. Anna Fosheim was experiencing some health issues and Emma was still struggling to raise her four kids and was pregnant with a fifth.

Raymond's nephew Jackie Norberg with his friends horse at 2620 Walnut Street in about 1942.

The news from both Asia and Europe was getting worse. Japan was occupying parts of China and rapidly building up its military. Nazi Germany had already conquered France and much of Europe and was beginning to look invincible to some. There was a large isolationist movement in the United States that still harbored bad memories from the Great War of 1918. It seemed like most of the population wanted to stay neutral and not get involved with another foreign war. Like other families the Fosheim's just wanted to live in peace.

Frank Marsh, John K. Fosheim, Ole Øvrum, Raymond and Olivia Fosheim, Martha Lyng, and Anna and John A. Fosheim at 2620 Walnut Street in 1941.

LaVern Fosheim.

Raymond was drafted on March 12, 1942 and was given a 'Leave of Absence Certificate' from the Lumber and Sawmill Workers Union, Everett District Council, from the Walton Lumber Company on April 3, 1942. It was signed by the owner, Clyde Walton. He was required to re-apply for his position within thirty days after receiving honorable discharge. The leave guaranteed him all seniority rights when he returned to his position if in able physical condition at the time.

Raymond expected to serve his country eventually as so many of his younger friends were either joining up or getting drafted. The Fosheim family was rather surprised though when both brothers John and Martin also were drafted at their age.

Raymond's Leave of Absence Certificate from the Everett Lumber & Sawmill Workers Union.

Chapter XII

The War Years

"In '36 I met a girl in Seattle; I worked there for a little bit and I liked her real well and of course when I went into the service, it ruined everything. But she still wrote to me after she got married and when I was in the service, and I thought that was strange. But I liked her a lot."

On December 7, 1941, on John A. Fosheim's thirty-fourth birthday, the Japanese attacked Pearl Harbor and America entered World War II. The war changed the lives of all the residents of Everett and it certainly changed the Fosheim family when all three brothers were drafted into the army. By the morning after the Japanese surprise attack everyone realized the seriousness of the danger to their homeland. Most Americans had no idea where Pearl Harbor was and many thought it was on the West Coast, maybe in California. Local Men were soon standing at both ends of the Broadway Bridge over the Great Northern Railway tracks, next to Hewitt Avenue, manned with shotguns in case of attack, and lookouts were stationed at Legion Park with binoculars scanning Port Gardner Bay for submarines or any suspicious activity. A lookout post was

quickly established on top of the Colby Medical Dental Building and nightly blackouts were immediately imposed on all. The citizens of Everett were ready to defend themselves against any Japanese aggression.

By the time America entered the War, the Fosheim family had survived the Great Depression, held on to their home on Walnut Street, and all the brothers and father John had fairly steady jobs in the sawmills. The three sisters were married and had families of their own. Raymond had his longtime girlfriend Frances and had sold his motorcycle to buy a used 1937 Ford. Now all that stability was in danger of changing as the impending war made the future unknown.

As expected, Raymond received his draft letter on March 12, 1942, shortly after the war begin and reported to the downtown Everett Armory on March 18th for his army physical. John A. Fosheim had already reported for his army physical on March 11, 1942 and Martin Fosheim was also drafted soon after even though he was thirty-seven years old. As the brothers joined the war effort things didn't look good as France had fallen to the

Germans almost two years before, much of Russia was over-run, and the Japanese had conquered vast areas of the South Pacific.

The 1921 Everett Armory at 2730 Oakes Avenue. *Everett Public Library.*

Raymond reported to Fort Lewis, Washington before being sent to the 80th Infantry Training battalion at Camp Roberts, California on April 27, 1942. After basic training, he was assigned to the Headquarters, 3rd Battalion of the 58th Infantry back close to home at Fort Lewis, Washington.

Raymond sent a postcard home to his parents on April 11, 1942 while he was waiting to leave Fort Lewis for his basic training:

> *"Dear Folks, Well we are just about ready to go now so I will send you my address when I get there. Most of us are going to the same place so I'll have most of my friends with me. I wish I was going farther east tho. I'm sure glad Johnnie got what he got and I hope he stays up here. Well tell everybody hello and take care of yourselves. As ever, Ray."*

> *"I was drafted and on April 4, 1942 I went in the infantry, just shy of four years. I served two years in the Aleutian Islands and then the rest in Europe; France, and up and down the Rhine River."*

58th Infantry Insignia, 'Love of Country.'

Raymond Fosheim and his dog Mac with his 1937 Ford Standard in the Cascade Mountains in March, 1942, one week before he was drafted. Notice his initials 'RMF' attached to the grill.

"I took my basic training at Camp Roberts, California. I was the only one of the three brothers that went in the infantry, the worst one. I was drafted into the infantry. And the other two were drafted into the Army Air Force, easy and that, but I got the dirty work. Of course, I was the youngest, you know, twenty-eight when I went into the military, and both my brothers were in their thirties, so that was a good place for them, in the Army Air Force."

Army basic training can be tough for an 'old' twenty-eight year old if one is mixed in with the young late teen draftees, but Raymond's group was mostly made up of older men. First there is the haircut and the issuing of the army clothes and gear. Then it's a matter of whipping everyone into physical shape and installing discipline.

Raymond Fosheim and friend at Camp Roberts, California at basic training in May

Raymond wrote a post card to his brother John on April 27, 1942 during basic training:

"Dear johnnie,

I got your address today and like to let you know that everything is ok with me. Hope the same with you. I'm glad you got to stay up there as it's sure hot down here and no place to go. We've been doing a lots of hand grenade and bayonet training the last week and I hope we get

to use our guns pretty soon now. Herb and Chet Lindstrom are over in a different division across the field from us. They mixed us up all over the fort. Drop me a card later. Ray"

Camp Roberts is located in the Salinas Valley just north of Paso Robles, California adjacent to highway 101. It was constructed beginning in 1940 in response to the war in Europe and the upcoming Japanese threat in the Pacific. Camp Roberts soon had the capability to house and provide training for 23,000 soldiers. Just under a half a million troops trained at the camp during the war years. Rows of wooden barracks were built to house the new troops, Churches, stores, a hospital, and even an amphitheater were soon added to make Camp Roberts a city of 45,000 during its height. When the war ended in late 1945 it suddenly became a ghost town. Today Camp Roberts is a California National Guard post.

Raymond Fosheim in basic training at Camp Roberts in May of 1942.

Camp Roberts, California. *Postcard.*

After basic training Raymond returned back to Fort Lewis, Washington, close to home and awaited his overseas assignment. The army doctors noticed Raymond was born with his neck permanently tilted slightly to the right and decided to send him to Madigan Army Medical Center close to the base for surgery. He blamed his hair loss in later years on the cast he had to wear during his recovery. After a short recuperation he was ready to rejoin his unit.

Fort Lewis entry in the 1930s. *Postcard.*

The newly built Camp Roberts, California in 1942. *Postcard*.

Camp Roberts, California basic training in May 1942. Raymond Fosheim is on the far right.

Raymond Fosheim recovering from neck surgery at Madigan Army Medical Center in 1942.

In May 1942, like many patriotic Americans, John K. Fosheim signed up to purchase United States defense savings bonds. A total of nine dollars was deducted every month off of his pay check for the duration of the war. This was quite a substantial contribution for the family at that time.

United States Treasury Department war bonds poster

Martin, John K., Anna, and John A. Fosheim, Olivia and Sandra Marsh, and LaVern and Deanna Williamson on a visit to Fort Lewis, Washington in the summer of 1942.

Between basic training and their first assignments all three Fosheim brothers were given leave to come home to Everett and visit the family. Raymond took dozens of photos of the Fosheim's enjoying some relaxing time together. John and Anna were both proud the three boys were serving their country but were understandably worried for their safety and about the future.

Everett citizens were experiencing the dangers of war firsthand at home when on Sunday morning, January 25, 1942 an army air force P-39 Airacobra fighter plane had mechanical problems after leaving Paine Field and plunged into the roof of the home at 1521 Grand Avenue in north Everett. It continued on and tore through a wood shed behind the house at 1518 Rucker Avenue before landing against a cherry tree. Luckily the pilot, Laune Erickson, who was on a training flight, had time to parachute out at about 1,500 feet and land in Port Gardner Bay. He was swiftly rescued near the General Petroleum dock by an observer in a small rowboat. Amazingly no one was injured on the ground. Unfortunately training accidents involving aircraft were quite common across the United States in the early 1940s as thousands of new pilots had to be quickly trained for the war effort.

Bell P-39 Airacobra similar to the airplanes stationed at Paine Field, Everett in 1942. *U. S. Army.*

By the spring of 1942 it seemed like everyone in Everett and the rest of the United States was involved in some way in the war effort. The first Ground Observer Corps Civil Defense program of the Army Air Forces soon had 1.5 million civilian observers at 14,000 coastal observation posts nationwide searching the coastlines with binoculars for enemy aircraft. There were also reports of submarine periscopes being spotted in Puget Sound along with false sightings of Japanese soldiers on the beaches of the Olympic Peninsula. The people of America eventually got past the early scares and were rapidly joining together as one to defeat the axis threat.

On the home front, many household goods were rationed during World War II including processed foods, meats, coffee, sugar, gas, tires, and clothing. Individuals were issued a ration book with sheets of stamps which were used to purchase these items. The buyer had to present the ration stamp and then was allowed to complete the purchase.

Raymond, John, and Anna Fosheim at 2620 Walnut Street taken in 1942 when Raymond was home on leave after basic training and just before being sent off to the Aleutian Islands. This is possibly the last photo ever taken of him with his mother.

John A. Fosheim with Jackie, Donna, and Dolores Norberg at 2620 Walnut Street in 1942.

Raymond Fosheim and Minnesota cousin Edna Lyng in 1942 at 2620 Walnut Street.

Anna Fosheim's May 1942 World War II Ration Stamp Book.

Scrap drives were a common practice. Many types of metal were collected to be melted down and recycled for the war effort. Even scrap paper was gathered up so it could be used for packing around military equipment and weapons. Engine oil and grease was saved and reused. Pennies were minted from zinc-coated steel in 1943 to save the much needed copper for critical use. Everett had paper, rubber, and scrap metal drives. Both adults and children went door to door throughout their neighborhoods collecting. Helping the war effort in any way gave everyone a sense of patriotism as family members were serving overseas.

It wasn't just the Fosheim brothers who got involved in supporting the war effort. Sister Emma Norberg, her husband Jack, and their five kids lived at 4325 3rd Street in Lowell during the war years. Like many women, Emma took a job supporting the war effort. All three of her brothers

Hollywood star Rita Hayworth in a publicity shot in 1942 for the scrap drive. *National Archives and Records Administration*

were overseas during the time she worked in the aircraft industry at Boeing in Everett. The Everett manufacturing building was located on California and Grand and produced parts for the legendary B-17 bombers.

The Boeing Airplane Company sub-assembly plant located at 28th Street and Grand Avenue in downtown Everett. The building previously was the location of J. K. Hart's Universal Machine Shop. *Washington State Archives.*

During World War II a major campaign was undertaken to encourage women to enter the work force to replace the thousands of men who had joined the military. Housewives were the main target of this campaign as they were considered the principal source of the replacement workers. Much propaganda was also focused towards husbands who were often reluctant to have their wives join the workforce. Rosie the Riveter was a key figure in this effort and appeared in posters across America. The number of working women increased significantly during 1942 and 1943.

Women workers at the Everett Boeing B-17 plant at 2804 Grand Avenue during World War II. *Everett Public Library.*

1942 Westinghouse poster. *National Archives and Records Administration.*

During the war years the cities of the Puget Sound area produced everything from airplanes to ships to tanks and most of the parts that went into building them. In addition to its booming lumber industry, Everett now had a rapidly expanding military ship building industry. The Everett-Pacific Shipbuilding & Dry Dock Company was established on Everett's waterfront in 1942, with resources provided by the U. S. Navy.

The Everett-Pacific Shipbuilding & Dry Dock Company on the Everett waterfront in 1944. *Everett Public Library.*

The Everett-Pacific Shipbuilding & Dry Dock Company was purchased in 1944 by Pacific Car and Foundry, and produced mostly smaller support vessels such as net layers, tugs and a variety of steel barges. The shipyard also produced large floating dry dock sections, some big enough to hold a battleship. Forty-nine launchings were made in the first 36 months of the shipyards operations but when the war ended the company couldn't make the shift from wartime production to peacetime operations and closed in 1950.

USS Ailanthus-class net laying ship built in Everett. *Everett Public Library.*

The Everett-Pacific Shipbuilding & Dry Dock Company employed over 6,000 workers and built ten USS Ailanthus-class net laying ships for the U.S. Navy during World War II. They were assigned to serve the fleet with her protective anti-submarine nets. The wooden-hulled ships were 195 feet long by thirty-five feet wide and weighed 1,190 tons.

The City of Everett had one military ship named after it during World War II, the Tacoma Class Patrol Frigate USS Everett, PF-8. She was built in Richmond, California and Commissioned on Raymond Fosheim's thirtieth birthday, January 22, 1944. She was 304 feet long by thirty-eight feet wide and weighed 1,430 tons. After the war she served in both the Soviet and Japanese navies before being scrapped in 1976.

The Patrol Frigate USS Everett PF-8. *U.S. Navy photo 2279-44.*

The Washington stove works moved to Everett in 1903 when the city's leaders, wishing to build a diverse industrial economy, lured the company from South Haven, Michigan with an offer of free land for their factory, as long as they employed twenty workers for at least three years. It turned out to be a win-win-win situation for the Mackey family, who owned the company, and the city of Everett.

During the war the galley of every Liberty Ship built on the west

The Washington Stove Works at 3402 Smith Avenue. *Everett Museum of History.*

Liberty Ship ranges manufactured at Washington Stove Works. *Washington State Archives.*

coast was equipped with a range manufactured by Everett's Washington Stove Works. The company also made ranges for the bigger Victory Ships and for many other military projects before the war ended. Washington Stove Works employees also participated heavily in War Bond drives.

Pouring a windlass bedplate at Sumner Iron Works. *Washington State Archives.*

Sumner Ironworks in Lowell, along the Snohomish River, was a manufacturer of mill machinery. Just before the War the company received a contract to produce anchor windlasses and steering engines for Liberty Ships. In the first two years alone Sumner produced more than 600 windlasses and 700 engines for the war effort.

1942 was not a good year for the Fosheim brothers to leave their Everett home to serve their country. Their dad John had suffered a stroke shortly after he had retired from working at Weyerhaeuser and was having a slow recovery. Anna Fosheim had been feeling weak and tired for months and her doctor wasn't able to help. The loneliness and depression of having the boys gone seemed to make her worse.

Washington Stove Works Advertisement from 1930s. *Polk City Directories.*

"She got leukemia, and the old family doctor, those old family doctors--everything was in their head...she went to him the last thing there, and no blood tests or anything, because he knew what was the matter with her. The doctor's name was Dr. Albert Duryea, he was a nice old man. I kept going to him after I come out of the service. My youngest sister saw my mother fade away and she finally got a younger doctor, Dr. Herbert Johnson, and he told my sister right away, she's got leukemia, just by looking at her. And the old family doctor, he said, 'No.'"

Raymond was stationed at Fort Lewis just two hours form home so his visited when he had leave. In the fall of 1942 his battalion was eventually loaded on a troopship and sent across the north Pacific to Dutch Harbor, Alaska, way out in the Aleutian Islands. It took about a week to get there. He was lucky, being put on a big ship that rode the waves well unlike the men on the smaller ships that were bobbing all over on the rough seas. Raymond was in the Aleutian Islands for almost two years. The weather was pretty harsh with lots of rain. In the winter the wind blew all the time and the icicles hung horizontally off the gutters. There wasn't a lot to do in Dutch Harbor particularly during the winter time when the average temperature hovered below freezing.

Raymond Fosheim enjoying a little Alaska sunshine while sitting in the snow by Dutch Harbor, Alaska.

Dutch Harbor became a haven for refugees evacuated from the Aleutian Islands. U.S. Army troops and civilian workers crammed into a bar named Blackies, the only one in the area. It had cheap beer and whiskey. The Five-hundred seat mess hall also served as a theater. The tickets for military were fifteen cents and thirty-five cents for civilian workers. By May 1943, twenty thousand sailors and soldiers were stationed at the remote base.

Sergeant T/4 Raymond Fosheim in Dutch Harbor, Alaska 1943.

In June 1942, the Japanese invaded Attu and Kiska Islands in the western part of the Aleutian chain. These islands were in a strategic location in the North Pacific between Alaska and the Soviet Union. The Japanese capture of Attu and Kiska

Dutch Harbor, Alaska bombing damage from Japanese attack on June 3, 1942. *U. S. Navy.*

WPA propaganda poster for the Thirteenth Naval District, US Navy. *Library of Congress.*

and the subsequent bombing of Dutch Harbor resulted in an immediate response by United States forces. The U. S. Navy blockaded Attu and Kiska Islands resulting in the March 26, 1943 nearby Battle of the Komandorski Islands. Finally in May, Attu and in August Kiska Island were recaptured and the Japanese threat to Alaska was defeated. Raymond's group stationed at Dutch Harbor supported these operations.

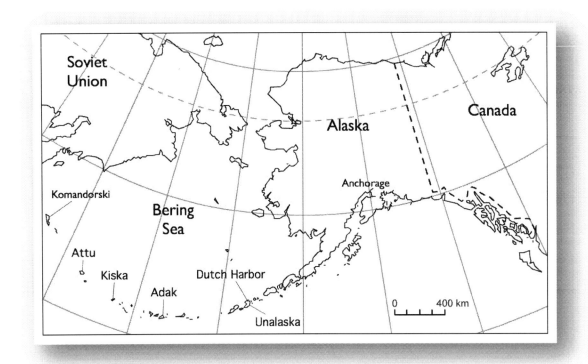

The Bering Sea and the Aleutian Islands with Dutch Harbor.

Raymond said the worst part of being in the army was doing what they told you to do all the time. He didn't like it at first but eventually got used to it. The vast variety of food was usually good even in remote Dutch Harbor and he met some nice guys and made a lot of friends, many whom he kept in touch with after the war.

Anna Fosheim

Raymond hadn't been in Dutch Harbor long when he received the sorrowful word that his mother, Anna Kristine had died at home on November 27, 1942. He immediately received a fifteen day emergency furlough for the long trip back home to Everett for her funeral.

"Two sisters were married at the time and I was in the Army up in the Aleutian Islands when Mom died. When she died, they gave me the news up there. I thought for sure it was my dad, because when I left, my dad had a light stroke. It took us two weeks to get home on an old, slow, small ship. We had so much foggy weather that we were delayed up in Canada for a long time. The military ran it

because we were with the servicemen coming home on furlough and stuff. I was only up there three months and my mother died, so I got to come home to her funeral. But that fog delayed us so long."

The three Fosheim brothers home on leave to visit their dad in 1942.

Raymond was very close to his mom so it must have been really hard on him. After the funeral he then had to turn right around and catch a ship back to Alaska for a long sad trip across the cold North Pacific as winter rapidly approached.

"From there, I went back to the Aleutian Islands and spent just shy of two years up there, just guarding the place, that's all we did. Then we came home in '44 and had our furlough and then they shipped us down to Texas. We were at two camps in Texas before they shipped us overseas to Europe."

Raymond Fosheim with his dog Mac at home in 1942.

```
              CHRISTMAS DINNER

Cream of Tomato Soup              Shrimp Cocktail

                 Roast Turkey
    Giblet Gravy                  Mashed Potatoes
    Whole Grain Corn              Cranberry Sauce
          Sage and Onion Dressing
          Lettuce and Tomato Salad

    Pumpkin Pie                       Mincemeat Pie
     Mixed Nuts                       Assorted Candy
                   Oranges

                 Fruit Juice
                  Hot Rolls
                Bread - Butter
                   Coffee
```

Raymond Fosheim's 1943 Christmas Menu for the 58th Infantry in Dutch Harbor.

Even though Raymond's Battalion was stationed in a desolate area, supplies were readily available and he enjoyed what appears to be a delicious Christmas dinner. He said it was terribly hard to be so far away from home during the holidays but he made numerous close friends during his time in the Aleutian Islands that he kept in contact with for many years.

John Fosheim missed his sons tremendously during the war. His wife Anna of almost forty years was gone but he did have his three daughters and a growing group of grandkids close by. He was healthy enough to ride the train and make one more trip back to see his brothers and sister in Fergus Falls, Minnesota in late September of 1943. He often wrote postcards to send to his boys overseas.

Dolores Norberg, John K. Fosheim, and Olivia Marsh at 2620 Walnut Street in

John Fosheim with Emma, Jack, Raymond, Sharon, Dolores and Donna Norberg and Olivia and Sandra Marsh in 1943.

Raymond was promoted from private first class to technical sergeant 4 on January 14, 1944 while assigned to Headquarters 3rd Battalion, 58th Infantry in the Aleutian Islands. He skipped past the rank of corporal.

For Easter of 1944 Raymond's commanding major sent out this letter to his troops:

"For the most of you this is the second Easter Day you have spent in Alaska. I know that all of you have suffered many hardships and privations for which all of you are better men. I consider the Alaskan soldier the finest of all because he has had to have sand and guts to face the hardships that Alaska has to give. You have not yet faced our enemies in combat, but you have lived an even more rugged existence, in that all of you are and have been patiently waiting for the opportunity to slug it out with them."

"Your duties in this theater of operations are just as important and will have just as much weight in determining the ultimate victory over our enemies as the duties of those soldiers who are in Italy, Burma, or the South Pacific."

"At this time I wish to extend Easter Greetings to all of you. It is hoped that by next Easter Day we will have helped to rid the world entirely of the cut-throats and gangsters that have caused the world so much heartache and suffering. Never forget the true meaning of Easter, for without that, we cannot survive."

Raymond Fosheim working on a GMC truck in the Dutch Harbor, Alaska motor pool.

The GMC model CCKW350 series, 2 ½-ton 6x6 trucks, nick-named the 'Deuce-and-a-half' by the GIs was America's standard truck during WWII. GMC built over 500,000 military trucks in the 1940s and Raymond got to know every inch of them. They had a ninety-two horsepower 270 cid inline six-cylinder engine with a five-speed transmission and were used in every theatre of the war.

GMC CCKW350 2 ½ ton. *U. S. Army.*

Raymond Fosheim with his 'Deuce-and-a-half' and sight-seeing in Dutch Harbor.

Raymond Fosheim's military motor vehicle operator's permit.

"I started out driving the officers around, then I went to the garage and started working on cars, motors and stuff. Then I ended up in charge of that; there was only about three months of that. Them days, everybody worked on their own cars, the old Model Ts and stuff. At home, I had a good friend, Clinton Hill; he was really good at motors and stuff, and I'd help him. That's where I first got my knowledge of car motors. And I did a lot of work on my own cars, and then I gradually worked up in the Army to bigger trucks and stuff, different equipment, more modern equipment, so it helped a lot."

Hollywood star Olivia de Havilland in 1942. *Henry Publishing Company*.

Visiting Raymond Fosheim in 1944.

Academy award winning actress Olivia de Havilland took time away from her busy filming schedule to visit Raymond's base in Dutch Harbor on a USO tour in 1944. She was one of the top Hollywood stars at the time. She appeared in 1939s Gone with the Wind and later won the Oscar for Best Actress for her performance in To Each His Own in 1946 and again for The Heiress in 1949. Raymond took the photo of her above and she also gave him an autographed photo during her visit.

The USO and the military put a lot of effort into bringing celebrities and entertainers to even the most remote outposts to lift the soldiers and sailors morale.

Olivia de Havilland photo autographed to Raymond Fosheim in 1944.

Disney Donald Duck USO poster from WWII. *USO Inc.*

The USO (United Service Organizations) was founded in February of 1941 when six service agencies (Young Men's Christian Association, Young Women's Christian Association, National Catholic Community Service, National Jewish Welfare Board, Salvation Army, and National Traveler's Aid Association) combined their energies to entertain and support servicemen and women stationed away from home. USO brought song, dance, and beautiful women to the men fighting on the front lines and USO clubs were established to help entertain wearied factory workers across the USA during the war.

The motor pool in 1943. Raymond Fosheim's desolate home for two years close to Dutch Harbor.

On a clear day Dutch Harbor and the Aleutian Islands could be a beautiful place but one can bet that Raymond and his entire battalion were more than happy to give up their heavy winter clothes and return to the USA. It must have been a shock to arrive in the warm clear California sun when Raymond's ship sailed into San Diego.

"Our whole outfit was kind of an over aged outfit. When we come back from the Aleutian Islands, they turned us over to the Marines down there in San Diego. We were at Camp Callan, San Diego, and they turned us over to the Marines for training, island training. But we were so old, they got rid of us; we weren't lively enough. But, of course, we did what we were told; we were a little slower. When you get in the thirties and forties, you can't keep up with the young eighteen and nineteen and twenty year-olds."

Raymond Fosheim next to one of the historic buildings in Dutch Harbor.

Instead of sending Raymond back to the South Pacific the army sent him for a paid tour of Europe. He was transferred to the 106th Infantry Division and Headquarters Company which had recently been formed for service in Europe. The 106th was the last of the sixty-six infantry divisions activated in WWII. It was made up of a motley group of new draftees and others from diverse

The entrance to Camp Swift, Texas. *U. S. Department of Defense.*

backgrounds. Raymond stopped at Camp Swift, Texas just east of Austin for a short time before boarding a troop train to Boston. He then was sent across the Atlantic by ship to England in November 1944.

"There were so many camps. Camp Swift was one of them. The other was a camp where the mountain troops were; I don't know what we were doing there, just fooling around until they shipped us to Europe. But then the war had pretty well gone against Germany at that time. I could never understand why they shipped us over there. But I am glad we got to go over there and see the whole country, but it was such a mess."

After only 19 days of training in England, Raymond's mostly inexperienced group arrived in France in December 1944 to join the Rhineland Campaign and then the Ardennes-Alsace Campaign. They were placed in a support position atop the Schnee Eifel on the German-Belgian border, hidden away from any expected combat. The Germans were pretty much beaten and the end of the war was just months away, or so they thought.

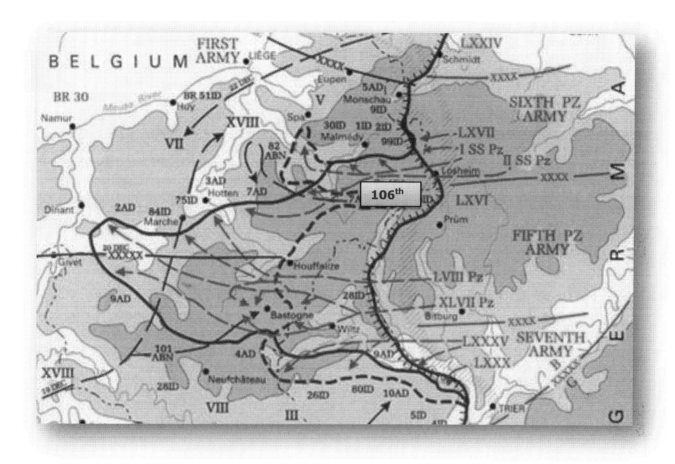

Map of the Battle of the Bulge during late December 1944. German advances from the east to the west into Belgium (red arrows with blue border lines). Most of Raymond Fosheim's 106th Infantry Division was trapped in the center of the attack.

No sooner than the 106th Infantry settled into its position on December 16th, it was overrun by the surprise German advance during the 'Battle of the Bulge.' Two of its three regiments were besieged and surrounded in the initial attacks and forced to surrender to German forces on December 19, 1944. The Germans took 6,000 American prisoners in the area of Schonberg in one of the largest mass surrenders in American military history, but luckily for Raymond he was with Headquarters Company, further from the German advance. Ultimately after heavy casualties on both sides the German attackers were turned back and the last German offensive of the war was over.

"It takes younger kids to be good fighting guys. But we got pretty close, when the Americans first went across the Rhine River, in the Remagen area. Otherwise, we never saw any action. We took care of prisoners of war, and we sure got lots of them, it kept us busy!"

The 106th Infantry Insignia, 'Golden Lions.'

Raymond Fosheim in Germany in 1945.

Raymond was reassigned to the 1st Battalion of the 159th Infantry Regiment when it was attached to the 106th to replace the two captured regiments. The division crossed the Rhine River into Germany in February where, for the remainder of its stay in Europe, handled prisoner of war compounds and participated in occupational duties. Finally the German army was beaten.

"We camped and were stationed all up and down the Rhine River. Beautiful countryside. But the towns were all demolished; bad, sickening. But the countryside was so beautiful.

1269th Engineer Combat Battalion crossing the Rhine River near Worms, Germany March 1945. *U.S. Army.*

We were guarding the German prisoners most of the time over there. It was quite a job, the poor things, they were out in the field, you know, cold and standing around while our head men were sorting them out. And then we'd have to transport them where ever they wanted to sort them out. But we took them all over to different camps."

"It kept us busy, hauling those prisoners. Of course we had to feed them, too. I was one of the truck drivers. They used General Motors two and a-half ton trucks to haul the prisoners. Otherwise, I was at the head of the mechanics for a while. I ended up in the motor pool, of course I worked in the motor pool all the time I went overseas, Aleutian Islands and in Europe."

"I saw a lot of suffering over there; it would make you sick. Those poor guys out in the field; we gave them blankets and everything. But we even had the nerve to take the cigarettes out of the food parcels for the German prisoners, we didn't give them any cigarettes. We didn't have any trouble with them, they were defeated. We took them to certain camps, the prisoners; went through certain towns, they had a lot of people waving at them and everything. They backed their soldiers up very well."

Raymond Fosheim enjoying his free time with German kids in Karlsruhe, Germany in 1945.

Just like in the Aleutian Islands, Raymond was assigned to the motor pool while he was in Europe. He took all the extra rations that were unclaimed and gave them to the German kids. He never smoked cigarettes so he also traded them for candy and food for the kids. Raymond had numerous photos taken of him with happy German kids standing next to him and sitting on his lap. They tried to follow him everywhere. It was a good respite from all the sad sights of destruction everywhere. Raymond gave away everything that he could find to help out the civilians and also the prisoners. That is just the way he always was. He would give you the shirt off his back if you asked.

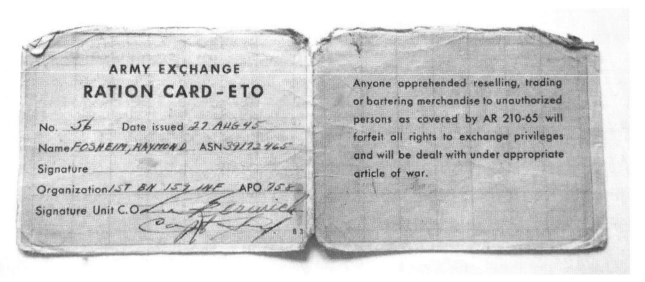

Raymond Fosheim's army exchange ration card from August 1945.

"They begged me for gasoline and stuff, for their cigarette lighters. If I found extra food, I'd give it to the prisoners. And the little kids, we'd chase them out of their homes, and go live in their homes; poor little kids. I'd take food out of the mess hall and give it to them. I'd even bring coffee out to their mothers; a lot of their mothers were there too, it was kind of rough. But then, it was the only way we could do it, I guess, instead of putting us out in the field."

By the winter of 1945 most Germans knew the war was lost and begin surrendering by the thousands. They had to be sorted out, interrogated, fed and housed.

German prisoners in 1945. *U. S. Army*

"I got well acquainted with a lot of the prisoners. Even wrote to them after I got home. Far as I know, they all liked Hitler and hoped he'd won. Of course, I always mention now, if Hitler would have laid low for a couple more years, he'd really have had an atomic bomb and everything. That's what ruined him, he went too fast. That's what some of the prisoners told me, too. I have to agree with them there."

"They knew the war was pretty much over by the time they were captured. They weeded out the bad ones, the ones that were guilty of something, the higher-ups did that. We had very few officers, they were no doubt separated somehow. Mostly just enlisted men. But I never saw any young kids, there were supposed to be a lot of them, but I never saw those young kids. They might have been captured farther north or something, the younger ones, and somebody else got to take care of them, I suppose, I don't know."

Raymond Fosheim on the left sitting in front of his jeep with a friend at their 159th Infantry camp in Germany in 1945.

"The camps were named after cigarette companies, in northern France. Lucky Strike and Camel, I don't know why. But we were all in there until we started heading into Germany. Then we were on our own battalion, traveling on our own. We were heading into Germany to take care of prisoners, I guess; they gave us that job. When they surrendered, they had them in this huge field, a hundred thousand, maybe. And we had to separate them. All our men had certain jobs, feeding them and taking care of them. 'Course we had the job of driving them, sorting them, taking certain ones different places."

"We fed them those little boxes of breakfast, lunch and dinner. Regular Army edition C Rations, we had them, too. There were three cigarettes in each one. They took them out, wouldn't give them to the prisoners. Where did the cigarettes go? I don't know. I suppose there was a lot of crooked work there, too. But I didn't smoke, but still I was rationed cigarettes, each person got so many cigarettes. I still got those cigarettes, but I had friends who grabbed them as fast as I could get them."

Raymond fulfilled his dream of seeing Europe and made the best of it under the difficult circumstances. He loved the historic sights and the architecture even though there was much destruction and chaos. On his short leave he went to Belgium at the end of the war and enjoyed exploring and spending time with the USO ladies.

While in Germany he made friends with a local restaurant owner's daughter, Rita in Eggenstein. As usual Raymond always had his camera handy to record his adventures.

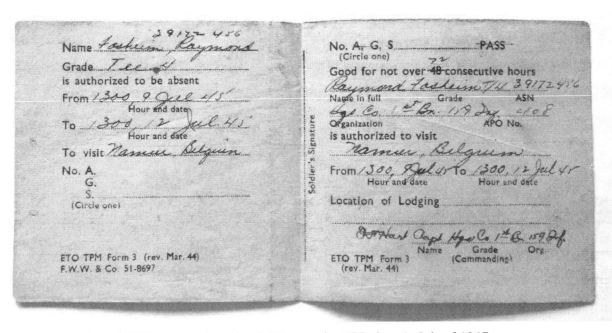

Raymond Fosheim's 72 hour pass to enjoy Belgium and a USO show in July of 1945.

Raymond Fosheim and his friend with USO ladies in Belgium and with German friend Rita in Eggenstein, Germany.

The 159th Infantry published a regular newsletter and in the August 24, 1945 edition, Raymond received a humorous mention:

MOTOR POOL VS CP

The scoop of the week for Hq Co came Tuesday when T4 (Souvenir Collector) Fosheim for the first time beat TSgt Frank Costello out in a hot race to the Mess Hall. Sgt Costello vowed that it would never happen again and up to this writing he is again holding his own.

> "I was there until the war ended, and then we waited our turn to go home. We went over on a big ship, thank goodness, we were going level with the other ones. My brother was on a little boat going with us, and he was bouncing all over the ocean. We went along pretty nice on the big ship, U.S.S. America. Coming home, we were on a smaller ship, but the ocean was just beautiful. From New Jersey, they flew us home on a little C-47, a regular passenger plane; they depended on that a lot and they flew us to Marysville, California and discharged us there. I took the train from there up to Seattle."

SS *America* renamed USS *West Point* (AP-23) during WWII. *Postcard.*

The 159th Infantry Insignia.

> "I was glad to get home, my mother died while I was overseas and my dad had had a stroke, so it was kind of rough, too."

On November 8, 1945 the 159th was inactivated and Raymond was sent home from Europe, never to return. Before flying to the West Coast, he spent a short time in Camp Kilmer, New Jersey where he met up with his brother Martin and good Everett friend John Solem.

> "The 159th infantry was mostly what I was in. Then when we got into Germany, I was in the Third Army, Patton's, that mean general. We kept so busy all the time, just taking care of prisoners. Kind of monotonous, but then, I felt so sorry for a lot of those kids and men. I mostly saw the older

fellows; they were probably the ones who surrendered easier, got tired of everything. But most of them were, I'd say, my age, early thirties."

Like many soldiers Dad had a pen pal during the latter part of the war from 1943 through 1945, Dorthy 'Dottie' Urich from Pennsylvania. The two continued to write for a short time after the war but they never met in person.

Pen pal Dorthy Urich from Pennsylvania.

Many men and women came home from the war with serious mental and physical injuries and many would not talk about their time overseas until late in life if ever. Raymond was one of the lucky ones that came home unscathed at least it always seemed so. He often talked with his brothers and his family about his war experiences. It took almost four years out of his life but it was something he had to do.

Like many organizations the Red Cross was active in fund raising to support the military during the war. Their truck was often seen on the streets of Everett. The funds raised were used to create Red Cross parcels containing mostly food, tobacco and personal hygiene items which were distributed to prisoners of war. Medical parcels were also delivered.

The 1944 Red Cross Caravan fund raising campaign on Hewitt Avenue just east of Colby Avenue in Everett. *Everett Public Library.*

The war in the Pacific was nearing its end in 1945 but the dangers of war had not ended on the home front in Everett. These dangers really hit close to home when on March 13, 1945 an unexploded Japanese balloon bomb was discovered in southwest Everett. Beginning in November 1944 the Japanese began launching the first of over 9,000 paper balloon bombs. The thirty-three foot diameter hydrogen filled balloons floated in the wind across the Pacific Ocean, some reaching the Puget Sound area. The Everett balloon was quickly disposed of by military men stationed at nearby Paine Field.

The existence of the balloon bombs was hushed up by the military so civilians would not panic, but unfortunately this policy may have led to the deaths of one adult and five children in Oregon when they discovered and accidently detonated a bomb in May, 1945. Over 300 balloon bombs landed in North America and as far east as Michigan.

Japanese Balloon Bomb. *United States Army.*

"I got sergeant's rating up in the Aleutian Islands; I was only up there about six months, working in the garage, and got sergeant rating, and I was the same rating when I was discharged. I put all the money I could in soldiers' savings and then got it when I got discharged. I had about fifteen hundred dollars, I remember, when I got discharged. I had to fix my car, a Model A, when I got home, it was in the garage. I had to get that fixed. I had to help my dad too, so that wasn't much, but then it helped."

Like his two brothers John A. Fosheim was drafted into the army shortly after the war started. He reported to the Everett armory on March 11, 1942 for his physical. After basic training John was assigned to the Army Air Force in the 69th Tactical Reconnaissance Group who flew North American F-6 Mustangs a derivative of the famous P-51. He was in France from February to March of 1945 as part of the Ninth Air Force. His group flew visual and photographic reconnaissance missions to provide intelligence for ground and air units. John was not a flyer though due to his age and spent most of his army years as a cook in the mess hall.

The United States Army Air Force insignia.

V-mail, short for Victory Mail, was a mail process used during WWII by service men and women stationed abroad. A V-mail letter would be written on small paper sheets, censored, copied to film, and printed back to paper upon arrival at its destination in America. The V-mail process ensured that thousands of tons of transport space could be reserved for war materials. As many as thirty-seven mail bags could be replaced by a single V-mail bag and the weight could be reduced from 2,575 pounds to forty-five pounds.

> Pfc. John A. Fosheim, 2620 Walnut street, has been promoted to corporal and has also been awarded the good conduct medal. He is serving in the army air corps, in the Louisiana maneuver area.

Notice in the Everett Herald newspaper announcing John's promotion in 1944.

John A. Fosheim shortly after the war in late 1945 with some of his many war souvenirs which he mailed home from Germany. He is wearing a German officers hat and holding two German swords.

John Fosheim was discharged as a corporal on September 17, 1945 at Ft. Lewis, Washington. Like many American soldiers in WWII he sent home several souvenirs from Europe. I found an army certificate listing his enemy military equipment: One German rifle, three German swords, one German canteen, four pistols, three German caps, two bayonets, one German belt, one gun holster, and one sword tussel. I would have loved to see his collection but he either sold it or gave it away before I was old enough to appreciate his historic treasures.

The Fosheim boys were very good at keeping in touch with their family at home in Everett. They all wrote numerous letters from England, France, and Germany during 1944 and 1945. They thought of their aging father, their sisters, brother in laws, and their seven nieces and nephews. The also wrote letters to one another, not knowing where they were but they did know they were all somewhere in Europe. The war was all too slowly nearing an end and all they could think of was coming home.

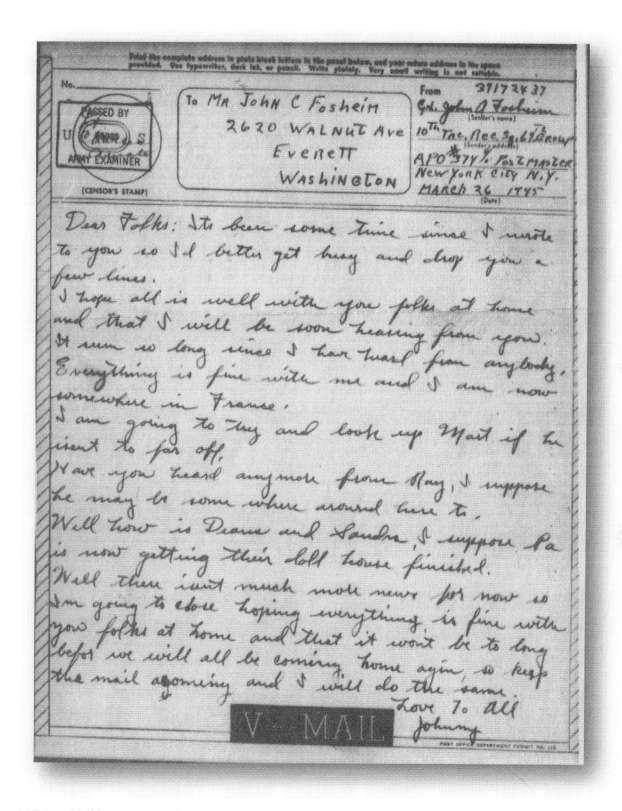

A Victory Mail letter From John A. Fosheim sent home from France on March 26, 1945.

John A. Fosheim with niece Deanna Williamson at home and in basic training in 1942.

Martin Fosheim and brother-in-law Frank Marsh at 2620 Walnut Street in 1942.

Martin Fosheim was drafted into the United States Army at thirty-seven years old. He reported for duty on July 7, 1942 and was eventually assigned to the IX engineering command 850th engineer aviation battalion, a service and support unit for the 9th Air Force which was activated on November 1, 1942 at Hammer Field, California. After months of training and construction duties in America, Martin's group sailed to Scotland in May of 1943. The men of the 850th immediately began construction on new facilities at various airports in England in a build up to support the upcoming invasion of Europe. It was hard work with 15 hour days and the constant threat of German air attacks.

The 850th left from Southampton, England and landed on Utah Beach on June 20th, just two weeks after D-Day. They went right to work and built a small airfield behind the beach. Martin was shocked to see the destruction along the roads of

Normandy from the huge battles that were still waging just a few miles away. From there the battalion proceeded to build airfields at Querville, Gaem, Iannes, Alençon, Vitry, Reims, Haye, Nancy and many other locations. Sometimes before the fighting was even done, Martin's group would move in to start rebuilding. By April, 1945, they had crossed the Rhine River where they completed five more airfields in occupied Germany. Martin was discharged after the war ended as a corporal technician 5th grade.

Raymond's younger sister LaVern married a navy man before the war. Perl Williamson joined the navy on June 12, 1934 as a seaman and by the end of the war in 1945 had been promoted to Lieutenant Commander. Much of his time was spent on the famous aircraft carrier USS Saratoga in the Pacific Ocean.

Martin Fosheim's group with a captured German HE-111 twin engined bomber in 1945. *U. S. Army.*

LaVern, Deanna, and Perl Williamson in 1942.

LaVern and Perl Williamson in 1945 after the war.

The Fosheim family had reason to be relieved that the long war was over. Everyone survived, unlike many friends from earlier days. Now it was time to get back to normal working lives and to continue raising families.

I was in my late teens when I first found out that Dad had been married for a short time while away in the Army. He, Mom, or the family never mentioned it. She was an Everett girl with a young daughter and a sister of a close friend of the family. The only thing Dad ever said was she didn't want to wait for him to come home from the war so they soon divorced.

Dad took lots of photos during the war and because of his position, was able to send home many souvenirs. Unfortunately people took advantage of his generosity and he gave away most of them. He gave me a German helmet when I was way too young to appreciate it and I traded it to a friend for a pet bird. I've regretted that all my life. I still have a great German mortar and a photo book of Hitler and a few other collectables.

Deanna Williamson after the war.

Captured Adolf Hitler book and German Mortar.

Kiley and her dad, Sergeant First Class Tyler Gene Fosheim just before a parachute jump in Alaska in 2008.

The Adolf Hitler book is a very high quality book with many glossy photos. Inside the cover, Dad wrote the following:

"To my son Gene. Taken from an occupied home in Eggenstein, Germany the summer of 1945 by Sgt. Raymond Fosheim. U.S.A. 106th Inf. Div."

I never followed in Dad's footsteps by joining the military. The Vietnam War was going on and I decided long before that I wanted to attend college instead. My son Tyler did enter the military and is currently a first sergeant. He has spent a year in Iraq, a year in Afghanistan, and has airborne, air assault, ranger and pathfinder ratings. He is the ideal solder. In some ways, he is more like my father than I am. We are very proud of him.

Raymond, John and Martin Fosheim late in the war.

When the three Fosheim boys came home from Europe there was never any thought of searching for a new home or settling in another community. They were Everett boys through and through and had no plans to leave.

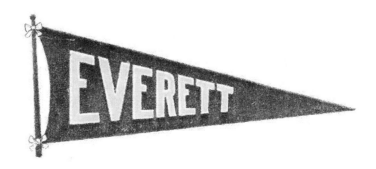

"All three of us boys were in the service, drafted. We all three were in the Army. Of course, when we got out, I went back in

the mill. I wish I'd tried to get another kind of work, but I didn't. And I was there until '59, and then they went out of business. So I went down to the bay and looked around, and got in at the Collins casket factory in 1960."

Actually Raymond worked at Eclipse Mill after the Walton Lumber Company. Eclipse burnt down and eventually he found the job at Collins. It's a shame that none of the Fosheim brothers took advantage of the new G.I. Bill for retraining. Because of their ages and other factors they all just went back to the sawmills. It was a decision that Raymond regretted the rest of his life.

The Servicemen's Readjustment Act of 1944, known to everyone as the G.I. Bill, provided a range of benefits for World War II veterans as they returned home. Benefits included low-cost mortgages, low-interest loans to start a business, tuition and living expenses for education, and up to one year of unemployment benefits. Within ten years almost eight million veterans used the G.I. Bill education benefits.

G. I. Bill choices. *Defense Council Records OSA.*

Chapter XIII

Back to the Sawmills

"Me and my brother, John, both went back to Walton's after we got out of the military. We both worked for the same foreman, Axel Nordgren. I knew a Clark that lived in Lake Stevens, and Clark Patterson, a grocery man."

Raymond came home from Europe and was given an honorable discharge from the army a short time after the war ended. The Walton Lumber Company honored his military leave of absence and gave him his former job driving the lumber carrier. John Fosheim also went back to Walton and Martin went back to his previous Weyerhaeuser job when discharged. When Raymond returned to Everett from Europe he moved back into 2620 Walnut Street with his dad and brothers. They all had the challenge of making the big adjustment back to civilian life.

When the three brothers returned home they found their father had aged visibly and was not a healthy man. He never recovered fully from his earlier stroke. He missed Anna his wife terribly. He spent his last year at home enjoying his grandkids and puttering around the home when his failing health allowed.

"He was seventy-two years old when he died and my mother was sixty-two. That's real young compared to his brothers and sisters, and her brothers; they were in their eighties and nineties."

Martin, Raymond, and John A. Fosheim with Lulubell at 2620 Walnut Street after a hard day at the mills.

John and Anna Fosheim's gravesite in Evergreen Cemetery in Everett, Washington in about 1948. The city of Lowell is below to the east along the Snohomish River.

Mac and John K. Fosheim at home in 1945.

The only known color photo of John K. Fosheim. Taken in 1941.

John Kristopher Fosheim died on Tuesday afternoon, June 25, 1946, five years before I was born so I never had a chance to sit on his lap or have fun doing a wood-working project with him. Considering what a wonderful family he raised, my grandpa must have been a hard-working and gentle man. I was told that John was a quiet man with a good sense of humor. I often visit Grandpa's and Grandma's graves in Everett's historic Evergreen Cemetery and wish I could have met them. I really missed out on some good times.

Post-war Everett enjoyed an economic boom like the rest of the country and much of the world. The Fosheim family members enjoyed full employment and even saved some money for the first time in their lives. The future looked bright as Everett's population grew with a building boom and new neighborhoods began popping up everywhere.

Raymond Fosheim and friend Herb Tobler on vacation in Flagstaff, Arizona in the summer of 1946.

Advertisements from the back page of the Everett phone book in 1946.

One of the strongest earthquakes on record for the Everett area, a 7.3 tremor centered to the northwest in the Strait of Georgia in British Columbia, Canada on June 23, 1946. It caused chimneys to fall and damaged the upper floors of buildings in Seattle. The first highly publicized sighting of UFOs was reported in Washington State on June 24, 1947. Neither the earthquake nor the 'flying saucers' were much of a diversion from the prosperous times of the late 1940s.

"When we started at Walton's, just me and a partner, we'd get a slip from the tally man and go out in the yard and we'd make up orders. We'd get different partners all the time. George Freed was one I still know and still see him, he lived in Lowell. He was the one that I was with most. We'd make up orders to ship out."

George Freed was an interesting man. He occasionally came to the Fosheim home to visit with Dad when I was young. Mom didn't care much to have him around but I sure loved his stories and I could listen to him for hours. I'm sure he was a bachelor all his life as he lacked a few social skills particularly with women. He was a real loner and spent every weekend hiking up in the Cascade Mountains. He was quite a climber in his younger years and hiked well into his old age.

I went hiking with George a few times when I was a teenager in the 60s and I could barely keep up. He drove an older Peugeot which was very rare in America at the time. I intently listened to his tales of hiking in the Cascades and climbing to the top of every mountain we could see. He said that he wished he had a nickel for every time he had driven the Mountain Loop Highway. One had to watch what you said around George as he could be very blunt and obnoxious at times. He was a real contrarian and I was always a little intimidated being around him.

Raymond Fosheim and nephew Jackie Norberg at 2620 Walnut Street in 1947. On the left side of the photo is the doll house that John K. Fosheim built during the war for his grand kids.

"This lumber was all dimensions, and then a lot of times we got to load cars or boxcars, it all depended. Loading cars, I kind of liked that, you put certain things. We loaded two by fours, two by sixes, and two by eights and one by fours and one by six, mostly like that. Hemlock, very few fir, some cedar. Then I decided I wanted to be a lumber carrier and I told the foreman. And when they got a break for it, I got a job running the Ross lumber carrier. That's when I went in the service. And then when I got out, I got back on the same job."

I faintly remember Mom and her brother, Uncle Buddy, taking me down to see Dad during lunch time at Walton's in the mid-fifties. I loved the big yellow lumber carrier he drove around the mill. He let me ride with him on it a few times. We sat up so high I felt like I was on top of the world and I still remember how scared I was when Buddy hoisted me up on the ladder to the top.

One day Dad was driving the tall lumber carrier through one of the old rickety sheds and hit his head on a rusty old spike that was protruding down from one of the overhead beams. He needed stitches and it could have been much worse. The doctor told us we were very lucky that he wasn't badly injured. Back in those days no one wore helmets or any other safety equipment.

Dad had lots of friends working with him at Walton's Mill. George Bonneywell was a nice and interesting guy whom I still remember. Dad would always end up being the car pool driver and would pick up many of his buddies on the way to work. Times were tight and Mom would be upset because some of the guys wouldn't give Dad any gas money, but then he would never ask for any.

Lumber carrier similar to the Ross that Raymond Fosheim operated at the Walton Lumber Company.

Raymond took a couple of weeks of vacation time from work in the summer of 1948 to drive back to Minnesota in his 1937 Ford and visit his relatives once again. He missed his dad terribly and wanted to see his aunt and uncles who were advancing in age. Raymond loved those scenic road trips across the mid-west.

Raymond Fosheim with his uncle Bernt Stene in Minnesota in 1948.

"And then in '59, the mill went haywire."

After Walton's mill closed Raymond was on the streets of Everett looking for a job just like in his younger days. He finally found work at the Eclipse Lumber Company down by the base of Pacific Avenue on the Snohomish River in Everett. The Eclipse Mill Company was founded in 1902

Bernt Stene loading his vintage folding camera.

in what was the Gould and Keene shingle mill. The mill was built on pilings, mostly over the Snohomish River so there was an easy access to logs that were floated in. The saws and carriages could handle logs up to seven feet in diameter and forty feet long. Most of the lumber they cut was Douglas Fir which was sold and shipped all over the country. The mill employed about 150 workers and cut over forty-five million board feet of lumber a year. The mill's name was changed to the Eclipse Lumber Company Inc. in 1948.

The Eclipse Lumber Company before the 1962 fire destroyed it. *Everett Public Library.*

Raymond was hoping to work at Eclipse until he retired but unfortunately his job at the mill only lasted a couple of years as the buildings disappeared in a fiery blaze. Although Everett sawmill fires were fairly common, the spectacular fire on the night of May 7, 1962 still stands out in the memory of the many who witnessed it. Its ferocity lit the sky throughout Puget Sound and the heat twisted the nearby railroad tracks like long stringy pretzels.

"I was out of work for a little over a year, but I worked around the mill doing a little clean-up work for some contractor, I don't know who it was. Then I got a job at the Collins casket factory in 1960 and I was there until I retired, running small machines. The little trim saws; it was all small work, mostly. And nailing up caskets, and working on the gluing machine and I finally ended up running a big machine there, the Linderman. I put boards together. It was a small business. I think right now there's only seven or eight people working at the casket factory. But Collin's whole outfit is gone, now it's just a small--I don't know what they call it now, but I know the people running it. And it's just a small thing. Collins is closed down. It's a different company now, in a different place."

In 1926, the North Coast Casket Company relocated to the large new wooden building built on pilings just south of the William Hulbert Mill Company. The location worked well as the caskets could be built from end pieces and scraps from the mill. In the early 1930s, North Coast Casket was sold and became the Collins

Casket Company. Ten to twelve different casket styles were assembled on the first two floors; sewing and the final details were completed on the top floor, where the caskets were also stored.

The historic Collins building in July 2009 before it was destroyed.

Many years later I was active with the preservation group, Historic Everett and much of the Everett community in trying to save and restore the wonderful historic Collins Building. The Port of Everett was set on tearing it down for the expansion of their boatyard area. We lost the long battle and now the big red building is gone and all that remains is a parking lot. It was demolished in 2011.

Chubby greeting Raymond Fosheim after a hard day at work in 1968.

A worker inside the Collins Casket Company in 1973. *The Everett Herald.*

"There was not a lot of industry down on the waterfront while I was working there, not like there used to be. There were a few little stores along there that weren't there before. Like the canvas factory there, making things for small ships and stuff, boats. When I was there, there was Northwest Casket, down by Nord's. Svensson owned it, but Nord's bought out that whole outfit."

"When I started working at Collins, I lived where I am now, 525 Pilchuck Path. The reason I started there, I knew my neighbor across the street worked at Collins. Steve Kerber, he told me to go down and see about a job, so I went down there and I finally got a job from Eddie Dams, and his partner was Johnson, those two owned it. I worked for him, nice fellows, both of them."

"Like I said before, I had to quit when I was sixty-two on account of the cedar dust bothering me so bad. I was getting short of breath, but then I got in the habit of exercising my lungs, so I think I'm pretty well good. But so many of my friends smoked heavy, you can't tell if it was the smoking or the cedar asthsma. They're all gone, the heavy smokers."

Dad never smoked cigarettes but on very rare occasions he would light up a big cigar. He also rarely drank alcohol. The only time I ever saw him drink a little too much was when watching the Washington Huskies on TV playing Wisconsin in the 1960 Rose Bowl. He lit up a huge cigar he'd been saving in the living room table's drawer and had a few beers by halftime and was pretty excited. I still remember how out of character that was for him. He did love his Husky football.

Often Dad would work his eight hour shift and then load our 1964 Chevrolet station wagon with wood from the Collins scrap pile. He brought home mostly redwood and cedar but also a few pieces of oak, pine, fir, cherry, and walnut. We always had stacks of lumber stored under our huge porch and up in the rafters of the garage. Every night Dad would make projects from the casket leftovers with his table saw in our basement.

Dad was an excellent carpenter and could build anything from a photo. He built everything from toy airplanes to kitchen furniture to our two car garage. When I got pretty good in my drafting and design classes, I made a drawing of a drafting table I wanted Dad to build for me, but to my amazement he had never read a drawing. I later found a photo of what I wanted and he built a real beauty in no time. Dad was an expert with wood. He could tell what any kind of wood was just by its look and smell.

My adjustable drafting table built by Dad.

Dad liked working at Collins better than some of his previous jobs in the Everett sawmill industry. He met some good friends there and the work was pretty steady. Before the Collins job Dad had suffered from decades of bad luck with sawmill closures, fires, and numerous labor disputes. Nothing was ever guaranteed but it was reassuring to have a steady paycheck coming in.

"I was making a little over six dollars an hour when I quit Collins. We got raises from the Union every once in a while."

The huge Linderman Automatic Dovetail Glue Jointer that Raymond Fosheim operated for years at the Collins Casket Company. *Linderman Machine Company.*

Weyerhaeuser Mill B in northeast Everett along the Snohomish River in 1957. The Fosheim home at 525 Pilchuck Path is at the arrow on the upper left. *Everett Public Library.*

Dad's oldest brother Martin was also a sawmill worker all his life. He not only worked at Weyerhaeuser Mill B for forty-six years but he stood in the same place, working on the same machine the entire time. It wasn't unusual back then to work for the same company for decades. As long as the company survived the employees were often more than happy to not look for another opportunity. Weyerhaeuser gave Martin a gold watch when he retired.

Uncle Mart spent a lot of time with our family. We would go to the Puyallup Fair together every year and he would come to our home to visit quite often. In later years he was the Fosheim family photographer and always took pictures of all the friends and relatives. He would make multiple copies of his photos so everyone would have an album. For years he used the latest Polaroid camera which took photos that developed instantly. We always had a fun time watching him patiently set everything up on a tripod, set the timer, and quickly run back to get in the photo with the rest of us.

The huge band saw in one of Everett's sawmills. *Everett Public Library.*

Uncle Mart bought me a sturdy metal tool box for Christmas one year when I was fairly young and every month or so for the next couple of years he would come by our home with a new hand tool for my growing collection. Dad had plenty of tools to borrow but it was fun having a set of my very own. Mart could be set in his ways and quite moody sometimes but he was a kind and generous person like all the Fosheim's. Unfortunately for Mart he was in a family who loved to play jokes and tease and he never quite got it. He was gullible and the target of many jokes.

Martin Fosheim and friend Jim Myers next to the historic Clark Park cannon in Everett.

Uncle Mart loved movies and went to the Everett Theater weekly to see every film that played there for decades. He could identify every movie star and could tell stories about all of them. As soon as he walked in our door he was asking Dad if he had seen the latest film. He would go on and on about which film had which stars in it. I loved it as a kid and listened to him obsessively say the same things over and over again.

Martin would only shop at Billy's Men's Wear on Hewitt in Everett. He bought all of his clothes there and usually dressed well. One could always count on Mart to be different. When Honda came out with their first little car in America he bought one. It was the tiny Honda 600 with a forty-five horsepower two cylinder engine. We of course teased him about the diminutive car which he didn't enjoy one bit. I ended up buying it when Uncle Mart couldn't drive anymore and kept it as a novelty for a couple of years.

Martin could be a little eccentric at times. Some of the family who knew him before the war said he just wasn't the same in later years when he returned home from Europe. Mart was drafted into the army like his two brothers. He was too old to see combat but he observed a lot of death and destruction from behind the front lines. Other family members attributed his sometimes quirky behavior to the typhoid fever he suffered from as a kid.

Martin Fosheim with Raymond's puppy Lulubelle in the late 1940s at 2620 Walnut Street.

Raymond Fosheim's cousins Alf, Leif, and Hjordes Østmo in the late 1940s.

Raymond Fosheim with his niece Dolores Norberg at 2620 Walnut Street in 1948.

Chapter XIV

Married Life

"I got married the last day of June, 1950. Married a girl from Minnesota, she was out here visiting her uncle, Andrew Nelson and I knew him. She was Swedish. A very nice girl."

Raymond was still living at 2620 walnut with his two brothers in 1948 when he met Mabel Oberg, my mom. They dated for a couple of years before getting married and immediately began looking for a new home in Everett. They finally found a cozy home at 525 Pilchuck Path in north Everett. It was small but in a nice working class neighborhood with a million dollar view of the Cascade Mountains over the top of the Great Northern rail yard and Weyerhaeuser Mill B.

Mabel Margaret Oberg was born on October 19, 1912 on the family farm in Rose City, Minnesota. Rose City was a small town with a beautiful little white Baptist church, a general store, creamery, gas station, and a restaurant. At the entrance to Rose City, there is an old weather-worn sign that says 'population 22.' Today that is quite optimistic as it is now just an intersection for two roads.

Mabel grew up in a family of six children; Irene, Emanuel, Richard, Elmer, Mabel, and Junette. A younger brother, Raymond, died in infancy. Mabel was a sickly child and it was even briefly considered having her adopted by another family to get through the tough times. The Oberg's were a religious Swedish family and Mabel loved attending the nearby Baptist church.

Mabel Oberg in the 1940s before she met Raymond.

Just as many Scandinavians settled in the Puget Sound region of Washington State they also were drawn to Minnesota and its neighboring mid-western states. Mabel's father, Sanfrid Oberg, came from Västergötland, Sweden and her mother Kathrine Nelson came from Jämtland, a farming and logging region of central Sweden. Many Scandinavians found the Alexandria, lake country, of west-

Västergötland, Sweden, Coat of arms.

Jämtland, Sweden, coat of arms.

central Minnesota to be similar to their home country. The Oberg's were farmers, hunters, and fisherman and found their new homeland to be the perfect place to work and raise a family.

Rose City Evangelical Free Church confirmation class. Mabel Oberg is on the lower right (see arrow) next to Mabel Rosell who married her older brother Richard. Mabel's younger sister Junette is in the front row right.

Mabel stayed on the Oberg farm for many years but never liked the rural farming life. She followed a friend to San Diego, California in about 1940 and worked as a maid for a well to do family. She also spent time with her older sister, Irene, in Denver, Colorado, in 1942 helping to take care of her young niece, Sonja Soderquist. She returned to San Diego to work for a few years and then moved to 2300 41st Street in Everett, Washington in 1948 to help babysit niece Delores for her uncle Andrew Nelson. Mabel was wonderful with kids and dearly loved her family but she really was ready for a family of her own.

A young Mabel Oberg with her mother Katherine in Minnesota and Mabel Oberg in the 1940s.

Andrew Nelson moved to Monroe, Washington from Eagle Bend, Minnesota and purchased a jewelry store in December, 1915. He married and settled in the area to raise his daughter Delores. In the late 1940s he met Raymond Fosheim through some mutual Scandinavian friends. He introduced his niece Mabel Oberg to Raymond while she was visiting him in Everett for the first time in 1948. After a quite persistent pursuit by Mabel, they were married on June 30, 1950. They lived their first few months together upstairs at the Fosheim family home at 2620 Walnut Street with brothers John and Martin Fosheim.

"Thank goodness, I didn't still have my motorcycle when I was courting my wife. We just took trips around in the car in those days. I was thirty-six when I got married and she was thirty-seven, and then we had the boy."

Andrew Nelson and his first wife Emma.

Andrew Nelson in his jewelry store which he purchased in Monroe, Washington in December, 1915.

Dad had never owned a home but once he and Mom were married they immediately started looking for a place of their own. Dad was an Everett man and there was no doubt that he and Mom would buy a home in the city. They found a comfortable home on Pilchuck Path in north Everett just above Weyerhaeuser Mill B. It was close to Hawthorne Elementary School, just a couple of miles from downtown shopping, and best of all it had a view of Dad's beloved Cascade Mountains.

Dad and Mom certainly did love travelling together and drove to Denver and then Minnesota on their honeymoon. Mom showed Dad off to all her relatives in the Alexandria area of Minnesota and enjoyed the tourist sites along the way. Then Dad had his chance to show off Mom in the Fergus Falls area of Minnesota to his aunt, uncles and cousins.

"My wife worked before we were married, doing housecleaning, but she never worked after we were married."

Andrew Nelson with his second wife Elsa and daughter Delores before the war.

Raymond and Mabel Fosheim at 2620 Walnut Street showing off the results of a successful salmon fishing date in 1949.

Raymond and Mabel Fosheim on their wedding day, June 30, 1950.

Raymond and Mabel Fosheim by Mt. Rainier in 1949.

Dad and Mom were married for almost forty years and lived at 525 Pilchuck Path for thirty-nine. They were a perfect pair. Dad was so easy going and Mom was pretty happy enjoying a simple lifestyle. They had what was considered a traditional 1950s marriage where Dad worked and Mom took care of the home. Mom never learned to drive a car so relied on Dad or her brother Elmer for transportation. Dad and Mom went everywhere together from shopping trips to an evening drive in the countryside.

"My wife and I took just short trips around the state, you know. That was our pleasure, mostly, just taking rides, and visiting around. Taking in all the, like Leavenworth every year, and Seattle a lot. The zoo and the parks and Seattle Center; we went there a lot. Just entertained ourselves like that."

Elmer Oberg, Raymond Norberg, Raymond Fosheim, Emma Norberg, Mabel Fosheim, Mabel's maid of honor Irene Gibson, and Olivia and Linda Marsh at 2620 Walnut Street on June 30, 1950 after the wedding.

Raymond, Mabel, and John A. Fosheim in the living room at 2620 Walnut Street in 1950.

Raymond and Mabel Fosheim with nephews Dale and Wally Soderquist in Denver, Colorado on their honeymoon in July 1950.

Two of Mabel's brothers followed her out to Everett to find jobs in the mills. They were both life-long bachelors and decided that farming wasn't the line of work that they wanted to pursue. Emanuel (Mandy) Oberg arrived in Everett in 1950 and soon went to work at the Nord Door Company on the Everett waterfront. Elmer (Buddy) Oberg was a few years younger than Mandy and had come out west earlier to visit his sister in Everett in 1948. He ended up coming back in 1950 and rented an apartment from the Bizeau family with Mabel at 1414 23rd Street #4. Raymond helped Buddy get a job with him at Walton's mill. Buddy was very close to his sister Mabel and fit right in with the Fosheim family from the beginning. When Raymond and Mabel bought their home he rented one of the bedrooms. Uncle Buddy ended up living with Raymond and Mabel the rest of their lives. Mandy eventually left Everett and lived with his older sister, Irene, in Denver, Colorado before living the last years of his life back in Alexandria, Minnesota.

Erik Adolf Nord emigrated from Sweden and came to Everett in 1924 to found a builders supply shop that eventually grew into one of the world's largest wood door manufacturing companies. The E.A. Nord Company sadly went bankrupt and was sold in 1986 due to labor union disputes.

Mabel Fosheim with her niece Delores Nelson and Uncle Andrew Nelson in 1949.

The E. A. Nord Company on 2202 Hewitt Avenue in 1929. *Everett Public Library*.

Elmer Oberg, Martin Fosheim, and Emanuel Oberg at Mt. Rainier in late summer 1950.

The Oberg family got along well with the Fosheim family. Elmer and Emanuel Oberg and Martin and John Fosheim were all bachelors and over the years they spent a lot of time together. When Elmer moved in with Raymond and Mabel Fosheim it worked out perfect for everyone. Having two income earners in the family made it easier to own a nice cozy home and for Raymond it was like having another brother. For me it was like having a second dad or an older brother.

Mom's brother Elmer Roscoe Oberg was born on April 17, 1911 and raised on the Oberg family farm in Rose City, just northeast of Alexandria, Minnesota. He lost a baby brother and his mother when he was young and survived the many hardships of the great depression. Buddy left school at an early age to help on the family farm with his two brothers Emanuel and Richard, and three sisters; Irene, Mabel and Junette. He was known as Buddy by his family and friends.

In 1944 Buddy left the farm and came west to work for E. J. Bartells Company in Portland, Oregon, installing insulation on Liberty ships during World War II. On April 21, 1945 he was drafted into the army at age thirty-four as an ammunition handler with Battery B, 63rd AAA gun battalion and Battery C, 485th AAA AW battalion and was sent to Okinawa just after the war ended. He

Elmer and Mabel Oberg on the family farm in Minnesota during the early 1940s.

attained the rank of Private First Class and was honorably discharged from the service on December 19, 1946. He received the Asiatic-Pacific service medal, the Victory Medal, and the Army of Occupation Medal (Japan).

Elmer Roscoe Oberg in 1945.

After his honorable discharge in 1947, Buddy worked at Jones Lumber in Portland for a short time before returning to Minnesota. In 1948 and 1949 he helped his brother Richard on the Oberg farm and attended agricultural school in Eagle Bend, Minnesota through the Veterans Administration training program. In 1950 Buddy followed his sister Mabel and moved permanently to Everett and got a job at the Walton Lumber Company with brother-in-law Raymond.

63rd AAA gun battalion.

Raymond Fosheim, Mabel and Elmer Oberg in the Cascade Mountains by Stevens Pass in 1950.

Buddy never really liked working in the sawmill and after years of strikes, layoffs, and various problems in the lumber industry, he changed his occupation and found a job as a custodian for the Everett school district in the late 1950s. In 1975 Buddy retired and began spending his summers on the Oberg family farm in Minnesota.

From the time Buddy moved to Everett to work and live with his sister he immediately fell in love with the Northwest and never thought of returning to Minnesota permanently. Raymond, Mabel and Buddy often traveled and enjoyed their family time together.

In 1950 the post WWII boom was hitting Everett in a big way. The population was growing and business was good. New businesses were opening up like the Sky-Vu drive-in movie theater on 34th and Pine

Elmer Oberg, Mabel and Raymond Fosheim at the Hope Island Inn just west of La Conner, Washington in 1950.

Elmer Oberg, Raymond and Mabel Fosheim in Darrington, Washington in 1950.

Street, the Rip Van Winkle Motel at 23rd and Broadway, and a new medical center on Hoyt Avenue and Pacific Avenue. Unfortunately downtown Everett was losing much of its beautiful historic character as many of its unique buildings were being lost.

Everett's Sky-Vu drive-in movie theater in about 1957 on 34th and Pine Street. *Jack O'Donnell Collection.*

The new 1950 Ford at Hutchings Motors in downtown Everett. *Everett Public Library*.

Raymond Fosheim and Elmer Oberg with Martin Fosheim's new 1950 Ford at the Hope Island Inn.

As the post-war economy improved Martin Fosheim could afford to buy a new 1950 Ford at Hutchings Motors in downtown Everett. Uncle Buddy bought a green 1949 Chevrolet and Raymond bought his black 1946 Plymouth. Even in the boom years one had to be careful with spending as there was always the possibility of a strike or a slowdown. That's the way it was in the sawmill industry. Raymond and Mabel were confident in the future though as they began to discuss having a family.

A post-war view of McGhee's Pharmacy in the Slack Block on the NW corner of Hewitt Avenue and Rucker Avenue in downtown Everett. *Jack O'Donnell Collection.*

Everett's 1952 Fourth of July Parade heading west on Hewitt Avenue past the Horseshoe Tavern and the Commerce Building.

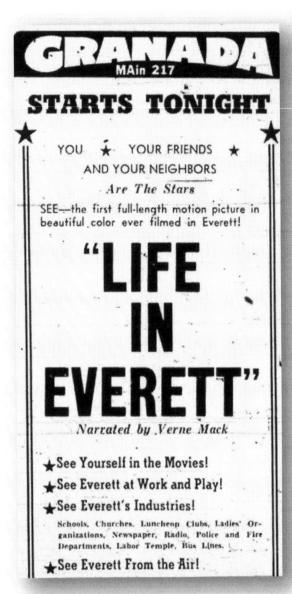

Everett's merchants were so proud of their community in 1946 that they teamed up with the Grenada Theater to produce 'Life in Everett' which showcased the prospering city.

Numerous new businesses opened in Everett during the post-war boom. The Monte Cristo Auto Company announced it's grand opening across from the Monte Cristo Hotel on Hoyt Avenue and Wall Street in December of 1946.

Chapter XV

525 Pilchuck Path

"My boy, Gene, was born on 525 Pilchuck Path. That's the only boy I had, the only child. He was born there, 1951."

The Fosheim family home at 525 Pilchuck Path in north Everett, was a very special place in a great middle-class 1950s neighborhood. I lived there with my parents and Uncle Buddy from 1951 until 1978. Mom and Dad bought the little 600 square foot daylight basement rambler in 1950 and it stayed in our family until we were forced to sell it in 1994.

Gene Fosheim, Suzanne and Annette Kerber, and Jean Hempel wait for Elmer Oberg to hook Raymond Fosheim's trailer to his 1946 Plymouth for a ride around the block at 525 Pilchuck Path in the early 1950s.

> "I moved in this house in 1950, at 525 Pilchuck Path. I was working at Walton's when we got married, then bought the house October, 1950. We paid $7,600 for the house. Others did the same; two neighbors paid a little over $7,000 for their houses, too. In twenty years, I had it paid for, fifty dollars a month. And then, I was out of work for a year and a-half while I was making payments. We had started a little bank account, and we had to draw just about all of that. 'Course we had to buy all new furniture and everything. But the house was fifty dollars, and I think all the furniture and that was probably thirty dollars a month, Slingerlend Furniture had the contract."

Our neighborhood on Pilchuck Path was built right on top of the remains of the old Everett Smelter site. Pretty much all the families who lived there knew it. In fact the old concrete foundations for the big smokestacks were in the back yard of the neighbor who lived right above us on Hawthorne Street. We were more concerned about the smell from the nearby pulp mill than any arsenic in the soil.

In 1894 a factory was built on a thirty-five acre site on the northeastern side of Everett just above the Snohomish River. It was used to produce gold, lead, copper, and silver. The Puget Sound Reduction Company was built to process ore mined from the Monte Cristo area in the mountains of eastern Snohomish County. A railroad was built to transport the ore. An arsenic extraction plant was installed at the Everett site in 1898. ASARCO, Inc. bought the smelter in 1903 and operated it until it was closed in 1912.

The Puget Sound Reduction Company smelter around 1900. 525 Pilchuck Path was very close to the center of this photo. *Everett Public Library.*

The smelter was demolished by 1915 and the above-ground structures, built of bricks were flattened and spread around the immediate area. The big slag pile was spread all over Everett as a base for the new streets.

Some of the foundations of the structures remained below the surface and were simply covered over with topsoil. The property was sold off over the years in various parcels. In the 1930s and 1940s, much of the area was developed into residential properties.

1951, the year I was born was a good year for Everett businesses. I was born at Everett General Hospital on April 23rd, the same month the new Safeway opened at 3700 Broadway and the huge B&M shopping center opened at 50th and Highway 99, now Evergreen Way. The new outdoor Everett Motor Movie also began to show its first films. In May of 1951 Rosemary the elephant arrived at the Forest Park zoo and in August Duffy Drugs had its grand opening at 16th and Broadway.

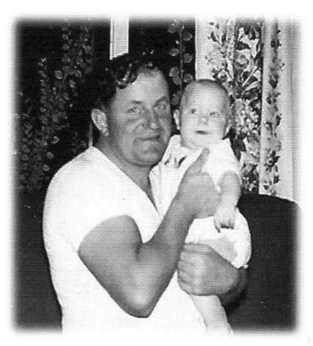

Raymond and Gene Fosheim in 1951

Raymond Fosheim was born to be a dad. I've always thought I had the best parents one could ever hope for. My birthday started out to be a great day for Dad. In those days the fathers were told to go to a waiting room during childbirth. Dad was so nervous he took a walk around the block at Everett General Hospital. He got lucky and found a brand new $5 bill lying on the sidewalk. That was a lot of money in 1951.

Everett General Hospital between 13th and 14th Street on Colby Avenue in Everett. *Everett Public Library.*

The Everett Motor Movie opened in 1951 at 75th and Evergreen Way. 1969 photo.

It would have been nice to have a brother or a sister but I'm an only child. Mom always said she was too old to have another kid. Mom was thirty-eight and Dad was thirty-seven when I was born and Mom had a difficult pregnancy with me so she was done. Money was another consideration. The economy kept going in cycles and a paycheck was not guaranteed in the lumber industry. Thank goodness we had Uncle Buddy living with us so we had a second income in the family.

Many of my fondest memories as a kid were spending time with Mom and Dad. They really spoiled me rotten. I don't know if I ever realized how spoiled I was until my latter years. Dad was always busy, usually building something out of wood or maybe working on a landscape project. With all of the exciting and fun projects going on around our home, most of the neighborhood kids usually hung out at our place. All the neighborhood kids loved Dad and he loved having them around. Even though he kept busy, he seemed to always have time for me and my friends.

On Saturday Dad would hook our little wooden trailer to the back of our 1949 Chevrolet and we would take a load of garbage to the city dump down by the Snohomish River. If there was room my friend and I would get to ride in the trailer with the load. We would drive into the dump and just unload the trailer anywhere. There were huge piles of stuff lying all over and some big rats too. The fun part of the visit was digging through the dozens of piles of garbage to see what we could find. We found bicycle parts and scrap metal and good pieces of wood to either burn or use for projects.

Raymond and Gene Fosheim with Mabel's oldest brother, Emanuel Oberg, at 525 Pilchuck Path in 1952. For a few years Uncle Mandy rented the little house at 523 Pilchuck Path just north of us.

It seems unhealthy and dirty today but back then, it was just fun. After we left, we would stop at one of the little corner grocery stores and get a bottle of pop and a candy bar. I still remember my first Dr. Pepper in the cool 10-2-4 bottle. I thought that it really tasted like it had pepper in it and I have been drinking it ever since. Mom used to get mad at Dad because if one of my friends didn't bring any money he would treat everyone. We just couldn't afford it back then. Mom was much more frugal than Dad. Often he was way too generous.

Gene Fosheim standing in the center with the neighborhood girls at 525 Pilchuck Path.

Dr. Pepper advertisement. *Dr. Pepper Company.*

Dad taught me how to swim at the downtown Everett YMCA. We went every Friday night and I got to take a friend or two with me. It was always a fun evening. One of the few times I ever saw Dad get mad was when I came up behind him and pushed him into the pool. He almost landed on a lady who was swimming by and he told me to never do that again. I really felt bad. After swimming, we all went down to Hewitt and had a milkshake at the counter of the Meadowmoor.

Dad would take my friends and I down by the waterfront and check where all the industrial waste was dumped just south of Nord's Door Company. We would find wood and other items to haul home for the fire or to build projects. The pile is overgrown with shrubs today but is still there, just west of Marine View Drive right on the water. That's got to be the most contaminated site in Everett but I never hear anything about cleaning it up.

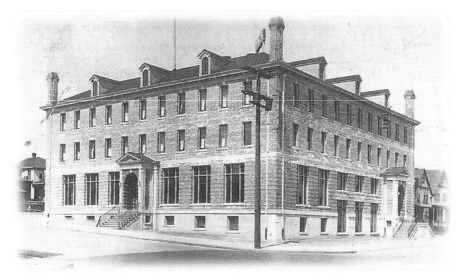

The Everett YMCA at 2720 Rockefeller Avenue. *J. C. O'Donnell collection.*

The highlight of a weekend was dressing up in our army surplus gear and taking the trailer across the Snohomish River to get a load of sand. My friends and I would all hop in the trailer and Dad would drive us over where Langus Park is now. He would back up to a dune and load the trailer full of the sand that had been dredged out of the river. My friends and I would hide in the sand pits, dunes, and brush and have our World War II battles. When Dad was ready to leave we would come out, surround him and take him prisoner.

Sometimes Dad would just take me alone across the river and we would target practice with his twenty-two rifle. Dad was an expert marksman from his army days. He was extremely safe with his gun and I remember we would always pick up all of the cans after shooting them. He was neat and tidy for his day and would never think of leaving behind a mess. One afternoon we had just arrived to do some target practice when a bullet whizzed close by our heads. I can still remember the sound and how scared I was. Dad immediately pushed me to the ground and stood up straight and tall so the errant shooters would see him and realize their carelessness. I sure thought that was pretty brave.

When the state put the freeway in, we had to stop our target practice in the sand banks by the river. The construction also put an end to many of our explorations on Smith Island as it pretty much cut the island in half. I remember Dad taking us for a ride on the new freeway when it opened between south Everett and north Seattle on February 3, 1965. It's hard to believe today but in the middle '60s we could drive all the way to Seattle and rarely see more than a few cars every mile.

One of our favorite stores to visit was Betts Variety Store on Everett Avenue. They had everything from candy to toys to comic books. I loved going there with Dad or on my bike with cousins John and Bill Williamson in our young days. The new I-5 freeway construction forced the wonderful little store to close in the early 1960s.

The new Interstate 5 cutting through the Riverside neighborhood on the east side of Everett in the middle 1960s. The left arrow is pointing to 2202 Cleveland Avenue, the right arrow is pointing to 2917 Leonard Drive and the top arrow is pointing to 2620 Walnut Street, the three Riverside Neighborhood locations where the Fosheim family lived. *Everett Public Library.*

Dad brought dozens of loads of sand home from the riverside to fill in our back yard and raise it up about six feet so it was level. He also collected numerous loads of broken concrete sidewalk pieces from around town to build up a six-foot high retaining wall. Eventually our entire property was terraced with retaining walls. Dad's experience growing up in Everett during the depression made him a hard worker and he was good at building various projects from whatever was available. He rarely had to spend money on lumber or landscape materials. Junk to others was a usable treasure to him.

Since neither Mom nor Dad had much of a formal education they put a lot of effort into making sure I was successful in school. I loved sitting on my chair in our living room drawing on my chalk board. Dad would ask me a question and I would draw out the answer. Sometimes we worked on arithmetic problems together. Uncle Buddy and Mom would participate too as they watched TV or read the newspaper. We spent a lot of time together.

Gene R. Fosheim

Gene Fosheim at Christmas time with his new chalk board and chair at 525 Pilchuck Path in the middle 1950s.

Dad loved trains. We could see them from our back porch. The huge Great Northern Delta switch yard was right below our home. There were hundreds of boxcars and various other cars from all over the country. It was fun to identify all the different railways represented. The variety of colors and names was wonderful in those days. We could hear the heavy boxcars banging all night long as they were repositioned behind the switch engines. Sometimes our whole house shook from the noisy couplings but after a while one just got used to it.

Great Northern EMD SW-9 Switch Engine

I barely remember the morning Dad took me for a walk down to the tracks to explore the yard. I must have been about six or seven years old. I always loved exploring with Dad whether it was up in the mountains or just around our town. We were standing along the tracks watching a big diesel switch engine come by when it stopped right next to us. Dad was pretty outgoing and friendly with everyone he met and soon started a conversation with the engineer. When the engineer noticed our enthusiasm for his huge machine he invited us aboard to see the brightly polished controls. I was really excited and who wouldn't be?

Dad and I climbed up the steep ladder to the engineer's compartment and checked out all the cool mechanisms. To our amazement the engineer asked us if we wanted to ride with him to Marysville, just a few miles north across the river and sloughs. We quickly accepted his invitation and off we went down the tracks and across the four low bridges along the way. As we came back across Steamboat Slough after our visit to Marysville the friendly engineer asked me if I wanted to take the controls. Of course I did! What fun we had as I gave the engine power and we smoothly sped down the tracks back to the Everett switchyard. When our ride ended we hopped off the engine and hiked back up the hill toward home where I could excitedly tell all my friends about my exciting adventure.

Like Dad when he was young I spent time down by the tracks mostly at the Delta yard below our home. My friends and I would explore and occasionally climb on the cars and pretend we were train workers. I never hitched a ride on a moving train as I was way too scared of getting hurt. I had heard many stories of kids falling off cars or tripping on the tracks and getting run over by the heavy train wheels. Mostly we just explored or often put pennies on the tracks and waited for a train to run over them. We were also afraid of the many exaggerated stories of the mean hobos that lived by the tracks though we hardly ever saw one.

Paul Bunyon mural.
Weyerhaeuser Archives.

Our home was on the bluff right above Weyerhaeuser Mill B and Mom and Dad enjoyed occasionally going down to the Big W cafeteria for dinner. I thought it was fun eating with some of the workers and going through the cafeteria line picking out my favorite macaroni and cheese and a piece of apple or berry pie with ice cream for desert. The best thing about visiting the Weyerhaeuser cafeteria was the imposing murals hanging high up on the walls.

The Weyerhaeuser Company hired local artist Kenneth Callahan to complete a huge series of murals which adorned the walls of the beautiful interior of the employees' cafeteria. The largest murals were on the ends of the cathedral ceilinged building and measured sixteen and one-half feet high by thirty-seven and one-half feet wide. Callahan had painted them between 1940 and 1944 in his Granite Falls studio on canvas before mounting them in the cafeteria.

The impressive murals depicted the step by step process of making finished lumber out of logs. The huge face in the mural represented folk hero Paul Bunyan assisting the loggers and the mill workers. I remember being scared to death on my first visit by the huge faces that towered above me but as I grew older the mural added to my growing appreciation for art. When the Weyerhaeuser cafeteria was unfortunately torn down the historic murals were removed and saved. They were donated to the city of Everett where they now hang in the top floor meeting room in the Everett train station.

Grading lumber mural, *Weyerhaeuser Archives*.

The 'Big W' Weyerhaeuser Cafeteria in 1950. *Weyerhaeuser Archives*.

"When I wasn't working, besides looking for work, I'd work around the house all the time. I did a lot of improvement, where I live now, quite a bit. That's about what it amounted to, maintaining the house and yard, and stuff. No hunting or fishing, at all."

Dad certainly made lots of improvements to our little home. The minute he and Mom moved in he started. First he enclosed all of the open eaves and built an enclosed entry porch on the north side up to the property line. In those days people either didn't need a permit for many things or just didn't bother getting one. Then he started the major project of building a full-length porch across the back of the house. This also became storage for all of his wood underneath. Over the years he put on a roof, enclosed the walls and eventually made the porch a huge room where we spent much of our time.

The interior of our home was constantly changing do to Dad's improvements. He put in all new kitchen cabinets and eventually moved the refrigerator to the now enclosed porch with a dining room. He installed built-in cabinet drawers in some of the closets and put in a large picture window in the living room. He enlarged or removed some of the interior doors and moved some around. Mom loved her new layout inside. When I think today how small our home was it's kind of shocking. We had one bathroom for the four of us and one bathtub.

The Weyerhaeuser Callahan mural in the Everett train station today. *Steve Fox.*

Elmer Oberg, Mabel and Raymond Fosheim at 525 Pilchuck Path in May 1958.

As the years went by Dad kept remodeling and adding on to our little home. In the late 1950s he constructed a two-car garage in back by the alley. He built the entire garage by himself with no help from others. It was a challenge to build the trusses and hoist them high up in place by himself. He found much of the wood and only had to purchase the bigger pieces. The foundation was built with eight inch by sixteen inch concrete blocks with a sand floor. He mounted one end of Mom's clothes line on a pulley high up on a mast on top of the garage roof and the other on our back porch so she could easily pull the clothes filled line out and then back in when dry.

I think the most impressive contraption Dad built was his elevator for getting fire wood upstairs. We had electric heat but we saved money by burning wood scraps Dad brought home from all over town. The wood was stacked under our porch and our wood stove was upstairs. He made a wood box that rose up on cables to bring the fire wood from below up to the level of the stove on the porch. When the wood box was lowered one could just walk on top like it was part of the floor. Not bad for a guy with only an eight grade education. He never owned a band saw or jig saw. Everything was made on his old Craftsman table saw.

Raymond and Gene Fosheim in the backyard sandbox at 525 Pilchuck Path in 1954. Raymond's stack of concrete blocks is in the background as is Happy Hooligan, our pet duck.

Dad always had time to build me something special. One of the first things I remember was the sand box in the back yard. I played in it for hours every sunny day. As I grew older the sand box kept growing bigger. Eventually he built me one that was eight feet by eight feet and a foot deep. It had room for all the neighborhood friends to play in. The only problem with the sand box was that Fluffy our cat liked to play in it too, and poop in it. Dad fixed that by designing a cover that we could pull over the top every night when we were done playing.

I have so many good memories about growing up in our home and in our little secluded neighborhood. Dad and Mom picked the perfect place for a kid to grow up. There were just a couple dozen homes on our street and the adjoining ones. Most of the families had kids and had lived in their homes for many years. The crime rate was pretty much non-existent, but we did have two families that caused a little trouble. The only neighbor that we kids were afraid of was Viola Oursler. If our ball or kite would accidently land in her yard, we would be too scared to go get it. If she saw us, we would really get hollered at!

Our long-time neighbors on Pilchuck Path with their addresses were: Wendel Muffly 450, Guy Pratt 502, Charles Doolen 520, Alton Svensson 521, Orville Beck 524, Stephan Kerber 534, Elmer Isaacson 535, Henry Schellenberger 536, Christensen 544, Jesse Towne 545, Fred Bauman 549, and Viola Oursler 551. We also had Eugene Mueller 514, Floyd Hempel 616, and Richard McAninch 620, but they didn't stay long. All of our homes were fairly small and simple except for the Svenssons. They owned Northwest Casket Co. on the waterfront by Nord's and had a huge home with a swimming pool and a four-car garage. I remember the Svenssen boys both had new late-fifties Studebaker Hawks. I never did see them as they pretty much stayed to themselves. The families all knew one another and everyone seemed to get along well.

We only had our local traffic on our street, so we spent a lot of time playing on the asphalt. When we were all very young, we would play hide and go seek, starting at the telephone pole. When we got older we played touch football in front of our house. My team mate was always young Dave Christensen, who became the head coach of the University of Wyoming Cowboys!

Gene, Raymond, and Martin Fosheim with Elmer Oberg at our annual visit to the Puyallup Fair.

By the time I was nine or ten years old I began spending more and more of my weekends with Dad's sister Aunt LaVern's family at 2525 Walnut Street in Everett. She had married a navy man, Perl Benjamin Williamson just before the war on July 13, 1940. They had three children; Deanna Pearl, John Kristopher, and William Dennis. Cousins John and Bill became two of my best friends growing up.

First Cousins Linda Marsh, Gene Fosheim, and John Williamson celebrating a birthday in 1955 at 525 Pilchuck Path.

Cousin John was four years older than I and was highly skilled at playing various games and building model kits. He was extremely creative and a big influence on me for many of my pre-teen years. We would spend weekends together playing games, working with clay figures, building plastic models and just having fun. John eventually moved on to his high school friends and I spent more and more time with cousin Bill who was a couple of years younger than I. I still think back to those days as some of my happiest.

Elmer Oberg and Raymond Fosheim's nephew Jackie Norberg at 2620 Walnut Street in 1950.

Sadly tragedy struck the Fosheim and Norberg families on September 23, 1956 when Raymond's nephew John (Jackie) Aron Norberg was killed in a one car accident four miles north of Snohomish on Highway 1A. Jackie had served just shy of four years in the army and was a corporal in headquarters Company of the 23rd Infantry in Korea before returning to Everett to work at Scott Paper Company. He lived in Lowell at 4315 5th Street and left his wife Patricia and two young sons, Johnny Gene and Loren Dale Norberg.

A few days after the terrible wreck Dad took me down to the junk yard to see Jackies destroyed car. The vision of his wrecked car haunted me for a long time. It was a sad thing to lose a cousin so young though I really never got to know him well. Dad loved his nephew and missed him terribly for many years after he died.

Dad's youngest sister, Aunt Olivia was my god mother and she never once forgot my birthday. I would always get a card and a little gift from her. She was very kind and wonderful with kids. Dad was very close to his sister and would drive us up to Arlington often to visit with her and Uncle Frank. They had two daughters; Sandra Ann and Linda JoAnn. Both cousins were older than I so we never spent much time together in our younger years. I remember not wanting to stay at their home very long when I was a kid because they didn't have any toys for boys to play with, just dolls. After Dad died it was Olivia to whom I became the closest. She was a wonderful loving lady. We talked on the phone every couple of weeks to get family updates and I would ask her questions about the old days.

Mabel, Gene, Raymond, Martin, and John Fosheim at 525 Pilchuck Path in 1958.

When I was young there were three days every year I really looked forward to: Christmas, my birthday, and the day of the Paine Field Air Fair. From its beginning in the summer of 1957 through the 1960s, Dad and I never missed attending the Air Fair. Dad would usually let me take a couple of friends with and we jumped into our old green 1949 Chevrolet and drove to Paine Field.

Attending the Air Fair was an all-day endeavor. We wandered around the airplanes, checked out the vendor booths, and watched the fly-overs. The Air Force Thunderbirds were the big attraction in the early years. I still remember being exhausted and sun burnt as we headed home at the end of the long day. We examined every airplane and eagerly climbed into the ones that were open for inspection. Dad knew a lot about the military airplanes and told us numerous stories from his time during the war and his younger days. Dad was such a great guy to spend the day with us like this. He loved the airplanes too and passed on his love of aviation history to me and my friends.

I couldn't wait for the Air Fair every year. I had my bedroom walls decorated with my big drawings of the fighter jets and bombers. I made a clay nose-piece for the front of my bicycle that looked like the nose of a Douglas

C-124 Globemaster II transport plane. I pretended to fly down the street as I furiously peddled past the front of our home. Dad helped me make a whole set of simple big wooden airplanes that we 'flew' through the grass of our back yard. One year, my friends and I even wore our WWII hats or helmets and army surplus gear to the Air Fair.

The Air Force Thunderbirds performing a low-altitude fly-by during the 1958 Pacific Northwest Air Fair at Paine Field in Everett. *The Everett Herald.*

An aerial photo of the first Pacific Northwest Paine Field Air Fair in 1957. *The Everett Herald.*

I studied all of the airplanes in the books at our school library and begin making plastic models of the jets in the late 1950s. We used to go to the grocery store at about 11th and Broadway and Dad would occasionally buy

Aurora Plastics Corporation P-40 model kit.

me a 1/48 scale Aurora airplane model, usually a WWII fighter plane. Every chance I got, I would draw pictures of airplanes, often instead of doing my homework. F-89 Scorpions were stationed at Paine Field in the 1950s but were replaced in March 1960 by the streamlined F-102 Delta Daggers. C-119 Flying Boxcars were also stationed there before being replaced by huge C-124 Globemaster IIs in the mid-sixties. The Paine Field Air Fair ended in the mid-nineties due to financial reasons. I still go to Paine Field and visit the wonderful new aircraft museums and watch the historic fly-bys but it just isn't the same. I will always have the memories of excitedly running around to see the big silver airplanes, and most of all, I remember Dad telling me stories about each one.

Dad used to love driving by and pointing out the tall Indian totem pole at 44th Street and Rucker Avenue. When he was young it was in the middle of the intersection of Wetmore Avenue and California Street close to the Order of the Redmen Hall. The eighty-foot tall cedar log was carved in five years by William Shelton as a memorial to Chief Patkanin of the Snohomish tribe. William Shelton (1869-1938) was the last hereditary chief of the Snohomish Indian tribe in Tulalip, Washington. He was also an author, a notable sculptor, and an emissary between the Snohomish people and the United States government. Shelton carved several 'story poles' as he termed them, based on legends told to him by elders on the Tulalip Reservation.

The Shelton story pole was dedicated on July 31, 1923 with an impressive ceremony. City of Everett Mayor W. H. Clay addressed the hundreds of people present. He explained what a distinction it was to have the pole to honor Indian heritage in Everett.

The William Shelton story pole at 44th and Rucker Avenue. *Postcard.*

Chief William Shelton carving a story pole in 1920. *Museum of History and Industry.*

Just as in Dad's younger days we still had the small corner grocery stores all around Everett when I was a kid. When we needed something in a hurry I would run down to the Millview Food and Beverage Store owned by the William Herschlip family at 728 Walnut Street only a block from our home. Other options on my bicycle were the two stores on the corner of 12th and Walnut Street.

Henry Schellenberger and Gene Fosheim on top of the fire wood fort built by Raymond Fosheim. Also shown is the huge enclosed porch that Raymond built on the rear of their home at 525 Pilchuck Path. Notice the forty-foot tall TV antennas on the roofs of the homes.

I grew up in a family full of love but not with a lot of money. I guess in those days we would have been considered middle-class Americans or maybe working-class. Since I was an only child, I never noticed a lack of money. We always had older cars but I had a nice yard to play in and plenty of toys. Dad would always build me things out of wood. I had a go-cart, a fort to play in, airplanes, stilts, and numerous other fun items. All the neighborhood kids hung out at our home. It was an exciting place to be.

As I approached my teenage years for the first time I became aware that my parents were older than most of my friends parents. For a short time I was embarrassed of my family, the way they dressed, the way they talked and that Dad was only a sawmill worker. I felt uncomfortable when Mom and Dad spoke Norwegian/Swedish in front of my friends. I regret those feelings today but one event stands out in my mind that made me feel wonderful at the time. Our family went to a big Boy Scout picnic at Everett's Legion Park. They had dozens of father-son events that day and we entered the three legged race. As Dad strapped his right leg to my left leg he explained the procedure to me. Teamwork was the key, not speed. Well the two of us got into a rhythm and we passed the numerous partners who had tripped and fallen down and we won by a mile. I was never so proud of Dad in my life. We were the perfect team.

Gene and Raymond Fosheim with their stuffed animals in the living room of 525 Pilchuck Path in 1958.

The big event in the Northwest in 1962 was the futuristic Seattle World's Fair, also known as the Century 21 Exposition. It opened just two days before my eleventh birthday on April 21, 1962 and ran until October 21, 1962 in an area just north of downtown Seattle. Though it made quite an expensive day, Dad drove us down and we enjoyed the fair several times that summer along with nearly ten million other people from around the world.

Construction of the Space Needle. www.*Seattle.Gov*.

During the months before the fair opened Dad, Mom and I would drive to Seattle on a shopping trip. While my parents were shopping at the huge downtown Bon Marche or Frederick and Nelson I visited Bob Hale's Hobby Shop or the great fishing store next door. On the way home we would always drive close by the Space Needle to see the progress of the construction. We marveled at how high it kept going up. Sometimes we would drive to the top of Queen Anne Hill for a better view. After the fair closed we still enjoyed many years of riding the Alweg monorail and going up in the Space Needle to see the impressive views as well as exploring the Pacific Science Center.

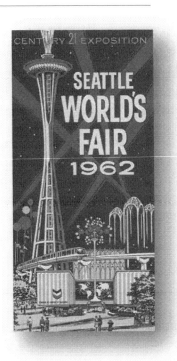

Raymond Fosheim, Elmer Oberg, Gene and Martin Fosheim in front of the one million silver dollars display at the 1962 Seattle World's Fair.

Other highlights of the World's Fair that we all enjoyed included the food circus with

The Seattle World's Fair Bubbleator. *Seattle Times.*

interesting cuisine from around the world. Dad and I also loved the big round glass Bubbleator. I wanted to ride it up and down every chance I could get. Uncle Buddy and Mart would usually go with and enjoy the people watching and the unusual sites. The fair also had a sky ride that crossed on cables over the thousands of people below. There was even a carnival area with games and entertainment.

The Philippine Pavilion was one of the many international displays at the Seattle World's Fair. Enjoying the day are Martin, John, and Gene Fosheim and Bill and LaVern Williamson.

    Mom and Dad always had a wonderful rose garden and grew vegetables and raspberries on the south side of the yard. We had shrubs and trellises and trees. Mom did the planting and Dad did the landscaping. He put in terraces and walkways all over the garden using pieces of broken concrete sidewalks held together by cement. Dad would mix yards and yards of cement in his old wheelbarrow. Ours was a great yard to hide in and perfect for playing army but we had to be careful not to destroy any of Moms garden. Dad built a nice covered swing in the front yard and that is where he, Mom, and Buddy sat on nice days, watching the neighborhood go by. Dad could build anything and I was very proud of him. Other kids didn't seem to me to have a dad as handy as mine.

Dad always kept in close touch with all his Minnesota relatives but he had a special relationship with his Aunt Martha Lyng who first came to America with Dad's father, John K. Fosheim. Aunt Martha made the long drive out to visit her Fosheim nieces and nephews in her 1954 Chevrolet in the late 1950s. Dad only got a couple of weeks of vacation a year, so he couldn't get back to Minnesota as often as he liked but he did drive back with Mom, Uncle Buddy, and I in 1968 and again during his retirement years.

Martha Lyng visiting her nephew Raymond Fosheim at 2620 Walnut Street in the late 1950s.

I got hooked on fishing in my early teenage years and I couldn't wait to take the drive up to Camano Island and spend a day at Uncle Ole's cabin on the weekends. Dad and Mom loved going there too, to play cards and talk. We would usually take one of my friends with and we would spend the day fishing while the older folks enjoyed their time together. Ole had a heavy wooden row boat that he had built himself and he let us use it. We also fished off of the tall Madrona Beach Marina dock. I learned how to catch pile perch and starry flounder on pile worms that I dug up at low tide. Dad was quite a fisherman in his younger days but he was a good sport and spent time with Mom and let us do the fishing.

It was fun just driving up to Uncle Ole's cabin at Madrona beach. Dad bought his very first new vehicle, a blue 1963 Chevrolet pickup truck so we had something fun to ride in. He built a cover for the pickup bed out of plywood and let us put down the tailgate and ride in back. We laid down on an old mattress and road backwards with a wonderful view all the way to Camano Island. One time when I luckily was not riding in the back a big gust of wind blew Dad's wooden canopy right off the truck and it landed in the bushes on the side of the road. We got out, picked it up and put it back on. Dad was the safest guy in the world but saw no problem with my friends and I riding in the back of the pickup or in our trailer. This was in the 1950s and 1960s though before laws were passed to prohibit this kind of fun.

Ole and Florence Øvrum at Madrona Beach, Camano Island.

Ole Øvrum and his nephew Raymond Fosheim at Madrona Beach on Camano Island in 1961.

I have many wonderful memories of my great uncle Ole. He was short, very chubby, and a good fisherman. With a beard, he would have looked just like Santa Claus. I heard in his younger days, he was quite a ladies man. Ole was quite old when I knew him so I didn't get to fish with him much, but I remember he would put out his crab traps and fish for smelt off the beach. Dad loved his uncle Ole and always helped him with his home and medical affairs. Ole's wife in America was Florence who was from England. She had a heavy English accent and Ole had his Norwegian accent so I was fascinated listening to them talk when I was young.

Ole Øvrum's eight children that were left in Norway: Alma Meistad, Randi Loveng, Ella Kristine Tiller, Alf Normann Øvrum, Jorunn Johansen, Helga Woll, Karen Lovhaug, and Odd Øvrum. The photo was taken in Norway in June, 1992 on Karen's seventy-fifth birthday. Compare this to the photo on page twenty-four.

Martin, Raymond, and Gene Fosheim, Ole Øvrum, Elmer Oberg, Olivia and Linda Marsh, Emma Norberg, John Fosheim, Erin Sherlock, Mabel Fosheim, and Florence Øvrum at Ole's cabin by Madrona Beach, Camano Island in 1958.

Mabel and Raymond Fosheim, Alf and Hjordes Østmo, Ole Øvrum, John Fosheim, Emma Norberg, and Florence Øvrum at Ole's Madrona Beach cabin in 1958.

Ole drove his car until late in life and was a terrible driver. Dad rode with him and was terrified when Ole passed cars on the blind curves on Camano Island's winding narrow two lane roads. Dad finally talked him into selling his car and giving up his driver's license. Ole's cabin was often the Fosheim clans gathering place for family get togethers. I used to love seeing everyone and hearing all the latest family news. Ole was born in Levanger, Norway on May 19, 1884 and died in Everett on April 27, 1979.

Dad loved the water and ships. Once a year we would drive down to Seattle and take one of the huge Washington State ferry boats on a ride across Puget Sound to see the Bremerton Naval museum and shipyard. We not only saw the active navy ships but the huge mothball fleet was also there. Everyone's favorite was the impressive battleship USS Missouri. I loved to stand next to the round plaque on the deck where the Japanese signed the surrender papers for World War II. We climbed all over the ship and posed next to the sixteen inch guns. Once again Dad loved telling his history stories about the war. Besides visiting the town and the shipyard it was really the ferry ride that was exciting. We often got to see one of the navy ships leaving port or on more than one occasion one of the big nuclear submarines passing right next to our ferry. They looked like a big black whale as they sailed by.

Mabel and Gene Fosheim on the Washington State ferry leaving Seattle for Bremerton in 1964. The Smith Tower looms over the historic ferry Kalakala at the next dock.

Dad and Mom would often go out of town on short road trips with their pickup. Dad had it fixed up with his homemade wooden canopy and a bed in back. Their favorite trips were either to the ocean or the mountains. They didn't have much money so they travelled cheap but always had fun. Of course our dog Chubby went with too.

Mabel Fosheim visiting the USS Missouri at Bremerton in the late 1960s. The USS Bremerton is on the left.

Raymond and Mabel Fosheim on a camping trip in the late 1960s.

Even though Dad had a family of his own after I was born he still enjoyed getting together with all this nieces and nephews and their growing families. He took dozens of photos and often had his movie camera handy. He would sit at the kitchen table in the evening for hours splicing film together and organizing his expanding movie collection.

Raymond's niece Dolores Norberg Sherlock with her kids, Bradley, Gregory, and Erin in about 1960.

John A. Fosheim with his 1960 Ford F-100 pickup at 2620 Walnut Street in the 1970s.

Raymond and Mabel Fosheim visiting the huge cedar stump at Smokey Point, Washington about 1960.

The giant Western Redcedar stump along Highway 99 in the late 1950s. *Postcard.*

Dad loved showing us the big cedar stump when we drove Highway 99 north to Arlington to visit Aunt Olivia and her husband Frank. The famous stump is a reminder of the giant trees which once forested the Puget Sound area. Over twenty feet in diameter and 200 feet tall, the huge Western Redcedar was more than 1,000 years old. It was killed by a fire in its hollow base in 1893 and a tunnel was cut through it two years after Dad was born in 1916. It was cut off at the bottom and moved to its location shown in the photos in 1939 and is currently at the Smokey Point rest stop along Interstate 5. Crown Prince Olav and Princess Martha of Norway once drove through the stump.

My Uncle Sven, Mom's brother in law from Denver used to love telling a story about Dad's kindness to animals. Because of our homes close proximity to the Snohomish River and the Great Northern Delta Yard we had a large variety of animals that would wander up our hillside. We often saw raccoons, possums, muskrats, and even an occasional porcupine. Mom used to beg Dad to set out traps for the rats and he meekly told her he would. One day when Sven was visiting Everett he spent some time with Dad down in the basement and the back yard. Instead of setting out rat traps Sven watched Dad hide food in his woodpile for the rats. He said he felt sorry for them.

Everyone on Pilchuck Path knew we lived on an old smelter site, but few cared. Whenever I dug a deep hole in the ground I struck bricks from the old collapsed buildings. My parents always had a garden and grew great vegetables in the soil.

Gene, Chubby, Raymond and Mabel Fosheim at 525 Pilchuck Path in 1967.

We were upset when all of a sudden someone 'discovered' the smelter waste which had been there for many decades. Like all our neighbors to the north of us on Pilchuck Path, Dad was forced to sell our home to Asarco in 1994. The price paid for the homes was fair but one couldn't place a value on an eviction. Families who had lived in the neighborhood for over forty years were forced to look for a new home.

Raymond Fosheim in his kitchen at 525 Pilchuck Path getting lunch ready for his visiting relatives.

525 Pilchuck Path from the alley. Raymond Fosheim spent forty-seven years improving his home from the full-width enclosed porch to the numerous concrete walls. He built everything by himself without any help.

525 Pilchuck Path looking east from the back porch. Raymond Fosheim's two-car garage and wood shed.

The destruction of our family home at 525 Pilchuck Path in the fall of 1997. It was a sad day.

Sadly most of the homes on our street were destroyed and the beautiful trees and shrubs were all taken to the landfill. The once handsome properties sat vacant and forlorn behind barbed wire fencing for many years. The last time I looked into the Svenssen's garage, I saw two pristine mid-1950s Packards sitting inside but they soon disappeared like everything else. Layers of soil were scooped off to remove any signs of pollution. Today the once charming hillside is crowded wall to wall with new condos occupied with people who more than likely have no idea what was there before.

Chapter XI

Retirement

"I do a little work on Gene's historic apartment houses; I'm working on that one over on 2017 26th street right now. I'm so tired and my legs are bad, so I just do a little work at a time."

Dad was never bored during his retirement years. He was always working on a woodworking project in our basement. Mom would have him make cabinets or chairs or he would build me something. He cut all his wood on a table saw or by hand. He never owned a jig or band saw until I bought him one in his later years. He was a real master craftsman and enjoyed every minute that he was in front of his saw. When Dad and Mom weren't working around their house they loved to travel with their dog Chubby.

Dad retired from the Collins Company at sixty-two in January 1976. He was always a fairly healthy man though he had a mild case of diabetes and was somewhat overweight. In his seventies he had some circulation problems and underwent a quadruple heart bypass operation. Dad recovered quickly and was back to chopping wood and working on his projects but he experienced some painful side effects from the various medications he was taking. He never complained other than saying he was often tired. Dad had a good disposition and was always happy and polite. He never asked for help with any project no matter how awkward or heavy.

"When I was out of work, I did odd jobs. I went down, Walton's was dismantling, and I kind of got a little job there, helping dismantle and stuff,

Raymond and Mabel Fosheim at Long Beach, Washington in 1971 just a few years before he retired.

thank goodness. But right after the war, I should have gotten a job away from the sawmills. I drove a lumber carrier most of the time. Before that, I made up orders; we were in the shipping department all the time."

Dad always regretted that he didn't have a chance to attend high school and go on to college. He loved working with wood but sawmill work was hard, dangerous, and often unhealthy. After the demise of the Eclipse Mill Dad applied for a job with the United States Post Office but that didn't work out and he was destined to end his career in the Everett mills.

"Then, we put our boy through five years of college. What we had in the bank, we had to take out of that for his college."

After I graduated from Everett High School in 1969 Dad and Mom wanted me to attend Everett Community College. I thought that was a good idea and completed two degree programs in three years before transferring to Western Washington University for a bachelor's degree in industrial technology. I wanted an engineering degree from the University of Washington but it was too expensive. WWU was a smart choice though as the Boeing Company hired me right after graduation as a designer on the 747 airplane program. My first hourly wage was more than Dad's at the time and one of my first paychecks went to the purchase of a huge television set for our home.

Raymond, Mabel and Gene Fosheim in 1973.

As I was starting my new work career and Dad was retiring from his the Everett area was going through some major changes. A Fred Meyer store opened in south Everett and a big downtown revitalization plan was nearing completion. Unfortunately our wonderful Woolworth building on Hewitt Avenue and Colby Avenue was destroyed and Everett (Robinson) Plywood and Weyerhaeuser Mill C both closed. Boeing, Everett's biggest employer, was experiencing some growth but would soon downsize again in the middle 1970s.

Everett effectively ceased being a mill town on March 29, 1992 when after 90 years the Weyerhaeuser Company closed their pulp mill just north of our home, the last of the six mills it operated in the 'City of Smokestacks.' There were still a few mills operating in the city limits but Everett now boasted that it was the 'Evergreen City' and its economy was dominated by Boeing and the aircraft industry.

The south Everett Boeing 747 plant was assembling airplanes for dozens of airlines during the early 1970s. *Associated Press.*

The Weyerhaeuser pulp mill in north Everett in the middle 1950s. *Everett Public Library.*

Dad and Mom spent most of their leisure hours together from shopping to sightseeing to playing cards. Mom was a Minnesota girl and really loved her card games, particularly casino and solitaire. Dad was a good sport and played every day with her and Uncle Buddy, though I'm sure he would rather have been in our basement working with his table saw. In his younger days Dad was an excellent poker player.

Dad and Mom loved to travel, at first with their small Aloha travel trailer towed behind their blue 1964 Chevrolet station wagon, 1971 Ford Torino, or later in their dark green Ford van. Dad bought a new green Ford Econoline van and carpeted the inside, put in a toilet and a bed and made a seat for our dog, Chubby. They never flew as Mom was afraid of airplanes and Dad loved driving. They visited relatives in Denver and Minnesota numerous times and drove up and down the coast all the way to see friends in southern California. Most of their trips were around Dad's beloved home state of Washington. His favorite trips were to Paradise Inn on Mt. Rainier and to the Washington coast to stay at Long Beach on the Pacific Ocean. Dad always bragged about his home state of Washington as being the prettiest place on earth.

Raymond and Chubby expanding the vegetable garden in our back yard at 525 Pilchuck Path in 1977.

Dad loved gardening as long as it involved building something. He dug a huge hole and built a concrete lined fish pond in our back yard. It soon became my favorite place for naval battles with both my wooden and plastic ships. Our yard was always the favorite hangout for all the neighbor kids. Dad built a huge sand box, a storage shed, and a two-story playhouse. He really enjoyed making kids happy. When I treated one of the neighbor kids badly he made it real clear to me never to do that again. He really was upset when I wouldn't let any girls in my playhouse so he tore it down. It took a lot to make Dad mad but it did happen occasionally.

Dad never had a chance to visit his father's homeland of Norway but two of his sisters did. Emma, Olivia and her husband Frank, and cousins Alf and Hjordes Østmo visited Verdal for four weeks in May-June of 1978. They met many of our cousins on Grandma's side of the family, the Øvrums. The previous year we had a visit from our Norwegian cousins here in Everett. It was exciting to have a huge Fosheim and Øvrum family reunion. This was when I first met my wonderful second cousin Rannveig Woll and we have been close friends ever since. I visited Norway myself in 2000 and in 2006. I wish Mom and Dad would have had a chance to go with. They would have loved the beautiful countryside and seeing the Fossheim farm.

Second cousins Rannveig Woll and Gene Fosheim in Norway in the summer of 2000.

Rannveig Woll, Hjordes Østmo, Randi Løveng, Elmer Oberg, Alf Østmo, Raymond Fosheim, and Kari Løveng standing in front of my 1973 DeTomaso Pantera at 525 Pilchuck Path when the cousins from Norway visited Everett in 1977.

The six Fosheim brothers and sisters spent almost their entire lives residing in the Snohomish County area so they spent a lot of time together. Birthdays and other special occasions were never forgotten and were always celebrated at someone's home. Olivia was the youngest sibling and the one who organized most of the family activities. They were always a close knit family and all got along well with one another.

Raymond, LaVern, John, Martin, Olivia, and Emma in the middle 1970s.

Raymond, John, and Martin Fosheim.

Emma, Olivia, LaVern, and sister-in-law Mabel Fosheim.

1978 was quite a year as I took a leave of absence from my design job at Boeing to attend college in Europe during the summer. Dad and Mom were pretty shocked and I was more than a little surprised myself with my sudden decision but I had always dreamed of studying art and history in Europe and that's what I did.

I'm somewhere in this crowd at the Everett Boeing plant for the August 4, 1981 rollout of the first 767 airplane. *The Boeing Company.*

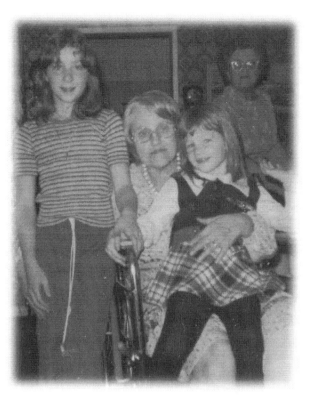

Mabel Fosheim in her wheelchair with her grandnieces Tanya and Tara Hitt in the fall of 1978. Cousin Hjordes Østmo is in the

The summer of 1978 changed all of our lives as I met Kelcey Lynn Snow, a Lake Oswego, Oregon girl and I fell in love. It wasn't a perfect year though as mom fell down in her garden and broke her ankle while I was away. She was confined to a wheelchair much of the summer but luckily she had a complete recovery and was soon taking care of her rose garden again. Kelcey and I returned to the United States at the beginning of the September and immediately started dating. I bought a house in south Everett and we were married in on February 10, 1979.

Dad and Mom were thrilled to finally have a daughter. They were equally thrilled when our two boys were born; Tyler Gene on August 27, 1981 and Grant Raymond Fosheim on May 12, 1983. Dad and Mom loved being grandparents and of course Uncle Buddy enjoyed having Kelcey and the boys around also.

Kelcey, Gene, Tyler, and Grant Fosheim in 1984.

Uncle Buddy had a girlfriend for a short period in the late 1960s and I was very jealous of the time he spent with her. But Buddy was happier living with us because he never asked her to marry him and she soon gave up the relationship. Buddy didn't have many hobbies or special interests but he loved kids and loved to travel. He went to the VFW or Eagles every Saturday night for years to visit with friends and he never missed watching Lawrence Welk, Hee Haw, or Big Time Wrestling on TV.

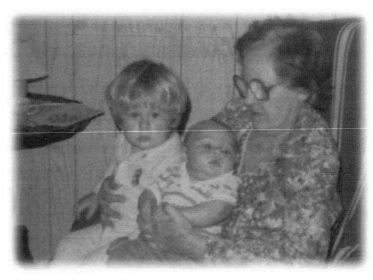

Mabel Fosheim with her grandsons, Tyler Gene and Grant Raymond Fosheim in 1983.

I was a very lucky kid having Uncle Buddy around. I remember riding on his back on the living room floor and wrestling with him when I was young. We used to play numerous games together. He was unbeatable at checkers and loved to win a good card game. I would go visit Buddy at his custodial job in the Commercial Building at Everett High School. He worked evenings so after school I helped him clean the classrooms. I loved cleaning under the gym bleachers and collecting the change that had fallen out of people's pockets. Afterward we would go into the cafeteria and the head custodian would get me a Popsicle.

Uncle Buddy, Grant and Raymond Fosheim having breakfast at 525 Pilchuck Path in 1984.

All my friends liked Buddy and it was fun having him to joke with us. For years every Saturday he would take me out to lunch and we would go for a ride around the countryside in his car. When I left for college he helped pay some of my expenses and I will never forget that. As my two boys grew up I got to enjoy watching them have years of fun with their Uncle Buddy too.

Buddy and I took many trips to Minnesota together, sometimes with Mom and Dad but usually just he and I in his car or by train. Twice Buddy took the train to the farm for the whole summer and I drove east to pick him up in September in one of my fancy sports cars. We had a fun time driving home together. Buddy was the best travel partner because he was so easy going. Some of the best memories of my life were from my time spent on the farm. I loved fishing with Buddy and his brother Dick. There was never a dull moment with those two particularly when we played the card game Rook. They really were a couple of funny characters. I could sit and listen to them talk about the old days for hours. In the last week before he died, Buddy thought of the farm and wondered who was milking the cows.

Uncle Buddy, Tyler Fosheim, and Buddy's nephew and my first cousin, Gary Oberg standing in front of a threshing machine in Rose City, Minnesota in 1986.

Uncle Buddy and his great nephew Grant Fosheim in 1984.

When I had a family of my own Buddy was always there to help. He loved my sons, Tyler and Grant. When I was a single parent he or Dad would come over every day after school to be with the boys, build a fire, take in the mail, and just spend time with them until I got home from work. It would have been hard to survive without their love and help.

Buddy had a content and simple life. He was always happy, never sick, and just satisfied to watch TV or sit and look out the window at the people going by. He never lost his temper and I can't remember him ever swearing. He had a sharp sense of humor, was honest, and was satisfied with life to the very end. He loved to tease people with a twinkle in his eye.

Dad's sister LaVern's husband Perl Williamson was intelligent, quiet, and self-assured. I got to know him quite well when I worked for the City of Everett during two summers while I attended college. Uncle Perl worked as a survey crew chief and I was lucky enough to get a part time job working on his crew with him. At first I was very intimidated by Uncle Perl and the other experienced guys on our crew but I received a valuable real life experience that helped me greatly in my future career. Plus I made good money to continue my education.

Dad's sister Olivia never forgot her roots and often talked about Norway and the Fosheim family history. In 1978 she travelled to Norway along with her sister Emma and established a close friendship with many of our cousins. For many years she would ask if I had heard anything new from Norway. When Olivia visited New York City and Ellis Island she found our Fosheim name on the wall of immigrants. I remember how excited and proud she was when she told me that story.

Olivia Fosheim Marsh in 2004 with her great grand-niece Kennedy Lynn Fosheim, the first girl born with the Fosheim name in eighty-six and one half years.

Raymond working on 2017 26th Street, Everett in 1992.

Shortly after Dad retired I purchased my first rental property in Everett and Dad was eager to help me work on the fixer-upper. Over the years I purchased numerous rental properties in the downtown Everett area and Dad helped rehabilitate every one of them. He loved doing all the finish work on the historic moldings. It was a real treat for Dad to get out and do what he loved. Many interesting people would stop by and compliment him on his work. Together we received numerous historic preservation awards including the prestigious William F. Brown Award from the City of Everett Historic Commission for our labors.

One of the most fun and satisfying projects was rehabilitating one of the oldest homes in Everett at 2017 26th Street. I bought the home and the one next to it at 2526 Broadway in 1980. It was in pretty bad shape. Dad and I worked on it for many years and helped restore it to its former glory. It was built in 1892 and designed by one of early Everett's famous architects, August Heide. We did a complete job from the foundation to the roof and took pride in our finished project.

2017 26th Street, Everett when I purchased it in April 1980.

Since we couldn't find any record of its early history and original owners, the historic preservationist with the City of Everett suggested the home be named the Raymond Fosheim House. The impressive home is now on the City of Everett Historic Register. We proudly placed a brass plaque on the front with the name and date it was built and when it was rehabilitated. It was easy to rent as people love living in preserved historic homes.

2017 26th Street, Everett after its rehabilitation in 1992.

Raymond Fosheim and his long-time family doctor, Jack Swander visiting 2017 26th Street in 1997 after the house was placed on the City of Everett Historic Register.

Our local newspaper, the Everett Herald interviewed Dad and I and ran a great story about our preservation efforts. Our home was also featured on the Historic Everett fall home tour. Our family doctor, Jack Swander read the story and came by to meet Dad and I for the first time in years and we gave him a tour of the home. It was fun to reconnect with Dr. Swander as he had been our doctor for almost thirty years.

The 1997 Herald newspaper story about our rehabilitation project on 2017th Street in Everett. *The Herald*.

Dad and I also undertook a major rehabilitation project on 2526 Broadway which was another one of the older homes in Everett, built in 1892. We spent hours jacking it up, repairing the siding, fixing the entryway, and restoring much of the remaining woodwork. Dad loved interior and exterior finish work but he also did some of the wiring and plumbing. He really knew how to do just about everything when it came to construction. I spent hours watching and helping Dad work and gained a lifetime of experience from an expert carpenter. Dad wasn't always a fast worker but he was really thorough in everything that he did.

Raymond Fosheim rehabilitating the front porch of 2526 Broadway, Everett in 1988.

Dad and I took a lot of pride in our multiple historic rehabilitation projects around the city of Everett but the crown jewel of our efforts was the work that we put into the Fosheim House at 2620 Walnut. My grandparents died in the 1940s and many of the Fosheim kids moved elsewhere. Emma Fosheim Norberg moved back into the home with her family for a few years in the 1950s. Brothers John and Martin Fosheim remained bachelors all of their lives and lived in the house until John died in 1983 and Martin moved to a retirement home. The once proud house stood vacant for the first time in a half century in 1984 when I decided that I just had to keep it in the family. I shuffled my finances around and made an offer to purchase it from the surviving family members which was gladly accepted.

Now the work really began. I had little money, I was working three jobs which took up most of my time, and now I had a vacant house to rehabilitate. I sat alone in the home and relived the many memories that it brought back. Dad visited his old home every day to putter around and tidy things up. I measured every room and began drawing up plans for a remodel that would fit the grandeur of the home without destroying any history. Most importantly I convinced a bank to put a mortgage on it so I could raise the money for the huge task ahead.

J. A. Juleen photo of 2620 Walnut Street on the left when new in 1910.

When I purchased the house it was close to the same appearance as when it was built in 1910 including the same checkerboard linoleum on the kitchen floor that I played on as a kid. There was only one light fixture hanging from the ceiling on the entire second floor with a fifteen watt light bulb that seemed as old as the house. I made the decision to have a separate living area upstairs since it already had a bathroom and that was the way the home had been used for years.

Dad and I stripped most of the inside right down to the studs so that I could rewire and re-plumb the entire house. I hired some help to do the heavy work and Dad lovingly removed the brittle molding away from the doors and windows. Inside one of the walls we found some real treasures; the original deed to the property and a child's coloring book from around 1910. Just by coincidence an elderly lady stopped by one afternoon as I was working and said that she used to visit her relatives in the house when she was young. I showed her around the home and let her see

Raymond Fosheim working on 2620 Walnut in 1984

the coloring book and to our surprise it was hers! She eagerly took it home with her to Ohio and sent me a wonderful photo of the home in 1910 when it was brand new. The photo was beautiful and taken by the famous local photographer Juleen.

Raymond remodeling the upstairs kitchen at 2620 Walnut in 1984. This is the room that was originally his bedroom for many years.

During the rehab Dad and I tried to keep much of the home as original as possible including reinstalling all the wonderful window and door molding. Dad particularly loved working upstairs where we installed a new kitchen in the area where his bedroom once was. We finished our rehabilitation of the Fosheim House by constructing and placing an octagon shaped stained glass window containing the letter 'F' for Fosheim in the front center on the second floor.

After we were done Dad and I took great pride in our work and happily showed the Fosheim family around our finished product before we rented it. Dad and I rehabilitated a quite a few historic homes in downtown Everett over the years but this job was by far the most fun and rewarding. In the ensuing years Dad couldn't wait to return to the home for a plumbing, electrical, or carpentry repair. He was the perfect partner to work with. I did the purchasing, financing, planning and design and Dad did all the finish work and whatever else he wanted to do. Mom also took pride in our historic homes but she sometimes hinted around that more needed to be done at their own home.

Raymond admiring the historic plaque on the Fosheim House at 2620 Walnut Street in 1984.

The Fosheim House, 2620 Walnut Street after our 1984 rehabilitation.

During the summer of 2001 I decided to do some additional rehabilitation work on 2620 Walnut Street through the City of Everett Community Housing Improvement Program to make the home even more appealing. I designed a new covered wrap around porch on the rear, a new roof, and a partial concrete foundation. I've rented the home to many happy families over the years and I always get a wonderful feeling when I step into the historic Fosheim home.

Dad had a chance to pass down some of his carpentry skills and work ethic to his grandsons, Tyler and Grant, while working on some of our historic homes. Our whole family was involved at times with Uncle Buddy gladly doing much of the clean-up work and mowing the lawns. Dad was running errands, making repairs and helping with our historic homes up to the last few days of his life. All together Dad helped me rehabilitate ten historic homes in the downtown Everett area. We feel we contributed to saving some of Everett's history and making it a better place to live. We were very proud of that.

"I lost her four years ago. We were married thirty-nine years, not quite forty."

After forty wonderful years together with Dad, Mom died after a thankfully short bout with cancer on February 2, 1990, leaving Dad and Uncle Buddy all alone. Dad and Buddy were different people in some ways but they both were gentle and easy to get along with so they always enjoyed being together. Dad was always busy doing something while Buddy was just content to sit and relax in front of the TV or read the daily paper.

Grant, Tyler, and Raymond Fosheim building a new garage at 2526 Broadway.

Mabel and Chubby Fosheim camping with their trailer home in southern California in the late 1970s.

"Since my wife died, life has been rough for me."

Dad missed Mom terribly in his last years but working around his home and our historic properties helped take his mind off of his loneliness. He and Buddy helped to care for my two sons, Tyler and Grant, when I was a single parent. They always helped around our home and spent every day waiting for the boys to come home after school. They took care of their dinner and helped keep things safe around the house.

Mabel and Raymond Fosheim at home in 1976.

For a few years the Fosheim household consisted of five bachelors and a dog. Kelcey and I sadly divorced after some tough years and I had custody of the boys. Those were some lonely times for all of us but we stuck together and made it through to happier times.

Raymond, Grant, Gene, and Tyler Fosheim with Uncle Buddy in 1991.

Dad overcame some of his loneliness by becoming involved with the boy's soccer activities. He went to every practice and never missed a game for years. He got to meet al lot of the boy's friends and their parents. Buddy watched the games too. The soccer years were some good times for all.

In the fall of 1992 after living single a few years I met Sue Dempsey. She's was a smart, friendly, easy going, Boston, San Francisco, and Seattle girl who got along with the boys real well. We dated for almost two years and got married in the summer of 1994. Dad, Buddy and the boys were excited having Sue and her dog, Murphy join our family.

Raymond Fosheim and Sue Dempsey with her pet bird in April, 1993.

Tyler, Raymond, and Grant Fosheim having lunch high up in the Cascades just off the Mountain Loop Highway by Big Four Mountain. Raymond passed on his love of the Cascade Mountains to his Grandsons.

Maka, Murphy, Bingo, and Raymond Fosheim on the porch of my home at 8629 Vistarama Avenue in Everett in 1995. Dad loved his dogs and they loved him.

8718 27th Avenue Southeast, Everett with the garage that Dad and I built for his woodshop.

Dad and Buddy spent the last few years of their lives living in a cute little three bedroom rambler I found for them at 8718 27th Avenue Southeast in the Eastmont area of south Everett just a few blocks from my home. Dad missed his basement woodshop so I designed and built a good sized garage with a shop in the back yard so dad could continue with his beloved woodworking projects. He also liked to heat his home with wood so he spent hours gathering scraps wherever he could. I took down some overgrown maple trees in my yard and he split them up to burn in his fireplace.

Dad and Buddy still helped clean up around my rental homes and mowed all the lawns. Buddy took great pride in his lawn mowing skills. All the tenants loved them both and they loved talking with the people they met. It gave them a good excuse to get out of their house. The two of them went out to lunch almost every day and were fairly healthy for eighty-year-olds. After never spending a day in a hospital Buddy had a few health problems in his last year and spent some recovery time in a care facility but soon returned to his own home.

Elmer Oberg died peacefully on January 18, 1997 in his bed at home after a long and happy life. All his material possessions fit in just one five-drawer dresser but he was one of the most content and kind persons I've ever known. I took Buddy back to the little Rose City Cemetery in Minnesota during a winter snowstorm to bury him next to his parents and brothers.

Dad died quietly in his own bed just a half year after Uncle Buddy on July 11, 1997. Dad was chopping wood and helping me with my historic homes just a couple of days before he died. He had a routine where he would come by our home and pick up our dog, Murphy, and take her for a ride around Everett in his Ford Ranger pickup. Then they would both go to Evergreen Cemetery for a walk. We had a small memorial service for Dad at our home for friends and relatives followed by a simple private service at Evergreen Cemetery in Everett.

Epilogue

Over the years Raymond Fosheim lived in seven different homes in the Everett area:

1515 Baker Avenue	1914-23	2917 Leonard Drive	1933-35
2202 Cleveland Avenue	1923-26	2620 Walnut Street	1935-50
East Everett	1926-27	525 Pilchuck Path	1950-94
2202 Cleveland Avenue	1927-33	8718 27th Avenue SE	1994-97

John Arthur Fosheim had a rough last few years of his life with illness and died on April 15, 1983. I had never really spent much time alone with Uncle John. He was in Providence Hospital recovering from extensive surgery on my wedding day in 1978 and I went up to visit him that morning. We sat and talked for a while. I cheered him up and he helped me relax before the big event.

LaVern Fosheim Williamson died in 1990 following a long illness.

Martin Fosheim was the oldest but outlived both his brothers and died on December 25, 2000, Christmas Day. He was ninety-five years old and barely had a wrinkle on his face.

Olivia Fosheim Marsh Died on the last day of December, 2005 after a couple hard years of illness.

Emma Fosheim Norberg had a hard life in her early years and raised five kids mostly by herself starting in the depression and continuing through World War II. She lost a son and a daughter but Emma had lots of support from her kids, grandkids and great grandkids in her later years. Emma died on November 27, 2009 the longest lived of the seven Fosheim siblings.

Raymond Fosheim and Emma Norberg.

Not a day goes by that I don't think of Dad. He taught me so many things from my love of history to my passion for building things. I was incredibly lucky to have him in my life for forty six years. He was the kindest and gentlest person I've ever known.

Raymond Margato Fosheim was a proud Everett boy all his life.

The Fosheim family members were laid to rest in Everett's historic Evergreen Cemetery with the exception of Olivia who rests in Arlington Municipal Cemetery. Uncle Buddy rests with his parents and other family members in Rose City Evangelical Free Church Cemetery in Minnesota.

In addition to Dad's and Mom's grave marker I placed a military cenotaph for Dad on his parent's grave and next to his two brothers.

The Author

Like his father, Gene Raymond Fosheim is a 'Mill Town Boy' and has lived his entire life in Everett, Washington. A 1969 graduate of Everett High School and a 1971 graduate in electronics from Everett Community College, he also has a Bachelor of Science Degree in Industrial Technology from Western Washington University. Gene studied at Oriel College, Oxford University and has a Master of Science Degree in Workforce Education from Southern Illinois University. During retirement Gene returned to college and recently completed a Master of Humanities Degree with honors from Tiffin University.

Gene began his working career in 1974 as a designer at the Boeing Commercial Airplane Company on the 747 and 767 aircraft. After eight years he followed his passion and left Boeing to become a college instructor, teaching in the architecture and engineering fields for twenty-five years. Gene also owns a business restoring and renting historic Everett homes and apartments.

Gene is a founding board member of Historic Everett, President of the Everett Museum of History and a former member and chair of the City of Everett Historic Commission. He also is active in numerous local and national professional organizations.

Gene enjoys travel in America and has visited forty-nine states. He also enjoys exploring and studying art and architecture in Europe. Gene loves hiking, reading, photography, fishing, model making, writing, and researching historic subjects. He also spends much of his time working in his two acre wildlife garden. His latest hobby is pretending to be a writer.

Made in the USA
San Bernardino, CA
09 March 2019